Being Rapoport

FOCUS ON AMERICAN HISTORY SERIES
CENTER FOR AMERICAN HISTORY
UNIVERSITY OF TEXAS AT AUSTIN
Edited by Don Carleton

Being **RAPOPORT**

Capitalist with a Conscience

AS TOLD TO **DON CARLETON**

WITH AN INTRODUCTION BY **BILL MOYERS**

University of Texas Press AUSTIN

Requests for permission to reproduce material from this work
should be sent to Permissions, University of Texas Press, P.O.
Box 7819, Austin, TX 78713-7819.

⊗ The paper used in this book meets the minimum
requirements of ANSI/NISO z39.48-1992 (R1997)
(Permanence of Paper).

LIBRARY OF CONGRESS
CATALOGING-IN-PUBLICATION DATA

Rapoport, Bernard, 1917–
   Being Rapoport : capitalist with a conscience / as told to
Don Carleton ; with an introduction by Bill Moyers. —
1st ed.
        p.   cm. — (Focus on American history series)
   Includes index.
   ISBN 0-292-77117-7 (cloth : alk. paper)
   1. Rapoport, Bernard, 1917–   2. Capitalists and
financiers — United States — Biography.   3. Philanthropists —
United States — Biography.   4. Jews — United States —
Biography.   5. Insurance companies — United States.
6. University of Texas System. Board of Regents —
Biography.   7. Democratic Party (Tex.) — Biography.
I. Carleton, Don E., 1947–   II. Title.   III. Series.
CT275.R2645   A3   2002
976.4'063'092 — dc21
[B]   2001052229

Contents

Preface

I have been keenly aware of Bernard Rapoport's political activities for at least thirty-five years. During that time, he has served as one of the financial godfathers of the Texas Democratic Party. However, I did not meet Bernard (or "B," as he prefers) until March 1992, when I was doing research for my book *A Breed So Rare,* a biography of Texas oilman J. R. Parten. At our first meeting, B and his wife, Audre, generously allowed me to interview them about Parten and the various political causes they had supported together. A few days after we completed the interview, B asked me to help him put his story on paper and, if the results seemed worthy, get it published. I was flattered by the offer and strongly interested in what I knew to be an important story. I had not finished my work on Parten, however, so I declined. I soon learned that B Rapoport does not take no for an answer. And I'm glad he is built that way. B was patient. He was willing to wait until I completed most of the Parten book. With that issue settled, we had an agreement.

B decided that his story should be told in his own voice in memoir style. My role was to research his life, largely by digging through his personal and professional papers at the University of Texas Center for American History. Using the information found in those papers, I constructed B's biographical outline and formulated questions to ask in our oral history sessions. Those oral history interviews were conducted in his business office in Waco, usually on Saturday afternoons, in sessions lasting from two to three hours. Afterward, I transcribed the interviews, checked facts and dates, and edited the transcriptions to produce a narrative of his life story. Follow-up sessions were used to fill in gaps and to clarify statements from the previous interviews. B was deeply involved in every stage of the process. He read, revised, and corrected the chapters as they were completed. This is in every respect his version of a life well lived, told in his own voice. The many hours that I have been with him have been among the most fascinating that I have ever spent. B is a life force on his own. It is as simple — and true — as that.

In addition to B's personal narrative, he and I decided to enrich the story with quotations from his professional associates, relatives, and friends. Those quotes are interspersed throughout the narrative, placed near B's related comments. With a few exceptions, these statements are taken from oral history interviews with the individual who is quoted. In some cases, they are from B's correspondence. Others are from public sources, such as press releases. A list of quoted individuals and the source of their quotes is included at the end of this preface.

I want to express my gratitude and sincere thanks to the individuals listed below who are quoted in the text. In addition, several individuals assisted me during the project. Dr. Mark Young, who served as my graduate student research assistant, dug through the Rapoport Papers with much energy and enthusiasm. His help was invaluable. Dr. Barbara Griffith conducted several oral history interviews that ultimately provided quotes as well as useful information. Ouida Hinsley, B's talented assistant, scheduled interviews, located photographs, and helped with many more matters large and small than I can list here. Dr. Jules Pagano arranged interviews for me in Washington, D.C. The staff of the Jerusalem Foundation, especially Teddy Kollek, Ruth Cheshin, and Alan Freeman, provided invaluable assistance to me during my research trip to Israel. I also want to thank Yael Levin, Yehudit Shalvi, Nafez Hamdi Nubani, and Benny Bittner for making my visit to Jerusalem such a memorable experience.

In the 1970s Dr. Thomas Charlton, professor of history at Baylor University, conducted an in-depth oral history interview with B Rapoport. Dr. Charlton's work proved to be a valuable resource for this book. I want to acknowledge that contribution.

Most of my work was made possible by financial support from grants administered by the Texas State Historical Association. I am grateful to Dr. Ron Tyler, director of the Texas State Historical Association, for his support. Evelyn Stehling, the gifted administrative manager of the association, was particularly helpful. I appreciate Evelyn's patience and good cheer. Thanks also to my professional colleagues and the other hard-working staff members at the Center for American History for their advice, help, and encouragement.

Most of all, I thank my wife, Suzanne, and our two children, Ian and Aunna, for their encouragement and emotional support during the extended period of time that I helped B get his story on paper.

DON CARLETON

Individuals Quoted in the Text

Unless otherwise noted, quotations are from oral history interviews conducted by this memoir project.

Morton Bahr
Ben Barnes
Hank Brown
Ruth Cheshin
William Clinton (White House press conference)
Charles Cooper
Alan Cranston (letter in Rapoport Papers)
William H. Cunningham
Thomas Daschle
Ronnie Dugger
Don Evans (University of Texas press release)
Alan Freeman
Hiram Friedsam
Vera Friedsam
D. B. Hardeman (diary, Hardeman Papers, LBJ Library)
Greg Hartman
Molly Ivins (*Texas Observer*)
John Kelly
Robert D. King (*Texas Observer*)
Teddy Kollek
Patrick Leahy
Ray Marshall
Garry Mauro
Maury Maverick, Jr.
Idel McLanathan
Eugene McCarthy
George McGovern
Jules Pagano
Audre Rapoport
Ann Richards
Fred Schmidt
Charles Terrell
Jim Wright

Introduction

Bernard Rapoport has written a love story.

Over a long life this man has lavished the affections of his heart, like his largesse, on his family and friends and on the causes and institutions that he believes will make the world a better place. It's as simple as that: What he loves, he nurtures.

Of course B himself is about as simple as a Texas twister. The young people who work with me in New York City still recall the first time he whooshed through our office. They had never before experienced such a force of nature. When I tell them now that Bernard Rapoport might be dropping by again, they batten down the hatches.

For the two of us it was kinship at first sight. Both of us had grown up in similar circumstances in Texas. We were very poor. We will not end up in similar circumstances, however, because B has become very, very rich. It's not that he wants to die rich, but he is up against an uncanny ability to make money as fast as he disposes of it.

He wanted to teach me the trick thirty years ago. "Come home and work with me," he said. "I'll make you a rich man." Both of us had studied history and literature at the University of Texas, but B had gone on to a postgraduate study of economics. "I know nothing about economics and less about the insurance business," I told him. "That's okay," he answered. "As long as we're in the same office we'll be able to talk about the same books." I didn't go, but it didn't matter. We became friends, anyway, and I've probably lived a lot longer than if I had been under the same roof with him.

Ideas are the forge of his loyalty and passions. Of the 60,000 new books published every year, I sometimes think that two-thirds of them must wind up in his study in Waco. The fax whirs in my office and coughs up yet another page copied from some book on which he has scribbled, "What do you think about this?" The mail arrives and if it doesn't contain the latest poem from his granddaughter, Emily, there's bound to be a book review or clipping heavily underlined. The phone rings: "Moyers, have you seen this piece in *Harper's?*" Most of the time I haven't seen or read the particular item he is recommending, but I've never gone wrong following the suggestion.

Looking back over his friendship, I realize that he has never asked anything of me but conversation and camaraderie. It's no secret he enjoys talking, but he listens too, and you had better be careful about the advice you give, because he just may take it. Like a baling machine in the hay field, he sweeps up everything in his path. Sooner or later he'll want to talk about it. The day's more interesting when B calls; his enthusiasms can be exhausting, but never dull.

Nor is his life. The poverty he knew in San Antonio was the equivalent of "dirt poor" in East Texas. It either broke your heart or it bit your ankles. Like a man with a bulldog at his heels, B scrambled up and out and never looked back. In the depth of the Great Depression he landed a job at Zales jewelry store at 619 Congress Avenue in Austin and worked his way — six days a week — through the university. There was no time for parties or football games on Saturday, but the campus was saturated with intellectual ferment and B soaked it up. The economics department, one of the best in the country and one of the most progressive, harbored not only New Dealers but also a genuine (although non-Communist) Marxist scholar.

A few blocks away, the State Legislature writhed in paranoia. A gaggle of cartel-loving, monopoly-boosting, on-the-take red-baiting rabble-rousers declared war on professors and students for their advocacy of labor unions, civil rights for black people, fair labor standards, antitrust laws, and corporate taxes. Back from Congress came the shameless Texas demagogue Martin Dies, to run roughshod over facts, reputations, and liberals. One of the students interrogated by his lackeys was a youthful B Rapoport, so patriotic he had "flunked German to spite Hitler." But the times were hateful and malice ran rampant, and patriotism was no guarantee against persecution. The State Legislature could make you "believe in the dictatorship of the proletariat," B wrote at the time, and Dies was simply an "awful man."

It was a defining experience for him. University regents passed a rule that the faculty could not attend professional meetings on state time and at state expense because of the dangers of mixing with "subversives and perverts" from out-of-state universities. Then they removed the John Dos Passos novel *USA* from a list of recommended reading in the English department. The UT president, Homer Rainey, fought back. The regents fired him, and the campus erupted, with 5,000 of his supporters parading down the streets. B joined the campaign to save Rainey's presidency. They lost. Then he and his bride, Audre, joined the campaign to elect Rainey governor, postponing a baby for the duration. They lost again (although McLennan County, which they managed, was one of the few Rainey carried). B and Audre have fought many a losing campaign on the right side ever since. They've lived to see a lot of them vindicated. It was a swell day almost fifty years later when B, by now a regent of his beloved university, delivered the keynote speech at the dedication of Homer P. Rainey Hall.

The educated man is empowered to argue against his own privilege— and morally obligated to do so, it seems to me, lest he forget his roots, take his good fortune for granted, and grow comfortable in the rarefied company of elites. B refuses to draw the wagons of wealth into a circle around him. Though the strength of his radicalism changed over the years, he never lost his commitment to improving the country where he prospered. He has been tireless in his support of social justice and progressive politicians committed to enlarging democracy's embrace. You will read in these pages how in the early days of his insurance company his sizable assets were structured in such a way that he couldn't tap them, so he continuously borrowed money to support his family. Even when he was living on debt, however, he managed to back candidates he liked despite the fact that their shared political ideology could threaten his own business. Glance at his resume and you would guess he is a conservative: degree in economics, jobs in retail jewelry, insurance salesman, head of a large corporation. Yet this is a man who studied Marxism in a state where a county sheriff finding a bootleg copy of *Das Kapital* in your glove compartment could be proclaimed a local hero for shooting first and asking questions later. Here's a man who finances the liberal *Texas Observer* despite the habit of its editors to expose the predatory excesses of the industry that made him rich. Here's a man who supports political candidates who promise to increase his taxes.

Don't get me wrong. Bernard Rapoport is no Texas-bred Jewish Mother Teresa. Many a pro playing poker with him went home in their underwear. When a business deal's on the table, his ideology isn't going to stack the deck in your favor. But I haven't met many rich Texas tycoons who believe society has not only the right but also the necessity to check and balance their own rapacious appetites. They rant, "Business good, government bad" (until, of course, government is good for their business). On the other side, though, B rejects the equally mediocre idea: "Government great, business evil." He's one of those people who tackle the contradictions and try to resolve them fairly. His capitalist instincts are powerful, but so is his social conscience. He believes in democracy, not in government or business.

Perhaps that's why he so loves our alma mater. B arrived at the University of Texas twenty years before me, but the imprint left on us by the place could not be more similar. Poor kids like us who attended the university in the middle decades of the last century could hardly believe it: All this *for us*? The people of Texas did this *for us?* Even the $40 tuition was beyond my parents' means. Yet there, spread out before us in a library larger than my entire high school, were stacks upon stacks of books, available for the asking. A cornucopia of courses stretched before us, too, many of them taught by minds afire with passion or puckishly bent on picking our pockets of banal preconceptions. In my day Gilbert McAllister taught anthropology. He had spent his years as a young graduate student among the Apaches. He liked to tell us how they used the same word for grandfather as for grandson: "Grandfather, grandson—the Apaches believed in the reciprocity of the generations, in both linking and locking one generation to another." Again and again in his classes he would look back over the sweep of time to point out that human beings have advanced more through having learned the value of cooperative caring behavior than through their ability to compete.

Robert Cotner taught my favorite history class. His message was that the building of this country was a social, not a solitary, endeavor. Yes, cruelty, exploitation, racism, and chauvinism deeply stained the record. Yes, a republic dedicated to the proposition that all men are created equal violently dispossessed the Indian and nurtured slavery in the cradle of liberty. But there was another strain in American life, Dr. Cotner would remind us. For all the chest-thumping about rugged individuals and the self-made man, the ethic of cooperation inspired a social compromise that gave us, in our best moments, the texture of a common endeavor. It was this talent for social cooperation that provided a resilient environment in which American capitalism flourished. Individual initiative succeeded only when it led to strong systems of mutual support. For this, the young die in battles for a peace they will never enjoy, the elderly plant trees they will never sit under, and men and women build universities for children not their own. The University of Texas, like the United States of America, is the gift to us of strangers: Pass it on. So we were taught.

With B, this notion of the social contract stuck. It's why he has bestowed on the university so much of his generosity. He knows that poor kids like us wouldn't have had a chance if others had not lived what we were taught and built what we could not afford.

With historian Don Carleton's help, B has finished his memoir, but there will have to be a sequel! As I write, he has sold one insurance company and bought another. He's just come back from taking his grandkids to Europe. Next week he will return to a school in one of Waco's impoverished neighborhoods to read aloud to the students. And he is still trying to figure out how the governor of his own state could lose the election and still win the presidency. His perplexity at this turn of events cheers me. It gives me hope that I may yet succeed in bringing him around to the one cause about which he remains ambivalent despite my years of hectoring — the radical reform of our campaign finance laws. In his heart he knows I'm right, but as a major player in the game, backing causes and candidates he believes in, he doesn't yet see the light.

So be it. If I fail once again to persuade him, our friendship will not be affected. Bernard Rapoport's friendship comes from some place deeper than politics. Call it that forge in the soul where sturdy affections are fashioned to last.

Meanwhile, there goes the fax again.

BILL MOYERS

Being Rapoport

1 ▸ *Beginnings*

I am the son of Russian Jews who immigrated to America in the second decade of the twentieth century. During my childhood, my father taught me Marxism and hard work. My mother taught me Judaism and compassion for humanity. Both of my parents taught me to love learning. To know these simple facts is to know much about who I am and why I have led my life the way I have.

Siberia to San Antonio

My father, David Rapoport, was born in Dvinsk, Latvia, which at that time was governed by czarist Russia. He was the son of lawyer Boris Rapoport and the grandson of a man who played an important role in the building of the first railroad in Russia. My father's family enjoyed a relatively affluent and privileged life despite being Jewish in a country deeply marked by vicious anti-Semitism. My great-grandfather Rapoport's involvement in the first Russian railroad made it possible for my grandfather and his brothers to enter professions from which most Jews were banned and to accumulate property and other assets such as a major interest in a salt mine.

I know very little about Papa's father and grandfather. I know nothing about the nature of my great-grandfather's contribution to the development of the Russian rail system. Separated from his parents at an early age, Papa never had the opportunity to learn about his family's recent past, much less his genealogy. When he was a teenager, Papa became a dedicated Marxist and an activist in the Russian Social Revolutionary Party. After the czar's military forces murdered several hundred peaceful demonstrators in the snow-covered streets of St. Petersburg on January 22, 1905 (the day known in Russian history as Bloody Sunday), Papa joined in the anticzarist uprising that rapidly spread across the country.

One of the most significant events in Russian history, the Revolution of 1905 ended when the czar agreed to accept certain governmental reforms, including the creation of an elected parliament. Months before the revolt ended, however, the police arrested Papa for distributing anticzarist propaganda. The usual punishment for crimes against the czar was death, but because of Papa's grandfather's contributions to the country and his family's well-known reputation as conservative subjects loyal to the czar, the government spared his life. He was saved from the hangman's rope, but not from harsh punishment. The Russian High Court of Appeals sentenced him to two years and eight months hard labor and banished him to northeastern Siberia for life. He was only seventeen years old.

Papa endured several harsh winters in Siberia, barely surviving the epidemics that swept frequently through the region. One of my most treasured possessions is a photograph of Papa in that bleak and bitterly cold country as he posed with fellow exiles and their armed guards. One day, after years of suffering intense and debilitating hardship, Papa decided that he had to escape or die. He walked away from his compound when the guards weren't looking. Papa told me that it was easy to leave the camp because there were no physical barriers to keep prisoners inside. The challenge was to survive outside. The camps were so isolated and the climate so hostile that the odds were heavily against anyone's surviving the trek back to the west.

Somehow, Papa beat those odds. He walked hundreds of miles across the Russian landscape, literally trudging much of that incredible distance through ice and snow. He also managed to sneak rides on passing freight trains. With the help of peasants and workers who fed and clothed him along the way, Papa eventually made it back to Dvinsk, where he hid for a brief time with his parents. There he learned that his older brother Raphael had fled Russia to avoid military service. He had immigrated to the United States and had settled in San Antonio, Texas. Facing arrest and a forced return to Siberia or even execution, Papa decided to join his brother in America. With money from his parents to pay the way, Papa traveled to Paris and then to Belgium, where he linked up with a group of exiled Russian socialists who helped him book passage on a steamboat to America. Before he left Europe, Papa's socialist "brothers" in Belgium gave him a letter of introduction to their comrades in the United States. I have that old document hanging in my office. When I show it to visitors I tell them that it is my father's Ph.D. degree.

It is fascinating for me to think about how the course of one's life is di-

B's father (standing to the extreme right), posing for a photograph with some of his fellow exiles and their guards in Siberia in 1912. CN 10494, Rapoport (Bernard) Photograph Collection, Center for American History, The University of Texas at Austin.

rected by a strange mix of conscious decisions, accidents, and sheer coincidence. For example, when my uncle Raphael departed from Europe on a ship bound for the United States, he did not know to what port the boat was going. It landed in Galveston, so that is how we all ended up in Texas. If the boat had docked at Ellis Island instead, it is likely that Raphael would have remained in New York and my story would be much different. But Raphael went to San Antonio from Galveston, and that is where my story began.

Papa departed from Europe in 1913 on a boat bound for the U.S. immigration processing facility at Ellis Island in New York Harbor. From New

B's father's "socialist passport" issued in Belgium in 1913. Author's personal collection.

York, he traveled by train to San Antonio. He could not speak English, so he did not understand that he had to pay for his meals while on the train. Papa's ship fare across the Atlantic had included all meals. He had not eaten well on the boat, so he was eager for some good food. He went to the train's dining car and ordered everything on the menu. When the waiter brought him the check, he realized for the first time that the meals were not included in the price of the train ticket. The train fare had exhausted his remaining funds, so Papa washed dishes all the way from New York to San Antonio.

After Papa arrived in San Antonio, his brother, who had changed his first name to "Foley," helped him get a pushcart so that he could peddle blankets door to door. Uncle Foley was a peddler and he just assumed that Papa would be one too, so that is how Papa supported himself for several years. He walked up and down dusty unpaved streets on the west side of town selling cheap blankets and clothes for 10 cents down and 10 cents a week to the poor Mexican-American families who resided there. He had to return every week to collect the 10-cent payment until the item was paid off. Because all of his customers were recent immigrants from Mexico, Papa knew Spanish before he learned English.

About three years after Papa settled in San Antonio, he met my mother, Riva Feldman. A native of Sevastopol, a major Russian port city on the Black Sea, Mama immigrated to the United States in 1908 with her parents, Chaim and Sarah, and two sisters, Frieda and Fania. She and her sisters had participated in the antigovernment protests during the 1905 revolution. They had escaped punishment, but as the months passed, Mama's parents worried that the girls might be banished eventually to Siberia. They decided to immigrate. Mama's brother, Morris, came to America first, settled in Fort Worth, Texas, and established a junk business that prospered and eventually became a major company called Commercial Metal. Morris sent for the rest of the family to come to Texas.

Mama's parents were Hasidic Jews—deeply devout and learned. Her father, Chaim, was a *shocket* who was part owner of a kosher butcher shop on East Fifth Street in Fort Worth called the Feldman and Coplin Meat Market. In the Jewish religion, there is a special ceremony that a *shocket* must perform when animals are slaughtered for their meat. That ceremony makes the meat kosher, which allows Jews who follow the Judaic dietary laws to eat it. Grandfather performed that particular function. I never really knew Grandfather Feldman because he died early, but his love for books and learning made a deep impression on Mama and her sisters.

My grandfather was an eloquent and wise man. Mama told me that he believed that for religion to be worthy it must be concerned with humanity and that it should be an agency for spreading knowledge among the people. She often quoted one of his favorite sayings: "Wisdom is the unspotted mirror of the power of God and the image of His goodness. Knowledge is the path to wisdom. Knowledge is the Messiah of humanity." That beautiful saying of Grandfather Feldman's made a powerful impression on my young mind. It guides me to this day.

My grandfather loved his adopted country. Mama and her sisters liked to sit on the front porch of their little house and sing Russian revolutionary songs. Chaim would tell them to sing their hearts out. "Here in America it's all right," Chaim would say. "In Russia you would be sent to Siberia for that."

My maternal grandmother was Sarah Aronson Feldman, whom we called Bobo. Although she resided in this country for about forty-five years, Bobo always lived as if she were still in a ghetto town in the Crimea. She lived into her early nineties, but she never acclimated herself to this country. She always spoke to me in Yiddish because she never learned English. Mama's youngest sister, Fania, was a poet who married Sam Kruger, a jewelry store entrepreneur in Wichita Falls. An internationally known poet and essayist, Aunt Fania personified the learned and introspective inclinations that characterized the Feldman family. Her best-known works are her books of poetry, *Cossack Laughter* and *The Tenth Jew*. Fania's daughter, Bert Kruger Smith, a distinguished educator at the University of Texas at Austin for many years, continued her family's tradition of scholarship.

Another of my mother's relatives who immigrated from Russia was a rabbi in San Antonio named Gerstein. It was he who invited Mother to come to San Antonio for a visit. She met Papa during that trip, and they soon fell in love. They were married in 1916 when they were both in their middle twenties.

From Buena Vista Street to West Woodlawn

I was born on July 17, 1917, a little more than one year after Mama and Papa married. They were living on Buena Vista Street on the West Side of San Antonio, which is the section of town where Papa peddled blankets. Mama and Papa named me after my paternal grandfather, Boris, which is "Bernard" in English. My sister, Idel, my only sibling, was born three years later.

I have few memories of Buena Vista Street because we moved to another neighborhood when I was about five years old. My father sold the Buena Vista Street house for a few hundred dollars profit. It was enough to allow him to make a down payment on a new house near his brother Foley's on West Courtland Place, completely on the other side of San Antonio from Buena Vista Street. This was a major step up the social ladder for us.

Not long after this happy move, however, my family's upward financial mobility ended rather abruptly. My father was unable to make the monthly payments on the house, so the mortgage company had to foreclose and evict us. The sheriff posted a foreclosure sign on the front door of our house. Several burly men soon followed him and unceremoniously moved all of our furniture out on the street. After this traumatic eviction from our new home, we found a rent house at 706 West Woodlawn Avenue, which is the place where the childhood of my surviving memories was spent. The house was a couple of hundred yards from some railroad tracks. As a kid, I had a lot of fun counting the hoboes who were riding the freight trains as they passed our home.

A Radical Heritage

Papa was not religious in the spiritual sense, but he did have a secular religion and that was socialism. He retained his political radicalism after he moved to the United States, which greatly irritated my politically conservative Uncle Foley. As a child, I deeply resented my uncle because he was always picking on Papa and criticizing his political views. You know how it is if someone seems not to recognize the virtues of someone you love, especially if it is your mother or father.

But Papa did not need his brother's approval when it came to politics. For ideological support, Papa could depend on his close friends from about a dozen Jewish Russian immigrant families in San Antonio. The members of this tiny group of Jewish intellectuals were very radical. None of them could speak English fluently—they spoke Yiddish primarily. The rest of the community never accepted them. As a result, my father never let me forget that coming from a Jewish revolutionary family meant that I would have to work twice as hard to get half as far.

We hear constantly today about how Americans are anti-immigrant. I must tell you that it was worse when I was a child, because people were much more obvious with their bigotry and prejudice. In the 1920s many people in Texas were quite suspicious of "foreign elements" in the country. I can remember how people in San Antonio laughed at my father and his friends because of their thick accents. Those Jewish Russians sounded strange to native Texans, many of whom would make fun of them in a rude and disrespectful manner.

Anti-Semitism was also a more overt problem in those days. The Ku Klux Klan had a large chapter in San Antonio, and Jews along with Catholics, blacks, and other so-called "undesirables" were their favorite targets. Our family was so unmistakably Jewish that we were frequently the object of anti-Semitic remarks and jokes. I honestly can't say that I had any frightening experiences. A typical incident would be some kids yelling "Jew boy" at me. Whenever we were with our non-Jewish acquaintances, we frequently had an uneasy feeling that someone would tell some stereotypical Jewish joke or make some disdainful remark. I try to eliminate unpleasant memories like that from my mind, so there might have been more of that type of thing than I care to admit.

> Barney and I were visiting our teacher at her house one after-
> noon after school. Barney and I got into a friendly wrestling
> match in the front yard of her neighbor's house. Barney in-
> jured his leg and had to be carried home. The neighbor was
> very upset because he was afraid that Barney's father would
> sue him because Barney had hurt himself in his yard. People
> didn't sue other people in those days like they do now, but
> this neighbor knew the Rapoports are Jewish and he believed
> the anti-Semitic stereotype. You know, "the Jews will sue me
> or something, they're always money-grubbing," and so on.
> —*Fred Schmidt, B's lifelong friend*

People were not as willing to reconcile themselves to ethnic and racial differences in those days as I believe they are today. There is no doubt in my mind that we have made great progress as a society when it comes to accepting people of different religious and ethnic backgrounds. We still have a long way to go, especially in black-white race relations, but we are much farther down the road to true tolerance and respect than we were in the 1920s and 1930s.

A heavy Russian accent, of course, was not the only reason my father and his friends remained isolated from the rest of the community. Papa and his comrades were proud of their socialist beliefs, and they were true believers in every sense of the word. Their eagerness to expound their socialist beliefs publicly won them few friends in San Antonio.

I have Papa's membership certificate in the Socialist Party of America framed in my office. He joined the party in June 1914, just a few months after he arrived in San Antonio. That certificate was one of his most prized possessions. My father's politics resulted from his intense and sincere idealism. That idealism permeated his worldview, and it totally defined my early thinking. This is difficult to believe in the context of today when personal agendas dominate public policy debates, but never was my father's idealism related in any way to self-interest.

In the 1920s and early 1930s, Papa and his friends firmly believed in the inevitability of a worldwide workers' revolution. For them, communism meant something totally different from what it does today. They were advocating the creation of a state based on a utopian type of communism, not communism as it evolved in the Soviet Union, China, and elsewhere. These were aesthetic people who were sincerely and profoundly concerned about the pervasive injustices resulting from an unregulated capitalist economy. For them, Karl Marx had the simplest answer to eradicating these very real injustices.

Soap Box Forums

We had a number of fund-raisers at our house for socialist political causes. I remember watching in awe as people who were tottering on the
sharp edge of poverty contributed their quarters to whatever cause Papa happened to be pushing at the time. Twenty-five cents was a lot of money to us.
You could buy a good meal for that amount. On those weekends when Papa
and his comrades were not raising money, they went to Milam Square across
from Santa Rosa Hospital and made speeches on soap boxes. I carried my
father's soap box to many of those meetings.

One of the strongest memories of my childhood is of Papa standing on
his box, speaking fervently (with a Russian accent!) about the coming socialist utopia, waving his fist at the small groups of curious people who would
gather around him. Papa's speeches often attracted the attention of Mexican laborers, men who had only recently crossed the Rio Grande in search
of a better life. On those occasions Papa gave his speeches in Spanish, a
language he knew much better than English. "Workers of the world unite,"
he would declare in Spanish, "you have nothing to lose but your chains."
Recalling this many years later, I am amazed that Papa was not beaten up or
arrested, because San Antonio was a very conservative place, with a heavy
military presence because of Fort Sam Houston.

Papa and his friends spent nearly all of their spare time arguing among
themselves about the world political situation. These immigrant Jewish radicals were the best-informed people that I have ever known in my life. They
formed a socialist bund, meeting every night (often at our house) to debate
the hot issues of the day. These discussions were always heated and emotional with a lot of yelling, but never to the point of fisticuffs.

I remember a particularly vehement argument one night when I was about
eight years old. I woke up the next morning and asked Papa, "Why do y'all
scream and yell so loudly? Why do you argue so much?"

Papa answered me in Yiddish: "Bloz twischen ses still," which translated
to English means, "Only among thieves is everything quiet."

Ever since then I have understood that intellectual discussion fired with
deep passion is good for the mind.

> Mr. Rapoport was a very emotional person. I can tell you that
> there was a lot of yelling in that house. —*Fred Schmidt*

> When I was in England I met a woman there. We were stu-
> dents together. We immediately had an affinity for each other
> because we found out that when we were little girls and had

dolls, our dolls did not go to parties. Our dolls went to political meetings. So political activity, community involvement, contributing to the world—I mean Bernard and I got that with mother's milk. I just do not remember a time that my parents were not having meetings at the house, were not involved in discussing the world situation, and what to do about this or what to do about that. —*Idel Rapoport McLanathan*

Sacco and Vanzetti and Shock Waves from Moscow

Growing up in such a politically charged environment, I cannot remember a time when I have not had an interest in politics and public affairs. During my early childhood in the 1920s there were countless political events large and small that generated intense discussion in our home, but the one event that I can remember having the most distressing effect on my family was the Sacco and Vanzetti affair.

Papa followed the tribulations of Nicola Sacco and Bartolomeo Vanzetti so closely you would have thought he was the one on trial. Of course, in that case he had every reason to feel a personal connection. Nicola Sacco and Bartolomeo Vanzetti were Italian immigrants and anarchists who were tried and convicted of the murder of two men during a robbery in Massachusetts in 1920. The controversial trial and the appeals that followed generated massive international interest. Their trial made a mockery of the American judicial system, and the prosecution turned it into an anti-immigrant and anti-leftist Inquisition. Having little evidence to connect Sacco and Vanzetti to the crime, the prosecutor systematically exploited their alien status, their poor knowledge of English, their unpopular political views, and their opposition to U.S. participation in World War I in his successful effort to convict them.

Papa felt that the prosecution's attack on Sacco and Vanzetti was an attack on himself, his radical friends, and any American who shared their immigrant, pacifist, and radical backgrounds. And he was right. The more I learned about the case while I was at the university, the more I understood how my father could feel so threatened by that affair. One of the vivid memories of my childhood was the night of August 22, 1927, when Sacco and Vanzetti died in the electric chair. It was just like members of my family had passed away.

The year 1927 was a deeply traumatic one for Papa in a political sense. The execution of Sacco and Vanzetti in August was followed in November by Joseph Stalin's expulsion of Leon Trotsky and Grigory Zinoviev from the Communist Party of the Soviet Union. To my father, Trotsky and Zinoviev had been heroes of the Bolshevik Revolution and the terrible civil war that followed, but now the Communist Party was saying that these heroic leaders actually were despicable counterrevolutionaries.

Until the late 1920s, my father, although never a member of the Communist Party of the USA, had been among those socialists who believed that the Soviet Union was in the vanguard of the historical process moving humanity toward the socialist utopia. The expulsions of Trotsky and Zinoviev, which were followed by the purge of several other old Bolsheviks, stunned my father and precipitated intense and emotional debates within his little circle of Jewish radicals. I believe that my father's disenchantment with Soviet Communism began with the purge of Trotsky. Unlike many radicals in the United States whose politics became more extreme after the Sacco and Vanzetti affair, Papa's views moderated. He became an evolutionary socialist instead of a revolutionary. But that transformation had nothing to do with the Sacco and Vanzetti affair. It resulted from the disheartening events in his native Russia.

Papa supported American Socialist Party candidate Norman M. Thomas for president in 1928. Thomas was a former Presbyterian minister who had succeeded Eugene V. Debs as the leader of the Socialist Party. My father was head of San Antonio's tiny Socialist Party in 1928, and he worked hard for Thomas's presidential candidacy. The 1928 presidential campaign was the first political campaign that I can remember well. Of course, Democrat Al Smith and Republican Herbert Hoover were the major candidates that year, and Thomas had no chance of winning, but that made no difference to Papa. He was accustomed to supporting losing political candidates as well as hopeless causes. When Thomas came to San Antonio during the campaign, he stayed at our house, a memorable event for my family. He and Papa discussed politics until late that night.

Norman Thomas was a civil libertarian (he helped found the American Civil Liberties Union) and pacifist who espoused a moderate, non-Marxist brand of socialism. In the late 1920s and early 1930s, Papa was not yet ready to jettison his Marxist view of the world, but he was strongly attracted to many of the ideas that Norman Thomas promoted. He again supported Thomas when he ran for the presidency in 1932. When Franklin Roosevelt launched all those wonderful New Deal programs that borrowed many of Norman Thomas's basic ideas, I asked Papa if he was sorry for not voting for Roosevelt in 1932. I have always remembered his answer to my question: "Son, if people like me hadn't voted and worked for Norman Thomas and put pressure on Mr. Roosevelt, he wouldn't be doing the things he's doing now." As I have gotten older and suffered through so many seemingly lost causes, that statement of Papa's has given me hope that it is not all in vain.

> Mr. Rapoport always thought that President Roosevelt had stolen the Socialist Party platform, all the things that the Socialists had talked about since the days when Eugene Debs had first run for president: unemployment insurance, work relief, and things of this kind. He sort of disliked him for that reason. It ruined Mr. Rapoport's revolution. —*Fred Schmidt*

In the mid 1930s, when Papa learned of Stalin's murderous purges, his doubts about communism turned into total disillusionment. He understood then that Stalin and his henchmen were the worst kind of barbarians. To some extent, I feel that Papa lost interest in life when that happened. The 1935 Moscow show trials and subsequent executions broke up his band of Jewish radicals. It just took the revolutionary spirit out of them. They continued to visit socially, but they quit having those lively, noisy, emotional, political discussions that so often had kept me awake at night. I think that Mr. Stalin killed a lot more people than the records will ever show. He killed the hopes of millions of people all over the world when he proved to be the murderer that he was. At the same time that this political disillusionment took hold in the late 1930s, Papa's old comrades started dying off. Their circle got smaller and smaller, and my father got lonelier and lonelier.

Surviving the Depression

The tough times caused by the economic depression of the 1930s are etched deeply in my memory. About a year and a half before the stock market crash of 1929, Papa gave up his peddler's business and took a job as an agent for an insurance company called Texas Life. Like all of the other children in school, I had to write on my enrollment form at the start of the year what my father did for a living. It was a big thrill for me when I could say that Papa was an insurance salesman rather than a pushcart peddler.

Papa sold low-cost, small-payoff life insurance. By the time the Depression fell on us, Papa could afford a car that he drove around selling these insurance policies. I sometimes rode in the car with him just to keep him company. Papa's sales fell to nothing during the early days of the Depression, and his clients could not pay him the money they owed. He in turn was unable to pay the people he owed.

> Mr. Rapoport worked all of the time. By the time I knew him, he had given up the pushcart that he had when he first came to this country and was in the insurance business. He had a little office in downtown San Antonio. The kind of insurance he sold was very common in those days. It was 25 cents down and 25 cents a week. He would go around collecting the 25 cents. It was real small stuff, and he was doing it largely on the West Side of San Antonio among lower income groups.
> — *Fred Schmidt*

I found out years later that Papa carried the payments for some of his clients when the economy hit bottom so that their policies wouldn't lapse. He was helping his friends even though we had so much trouble paying our own bills that it seemed as though the utilities were cut off at our house as often as they were on. I remember the sharp embarrassment that it caused me more than anything else. Whenever one of my friends asked to use our telephone, I would tell him to wait until I looked into something. Then I would slink over to the telephone to check if the line was dead. If it was, I made up some story about why the telephone was unavailable. Of course, it was even more embarrassing when friends visited and the lights wouldn't go on when they flicked a wall switch. There was no way to hide the darkness.

That is what I remember the most about the Depression, the embarrassment that it caused me as a child.

> The family was poor and Mr. Rapoport was very tight with what little money he did have. Barney and his sister had no toys, nothing like that. Mr. Rapoport had no time for frivolities. There was no such thing as going out on a family picnic or going to a show together. — *Fred Schmidt*

> There was so little money in our family, Mama would have to save for a year or two to buy one of us something. I still remember the day that my brother came home on the trolley carrying a new scooter. Mother had it put in layaway at the store and then saved for months to pay for it. I remember this was the grandest thing I had ever seen in my life. That was really a high holiday in our house. That is the kind of thing Papa never did. — *Idel McLanathan*

Although there wasn't much that I could do as a child to help out the family in the financial sense, I did work part-time jobs to bring in a little extra money. I was ten or eleven years old when I got my first job selling *Liberty* magazines. Later on, the man who owned the grocery store up on the corner hired me to distribute advertising circulars. He gave me 25 cents a day to deliver them to the front door of the houses in the neighborhood.

One time I was delivering the circulars and I got bored with the job, so I decided that no one would know if I didn't deliver all of them that day. I threw a batch of them in the creek close to our house, returned to the store, and got my quarter from the owner. I don't recall how, but Papa found out about it. He was absolutely furious. He told me that I had cheated the store owner and that I had committed a terrible sin. What was the sin? I had agreed to do a job for someone and I had not done it as well as I knew how. That simply was unacceptable to my father. He made me take the quarter back. I was deeply humiliated and ashamed. It took some time before I could look him in the eye again without feeling bad about what I had done, but that was a good experience because it taught me a lesson that has stayed with me all of my life.

I honestly don't know how people kept body and soul together during the worst part of the Depression. Somehow, Papa managed to bring home two or three dollars a day, and in those days two or three dollars was a lot of money, so we were able to live. Although the food wasn't bountiful, we had enough to eat. We didn't live well, obviously, but although we were poor financially, we were rich culturally. My parents had a wonderful collection of records that we loved to play on an old Victrola that we had to wind by hand. There was a supply of recordings of great symphonies and operas. We had a deeply cultural home, and in some important ways that alleviated the problems resulting from our lack of material things.

> They lived in a little bungalow of a house. It had a front bed-room and a little living room and dining room. Mr. Rapoport had turned the other bedroom into a study, and under the locked bookcase he had all of his books in Russian. In back, they had a porch where Barney slept. I spent a lot of time sleeping there, too. His sister, Idel, had a little cubicle also in the back of the house. There were no frills. They had linoleum floor coverings, no carpet, and no finery. — *Fred Schmidt*

The most important element in our cultural and intellectual lives was our reading. Throughout my life, Papa constantly admonished me always to protect my good name, always to maintain a sense of outrage at injustice, and never to be without a book in my hands. To him it was a crime not to read a book every day. My father had one of the brightest minds that I've ever been around. He had a tremendous library from which we read Tolstoy, Turgenev, Dostoyevsky, and Pushkin. By the time I was fourteen, I had read all of the Russian masters. Then, of course, we had the writings of the communist theoreticians, including Bukharin and Sorel, as well as the works of other revolutionary writers. They all played a prominent role in our library because Papa remained a political radical for most of my early childhood years, and they were the philosophical base of his worldview.

> **Books really were the center of the Rapoport household. Books were shelved and even piled all over the place. Mr. Rapoport was a very literate man who read everything that he could get his hands on.** — *Fred Schmidt*

Not all of our reading was serious. I have special memories of the fun I had reading A. Conan Doyle's Sherlock Holmes stories. We also were avid newspaper readers. There were three newspapers published daily in San Antonio when I was young, and we read them all. We also subscribed to three weekly Jewish newspapers: the right-wing *Tag* (for my grandmother), the socialist *Jewish Daily Forward,* and the leftist *Freiheit.* All three came to our house on a regular basis, so our family always knew what was going on in the Jewish community in the United States and throughout the world.

Maverick

Mama and Papa also were well aware of the issues and problems in San Antonio, but they did not participate in local election campaigns because they didn't think their views would be taken seriously. One exception, however, was when Maury Maverick, Sr., ran for Congress from San Antonio in 1934. Maverick was a descendant of Samuel A. Maverick, the Texas pioneer whose habit of letting his unbranded calves wander loose gave the English language the word "maverick," a popular term for a person who refuses to follow the pack.

Maury Maverick certainly lived up to his name. He was an outspoken liberal who thoroughly enjoyed his role as an agitator and dissident. In Congress, Maverick was the only Southerner to support the federal antilynching bill. He was one of the most progressive men ever to have served in the Texas delegation in Congress. In my opinion, Maverick was one of the great men in Texas, one of the most unappreciated public servants in Texas history.

Despite being a Democrat and not a Socialist, Maverick was Papa's kind of man. Not only did Papa support Maverick but he also worked hard for his election. Papa had influence in some of the Mexican neighborhoods. The people who lived there were his friends because they were the people he dealt with in his blanket and insurance business. I remember Papa walking up and down the streets on the west side of town handing out Maverick bumper stickers and pins, knocking on doors to talk to his Mexican-American friends about voting for Maverick. In those days it was common practice in San Antonio for politicians to buy the votes of these poor people. They would give Mexican voters a dollar bill with a slip of paper listing the name of the candidate for whom they were supposed to vote. Papa pleaded with his Mexican friends not to sell their votes.

Papa helped Maury Maverick in every one of his campaigns for Congress; he won in 1934 and 1936 but lost in 1938. Maury was the first professional politician that I ever met, and he was the first political leader to pay any attention to my mother and father. While he was still in Congress, Maury visited me in Austin, where I was going to college. As a courtesy to Mama and Papa, he came to the jewelry store where I worked to see how I was doing. Later that evening I met him for dinner at the Stephen F. Austin Hotel on Congress Avenue. Maury bought me the first charcoal-broiled steak dinner I ever had. I can still see that steak sizzling on the platter. I didn't think there was anything in this world that could taste that good. He was exceedingly kind to me and my family, and I never forgot it. His son, Maury Junior, later became a close friend and political comrade of mine.

The Accident

I was lucky to have some gifted and caring teachers at almost every level of my schooling in the San Antonio public schools: Beacon Hill Grammar School, Mark Twain Junior High School, and Thomas Jefferson High School. I don't remember much about my elementary schoolteachers except that they were good. At Mark Twain Junior High, Mrs. Byers, my Latin teacher, and Helen Upshulte, my social studies teacher, were tremendous influences on me. Miss Upshulte was the first really pretty teacher I ever had, and since I was about thirteen or so, that made an impression on me. She and Mrs. Byers both gave me special attention, and they made me more of a social animal than I had ever been before. They realized that I was a little bit backward in the social amenities, and they helped draw me out of my shyness. Mrs. Byers chose me for the class play, which was my debut as well as my finale as an actor. Although acting wasn't my forte, the experience helped me to develop some social skills.

My socialization was slowed, however, by a traumatic incident that occurred when I was in the ninth grade. Like most kids in the 1920s and 1930s, I was crazy about major-league baseball. I followed the team standings and read the box scores of games in the sports pages every morning. The most memorable baseball season for me was 1930, largely for a reason having nothing to do with the pennant races or the World Series.

In 1930 the St. Louis Cardinals won the National League championship by two games over the Chicago Cubs. Connie Mack's awesome Philadelphia Athletics easily won the American League title. That was a great season. The Cubs' Hack Wilson hit 56 home runs, and the New York Giants' Bill Terry won the batting championship with a .401 average. The World Series that October was the most anticipated event in my thirteen-year-old life. The Cardinals, featuring such baseball luminaries as infielder Frankie Frisch (the Fordham Flash) and pitcher Wild Bill Hallahan, were facing a tough Philadelphia team led by pitcher Lefty Grove, catcher Mickey Cochrane, and outfielder Al Simmons—each one destined for the Hall of Fame.

Happily for me, the series was broadcast over the radio in San Antonio. In those days the games were played during the daylight hours only, which meant that I had to get home as quickly as possible after school to catch the last few innings. I heard the end of the opening game on October 1, which Philadelphia won 5 to 2.

The second game, however, was played on October 2, which happened to be Yom Kippur. Because of this important Jewish holy day, I was allowed to miss a day of school to attend synagogue observances. That also made it possible for me to get home earlier than usual and hear the game. After the services that afternoon, I rushed from the synagogue and jumped on the city bus that went by our house on West Woodlawn. When the bus stopped at my house, I was so eager to get to the radio that I dashed into the street without looking for oncoming cars. When I got about six feet from the curb in front of my house, a car hit me. The force of the car's impact tossed me into the air, and I landed on the street pavement bruised, bloody, and unconscious. The driver was an eighteen-year-old kid named Elliott Hovel. He tried to avoid me, but I ran out in front of him too suddenly. After striking me, Hovel's car swerved into our front yard and knocked down a tree. He must have been speeding, because the police arrested him on the charge of aggravated assault with an automobile. I don't know what happened to him after that.

Some of the neighbors ran out and picked me up off the street. I regained consciousness as they carried me into the bedroom of my house. I vividly remember the excruciating pain in my right leg and the profuse bleeding from my other leg. Mama was by my side crying her head off. I don't know how Mama lived through it. She was crying so much while we were in the ambulance on the way to the hospital that I told her jokes to make her feel better, even though I was in a lot of pain. At the hospital, the ambulance driver told a reporter about my attempts to cheer up Mama. The next day the headline on the news story in the *San Antonio Light* declared, "Boy Victim Jokes for Mother."

The ambulance took me to Central Clinic on St. Mary's Street. I received very poor medical treatment there because my family had no money. Dr. Paschal, the attending physician, was not an orthopedic specialist. Actually, I don't think he was much of a doctor for any purpose. I later learned that his main business was conducting examinations for insurance injury claims. This doctor mishandled my case rather badly. He wrapped adhesive tape around my legs, which did me no good. A few weeks later, when I tried to stand up for the first time by using my crutches, the bone in my leg shifted at the point where the break had occurred. The pain was incredible. That really set me back.

> My brother's accident was a really critical event in our family. Although he was in great pain, his main concern was for Mama. He didn't want her to be so frightened. We had a doctor who really did not take care of him. The whole terrible thing seemed to go on forever. But I'll never forget that one of the first things he said after he woke up and realized what had happened was that his career was lost. He meant that he would be a year behind in school and that might somehow keep him out of college. He said nothing about how it would affect his playing with the other boys or anything like that. He was only thirteen. I mean, he always had this seriousness about him. I was terrified for him. *— Idel McLanathan*

Frustrated by Dr. Paschal's incompetence, Mama somehow persuaded an outstanding physician, Peter McCall Keating, to take my case. Dr. Keating treated my injury properly. He moved me to Santa Rosa Hospital, which was a better medical facility, and then he put metal tongs in my leg to keep the bone sections together and placed weights on my feet to hold my legs steady in bed. Within two days I could feel the improvement, although I remained bedridden.

Because of the mishandling of my broken leg initially, the recovery took several months. I was forced to stay in bed until December, and I was unable to return to school until April 1931. Mother had a wonderful tutor named Miss Easterling come to the house, and she helped me keep up with my classmates in school. I was always a pretty good student, so I really didn't have much trouble with my lessons, but it was difficult being in bed for more than two months. I remember waking up every morning at about 5:30 and just lying there waiting to read the newspaper. I missed my friends and the social contacts that a kid needs. It was so frustrating, because I could hear children laughing and playing outside while I was in bed. Fortunately, I had some good friends whom Mama invited over every Saturday and Sunday to have lunch and visit with me. We had a big dining-room table where I played board games and card games with them. It was frustrating for a teenage boy, of course, but thanks to Mother, I never felt lonely.

When I was ready to get back on my feet, Dr. Keating put a leather and metal brace on my leg to provide the necessary support to allow the bone to continue to heal properly. The brace was flexible enough to allow my leg to bend at the knee. It gave me mobility, made me feel much better, and allowed me to get back in school, where I quickly became known as Peg-leg Rapoport. That nickname sounds humorous now, but it was anything but funny to me at the time.

Dr. Keating did a magnificent job. Over the years, I have often wondered if Mama and Papa ever paid him. If they did, I don't know how. My leg injury was such an ordeal that sixty-five years later I can still mentally feel the pain from that broken bone. As a result of the accident, my right leg is an inch and a quarter shorter than the left.

That accident did two good things that have stayed with me all my life. When I finally recovered, Mama got me a tennis racket so that I could play a noncontact sport. I learned to play tennis, a sport I love and still play daily. I have gotten much enjoyment as well as exercise from my tennis playing, but I doubt that I would have learned the game otherwise. More important, however, the accident taught me at an early age just how precious and precarious life really is.

High School Days: Fred Schmidt and Pecan Shellers

The truly meaningful friendships that I had during my high school years were with two boys, Louis J. Manhoff Jr. and Fred Schmidt. I had known Junior Manhoff since elementary school. We were inseparable. We played together every day, and we just had an existential kind of love for one another. His personality at that age was pretty much like mine: quiet, shy, and serious. He was a brilliant physical scientist in high school, and he eventually became a very fine medical doctor in San Antonio.

Fred Schmidt came out of a childhood that was not as happy as mine, so I felt like he needed our family. Because the need was there, it created a special kind of closeness enhanced by mutual respect and compatibility.

> I met Barney in Thomas Jefferson High School in San Antonio in 1933. I don't remember how we met. It just seems like we've always been together. But Barney befriended me. I didn't have any parents, and I was living alone in high school. Barney and I spent a lot of time together. I hung around his house a lot. He taught me to play chess and things like that. His mother was a saint. I'd go over to his house for a hot meal. Mrs. Rapoport was always putting an extra plate down when I was around the house. —*Fred Schmidt*

> Fred Schmidt was one of Mama's boys. His mother had died and his older sister was taking care of him. —*Idel McLanathan*

Fred planned to be a Presbyterian minister after college. I went to church with him on Sunday mornings several times. He would take me up to his minister after the services and we would talk about religion. Fred worked hard to win me over to Christianity, and he actually had me on the brink of converting at one point. I kept a diary during my late teenage years. When I read it recently for the first time in decades, I found this entry from June 1936: "Fred inspires me to such clean thoughts. He tries awful hard to make me religious but I don't believe he ever will."

Papa had the Marxist view of religion as "the opiate of the masses," so he didn't look on my churchgoing with any satisfaction. Mama was much more of a spiritual person, however, and she wanted her children to be exposed to various religions. She was very broad-minded about things like that.

> I was very much involved in the Presbyterian church in high school. I belonged to the young people's group that met every Sunday at our church. I tried to proselytize Barney. He chides me about that to this day, and he likes to remind me about how when we were on the debating team I would sometimes say, "Well, let's stop and hold hands and pray before we go into this debate." That's how fervid I was. —*Fred Schmidt*

I didn't realize until many years later, however, that the religious education was not all going in one direction. Fred learned as much from me about Judaism as I did about Christianity from him.

> I celebrated all of the religious holidays with the Rapoports, and I learned a lot about their culture. I don't know that they went to temple. It was more of an observance of the High Holy Days and the cultural side of Judaism. And the food—you know, the matzo balls, the beet soup or borscht—I ate a lot of that. —*Fred Schmidt*

After Mama and Papa, Fred Schmidt probably was the most important single influence on my life. He was one of the few people that I knew in high school who thought deeply. Fred was the kind of guy who would challenge my mind with provocative or difficult ideas. In that way, he was a profound influence on me intellectually. I believe that my parents and I served as the same kind of catalyst for him. Fred was very liberally inclined in political terms, and he enjoyed hearing Papa's radical views.

> Barney took me to the Socialist Party meetings in San Antonio —this was right in the depths of the Depression in 1933 and 1934—and introduced me to a lot of radical thoughts. That was pretty amazing actually, because Jefferson High School at that time had a lot of rich kids, not many minority students and not many poor kids, because it was the North Side of San Antonio. The poorer kids went to Breckenridge High School or to the trade school or Catholic high school. Jefferson was not the place where one would expect to find anyone with thoughts even resembling socialism, and here was this shy Jewish high school kid with all of these Socialist connections. —*Fred Schmidt*

One of our high school social studies teachers also served as a significant influence on my political and intellectual development. Her name was Olga Vogel. She was the person who introduced me to the modern American liberal thinkers, especially Thorstein Veblen, whose ideas have had a profound influence on my life (but more about that later). Miss Vogel, who taught me during my junior year, was one of the most dedicated and gifted teachers I have ever known. She often had Fred and me over to her house in the afternoons after school to discuss the social and political issues of the day.

Miss Vogel was very liberal politically, and she encouraged us to look at the social and economic injustices in our own back yard. One of the worst cases of labor exploitation in the United States existed in pecan-shelling workshops in my old neighborhood on the West Side of San Antonio, where most of the city's poor Mexican Americans resided. I went with Miss Vogel to look at working conditions in the shops. The owners of the pecan companies brought pecans to shops where groups of poor Mexican families would assemble to crack and remove the shells so the insides could be used commercially. I saw whole families—mother and father, grandparents and children—sitting for long hours on hard benches in hot and filthy work sheds diligently shelling pecans for pennies a day. A large number of children had to work in these factories instead of going to school. Even with the entire family working, they couldn't make enough money to lift them out of the bottom rank of poverty.

Papa's lecturing about capitalist exploitation of labor was one thing, but this was the first time that I had seen it with my own eyes and recognized it as such. Miss Vogel persuaded me to write a term paper about the pecan shellers, and the assignment became the first time that I had ever seriously analyzed economic and social injustice based on personal observation.

In 1938 the pecan shellers finally went on strike and shut down 130 of the pecan shops, sending shock waves through San Antonio's conservative business establishment. The strike leader was a fiery young Mexican-American woman named Emma Tenayuca, who earned from admiring workers the title "La Pasionaria de Texas." Tenayuca was a hardworking and dedicated labor organizer. She also was a Communist whose involvement in the strike made headlines across the country. By the time of the strike, I was away at the University of Texas, but I paid close attention to the event.

I knew Emma, although not well. She had been a member of the student debate team at San Antonio's Breckenridge High when I was at Jefferson. Fred Schmidt and I were on Jefferson's debate team, and I remember that Emma had been a tough opponent in our debate contests against Breckenridge. Ironically, the debate issue that year was whether the electric light and power industry should be owned by the government. It was ironic because Emma had to take the negative side in the debate, and she and her partner really stuck it to us. I remember that we had a hard debate, but after all these years I can't remember who won. My guess is that Emma's team beat us, because I wasn't a good debater. I do remember, however, that Emma was as pretty as she was tough. Fred and I liked her.

I was delighted when Emma and the pecan shellers won a few concessions to end the strike in March 1938. The victory proved to be a hollow one, however. The labor problems persuaded the pecan owners to replace the workers with shelling machines. Of course, mechanization (later called "automation") would ultimately do grave damage to the entire labor movement. Emma continued her work as a labor organizer and Communist Party activist. She was married at one time to Homer Brooks, the head of the Communist Party in Texas. I lost track of Emma for many years, but I understand that she renounced communism and retired as a labor organizer. She died in San Antonio in 1999.

Although I was not the best of debaters, that was no fault of our coach, E. C. Barksdale, another wonderful teacher. Barksdale later became a history professor at Arlington State University (now the University of Texas at Arlington). He did more than just teach us to debate; he made us understand what the subject matter was all about. This man would spend hours and hours after school with Fred and me. He was so good that we somehow made it all the way to the semifinals in the state championship in Fort Worth, where we won a silver cup. Barksdale was one of those guys who would tear a little piece of his gut out and give it to you. I'm sure that anybody who had contact with him feels the same way I do. He just stands out in my mind.

I had some excellent teachers, such as Olga Vogel and E. C. Barksdale, but I didn't have a lot of fun in high school as far as my social life was concerned. I had a few dates, but I never was a man about town. For one thing, I never had any money to spend on girls. And I didn't know how to dance because that was considered to be a lot of foolishness around our house. I had fewer dates than most young people had during those times.

> Barney and I didn't go to the dances. We didn't have a car. We didn't have any spending money. That left us out of the social and athletic activities of high school. — *Fred Schmidt*

I've always been too serious, and it's because of the circumstances in which I grew up. Papa had no sense of humor. There was virtually no levity with him; everything was extremely serious. I never read the funny pages in the newspaper because I knew that Papa disapproved. I did read the sports pages, but never when Papa was around. He felt that it was a big waste of time. Papa frequently warned me that there is no time tomorrow to get anything done, you have to get it done today — and he lived his life that way. Papa regularly left the house by four-thirty in the morning for work, and he wouldn't get home until eight or nine at night. Among my most enduring memories are the many telephone calls over the years that I received from Papa at 5 A.M. I would be jolted awake by the ringing of the telephone, and when I mumbled hello, Papa would demand to know what I was doing.

"Papa, I was sleeping," I would answer, knowing full well what was coming next.

"Son, do you want to be a bum *all* of your life? Get out of bed and start reading a book right now!"

It is a joke with my husband. I still get up most mornings around four o'clock, and he will ask, "Why are you getting up?" Then as a joke I will say, "Because I have not accomplished anything yet today," but it is not exactly a joke. I mean, it was very important to my father that I did something constructive, and this was just part of what a person does. —*Idel McLanathan*

Barney's father wasn't very communicative. He had a scowl on his face all of the time. He was tough. I can remember one time when Mr. Rapoport's car battery had gone dead. What you did with batteries in those days was put them at a filling station and recharge them. It would take two or three days, and it was 10 cents a day. Mr. Rapoport got in a huge argument with the filling station attendant when he picked up his battery, arguing about whether it was three days or four days. They had this big battle over 10 cents, and I think Mr. Rapoport won that argument. He was extremely forceful on things like that. —*Fred Schmidt*

Bottle Washer for the NYA

I graduated from high school in 1935 in the top 1 percent of my class and as a member of the National Honor Society. My election to the National Honor Society was my first meaningful recognition. I was always an especially good student, but I don't really deserve a lot of credit for that. My family background compelled me to be a good student. My parents had a deep commitment to education, and good grades were just all-important. Mama always told me I was the smartest boy in the world, so I had self-confidence in the classroom at an early age.

One thing about the old immigrants (or greenhorns, as people like my parents were called back then), they lived their lives through their children. Maybe they did it to a fault, but that was the way they lived. Their children's success was almost the only personal satisfaction they could enjoy. In conversations with her friends, all Mama would talk about was my sister and myself. We were her entire life. Idel and I loved her dearly. This passage in my diary from May 1936 (I was eighteen years old) tells all you need to know about my feelings for Mama: "Today is Mother's Day. OK God, you blessed me with an angel. I love her better than life itself."

Idel eventually became a professor of psychology at St. Mary's University in San Antonio, where she taught until her retirement in 1984. In Mama's later years, whenever she was asked about her children, she would always say proudly, in a clear and strong voice, "My daughter, she's a professor." Then, in a muted tone, she would say, "My son, he has an insurance company," adding in her louder voice, "but he's a very learned boy!" I came out of an atmosphere that told me that education was the only thing that counted.

Because of my family's obsession with education, it was just as natural for me to go to college as it was to sit down and have breakfast in the morning. Almost from the day I was born, I knew I was going to college. That's all Mama and Papa talked about when they discussed my future. There was never any discussion of "if" I was going; it was always "when." The problem, however, was money—our lack of it. There was a will to go to college, but there was no obviously apparent way.

I don't remember the details now, but in those days a member of the National Honor Society automatically received a book and tuition scholarship to Drake University in Iowa. I couldn't accept it, however, because I didn't even have the money to travel up there, much less pay for my room and board. Truthfully, the Drake scholarship didn't appeal to me anyway, because I had a deep yearning to go to the University of Texas in Austin. My family's financial difficulties meant that I would have to work at a night job in Austin to pay my way through college. Unfortunately, jobs—even part-time positions—were scarce. I failed to find work in Austin. I had better luck in San Antonio, where I discovered that the National Youth Administration (NYA), one of Roosevelt's New Deal agencies, would pay me 25 cents an hour to wash chemistry bottles if I enrolled in San Antonio Junior College. Postponing my dream of going to the University of Texas at least for one year, I accepted the NYA job and registered for classes at San Antonio Junior College.

My friend Fred Schmidt was more successful. He received a full scholarship to study for the ministry at Austin College, a small private denominational school in the north Texas town of Sherman. While he was away, we kept up a correspondence in which he would argue for a kind of Christian liberalism while I continued to proselytize for my rather confused version of noncommunist Marxism. I have often said that I won that intellectual battle, but that really isn't true. Through his own intellectual development, Fred dropped his Christian advocacy and became a Marxist. It caused him to leave Austin College after one year to enroll at the University of Texas. In some ways, Fred became more radical than I was.

To me, San Antonio Junior College was really a glorified high school. I resented having to spend a year there, but there was nothing I could do about it. My job as a bottle washer added to my unhappiness. It was tough because I had to wash some harsh and corrosive chemicals out of the glass tubes and bottles. None of us wore gloves while we worked, and the chemicals irritated our hands so severely that the skin often blistered and peeled off.

A Devout Communist

The year I spent at San Antonio Junior College was not a complete waste of time. I met a brilliant young Jewish political activist there by the name of Nathan Kleban, who challenged me to examine my political views in more depth than I ever had before. When I first met him in April 1936, Nathan had decided to become a member of the Communist Party of the USA. He and I spent many hours discussing the merits of communism and the evils of capitalism. Although I had long thought of myself as a noncommunist Marxist, my discussions with Nathan caused me to look more favorably on communism. Because of Nathan, who was more radical than any of my other friends in those days, I experienced a period of intense self-examination and some inner confusion about the nature of my worldview. My diary entries from that spring and summer reveal the intellectual turmoil I was experiencing:

> [APRIL 26] Met Nathan Kleban. He's an atheist and a communist. I don't know what I am. I wish I did. This mental frame of mine is terrible and I hate it.
> [JUNE 16] Nathan Kleban came over. We talked about Communism. I believe Communism has good ideals. I don't know of the practicality of it. I'm not going to say what I am until I have definitely made up my mind. Kleban [is] a brilliant boy; I would like to know him better. He's like [Fred] Schmidt except he's on the other side.
> [JULY 4] Today is Independence day. Nathan Kleban came over. I surely like to talk to him. My sympathies are more than ever with the working man but in a more practical way.
> [JULY 16] Nathan ate supper over here. I am beginning to get idealistically communistic. I would like to join the party. It is the only sensible plan, a plan which protects all the people. I believe it is far superior to any other system.
> [JULY 20] I am becoming more and more interested in Communism. I have to consider if the fact that the communists

advocate force and violence is enough to make me a socialist. That's a very serious question.

[JULY 24] I sure am interested in dialectic materialism. I believe I am a devout communist.

After I moved to Austin to go to the university in the fall of 1936, Nathan and I kept in touch. We got together whenever I made weekend visits back to San Antonio to see Mama and Papa. When I came home for the holidays in late December, Nathan told me that he had made a critical decision. He had taken a job as a labor organizer for the Communist Party, an action that had resulted in his breaking off relations with his parents. He was moving to Houston to organize dockworkers at the ports in Houston and Galveston. He urged me to do the same. I was stunned. I told Nathan that I was becoming "more and more communistic" and that I believed communism was "the only form of government that is desirable," but I could never break away from my family. I also wanted to stay in school.

Nathan moved to Houston, where he was known as Jeff Kleban. He became secretary of the Houston chapter of the Communist Party and served as its unofficial spokesman. In 1938 Nathan ran on the Communist Party ticket for attorney general of Texas. Emma Tenayuca was on that same Communist ticket as the candidate for Congress. I saw Nathan a couple of times after that, but we gradually lost touch with each other in the early 1940s, and I don't know what became of him. By then, however, I had lost my fervor for communism and for Marx, as had Fred Schmidt. As we became intellectually mature, we were better able to recognize the fallacies in Marxism. My intellectual growth, however, was the direct result of my exposure to some outstanding professors in the department of economics at the University of Texas.

As I have often stated, it was at the university that my life really began.

When My Life Began: The University Years

Morris Zale, one of the top retail jewelry entrepreneurs in the history of American business, made it possible for me to attend the University of Texas. In August 1936 he told my cousin Sol Kruger, who managed the newly opened Zales jewelry store at 619 Congress Avenue in downtown Austin, to give me a job. The income from that job would pay my living expenses, tuition, and books. When I heard this wonderful news I scribbled a hasty note in my diary on August 15, 1936: "Hooray and hallelujah! I have definitely got the job. It means my college education. Bernard, please, please make the most of it."

Morris Zale and I weren't blood relatives, but his family and my mother's family were very close. Morris's mother was Leeba Kruger, who was the sister of Sam Kruger, the husband of my aunt Fania. The Kruger and the Zale families had both immigrated to Texas from Shereshov, Ukraine, in the early 1900s. Morris and his brother William started a jewelry business in a drug store in Graham, Texas, in 1922. Two years later, Sam Kruger loaned Morris funds to open his first Zales jewelry store, which he located in Wichita Falls, the center of an oil-boom region awash in new money. He understood that the newly affluent would be eager to spend some of their money on luxury items such as jewelry. As a child, I got to know Morris well because Mama and I often visited his store during our frequent trips to Wichita Falls to see my aunt Fania.

After that humble beginning in Wichita Falls, Morris Zale eventually transformed the jewelry industry worldwide. From the start, Morris believed that selling jewelry could be a mass volume enterprise like clothing and groceries. Before Morris Zale came along, the jewelry industry had catered only to the wealthy. Sales were strictly on a cash basis. Morris decided to go against the grain. He made it easy for consumers to purchase his products on credit, which made quality jewelry available to the middle class. He also was a marketing innovator, pioneering the use of newspaper advertising to promote his jewelry business. That his company made a profit throughout the Depression selling diamond rings and gold watches was evidence enough of his entrepreneurial genius. The Zales corporation eventually expanded throughout the United States, with more than 1,500 stores, and it operated its own jewelry design and production shops.

To be honest, Morris was more interested in getting me involved in his jewelry business than he was in helping me go to the University of Texas. He was expanding his business, and he wanted the trusted members of his family and its kinship network in charge of as many stores as possible. Having quit school in the seventh grade, Morris at that time didn't see the value of a college education. He told me that I was wasting my time taking classes in history, literature, and economics. To Morris, all that effort in class just got in the way of the real education that I would get at his jewelry store. I ignored his advice, but I was thankful for the job.

So after attending classes at San Antonio Junior College for one year, I packed my clothes on Sunday morning, August 16, 1936, and moved away from home for the first time in my life. I recorded in my diary the mixed feelings I had about leaving the family nest: "Gosh it was hard leaving. I know everything is going to be perfect, that is if I make the best of everything. I must write mother every day."

Austin was only 75 miles north of San Antonio, but it seemed much farther to me the day that I kissed Mama good-bye and boarded the bus bound for the state capital.

Flunking German and Spiting Hitler

Soon after I arrived in Austin, I found a room to rent at Miss Brydson's rooming house at 1911 University Drive. To keep myself afloat financially, I had to work six days a week at Zales. I attended my classes in the morning from eight until eleven, and then I worked from eleven-thirty to seven every evening. I worked all day on Saturdays until nine-thirty. I went to the University of Texas for four years and never saw a football game because of my Saturday schedule. I learned early on that it wasn't a good idea for me to plan any social activities after work. For one thing, I really needed a few of those hours at night to study, but also I was usually so tired after work that I just didn't have the energy to go to parties.

I do remember going to one dance party in Gregory Gymnasium on a Friday night after I got off work. My date was a lovely girl named Minette Tobolowsky, who had come to the university from the little town of Alvarado, Texas. Minette and I weren't at the party for more than ten minutes before I got so sleepy that I couldn't keep my head up. I was completely exhausted. I excused myself for a few moments and walked outside to get some fresh air. Finding an unlocked car parked by the gym, I climbed into the back seat and fell fast asleep until the party was over. Minette was not pleased. I have to admit that I wasn't much of a partygoer. Parties, especially dances, still put me to sleep, but at least now I can sleep in my own car.

Don't try to find my picture in any of the old university yearbooks, the *Cactus.* It isn't there. The simple reason is that it cost too much. My salary at Zales was so low that I had no extra money for such frivolities. To save money, I usually skipped breakfast. I bought a toaster, and before I went to the store, I made two grilled cheese sandwiches for lunch. That saved me 15 or 20 cents, which I could then apply to dinner. Sometimes I splurged and spent 40 or 50 cents for dinner. This diary entry from October 1936 was typical of my financial plight: "I sure would like to have a date, but God, I am too broke. I don't know what I will do for food tomorrow. Well, anyways, I can always starve."

I wasn't actually in danger of starving, of course, but it was rough in those days for nearly everyone. Nevertheless, they were good days because I was young and the university was an exciting place. They really were the best days of my life.

The most disappointing result of my work schedule at Zales, however, was not its effect on my social life, it was the toll it took on my grades. I had graduated from high school with an A average, but at the university my grade average was never higher than a B. Not making all A's was a terrible blow to my fragile ego. I always made good grades in economics and government because I was particularly interested in those subjects, but my grades in the other courses were not good. I could not be the kind of student that I was capable of being because I simply did not have time to study as much as I needed, and I didn't care about my grades in subjects in which I had no interest. The former problem was beyond my control, but the latter was the result of my lack of intellectual discipline. I'm not proud of that part of my university life.

Naturally, I worried what my mother would think when I made bad grades. I desperately wanted to please her. But she was always supportive, never critical. I flunked German one semester when Adolf Hitler was dominating the newspaper headlines because of his anti-Jewish laws and the brutal pogroms his policies spawned. Mama, instead of being aggravated and chastising me about the failed grade, just smiled and said, "It just shows what a great son you are. You flunked German to spite Hitler." Here I was distraught because I had flunked the course, and she told me that it had been a political statement!

*B as a student at the University of Texas at Austin in
1938. CN 10754, Rapoport (Bernard) Photograph
Collection, Center for American History, The University
of Texas at Austin.*

After a few months at Zales I was earning enough money to allow me
to reduce my work hours, which would give me more time for study. My
sister's situation soon complicated matters, however. She had entered the
university in 1937 without adequate financial backing. Papa was so difficult
when it came to money, she could not expect any help from him. Without
my support, she could not stay in school. I really had to help her, so that
ended any thought of my getting more time off.

Because I had to work my way through school I was not able to take an
extra course or two or to read all of the books that I could have read otherwise. From that perspective, I don't believe that I got the full educational
benefit of my four years there. Nevertheless, as far as my intellectual development was concerned, my years at the University of Texas were the most
important of my life. It was there that I developed my capacity for open,
critical, and independent thinking. At the university I was exposed to some
truly gifted teachers and intellects who stimulated my interest in the world of
ideas and taught me to question conventional thinking. I went to the university without a developed sense of dignity; I left with an outstanding general

education and my self-esteem much enhanced. I don't think any Harvard student ever got a better education than I received in Austin.

During my time as a college student, I also developed a better sense of my own religious heritage, not in a mystical or spiritual way but in larger cultural terms. I had more Jewish friends at the university than back home in San Antonio, and although my work schedule interfered, I got involved in Jewish organizations on campus. In my junior year some of my friends and I formed a Jewish rooming cooperative called Esquire House, which was on Wichita Street, near campus. Esquire House provided affordable room and board for Jewish students who had little or no financial support from home. Fourteen or fifteen dollars a month was all a student needed for room and board. I moved into Esquire House and served as its president for one year. About eight or nine months after we opened Esquire House, a fellow who was gung ho on fraternities persuaded me to help him start a fraternity for poor Jewish students called Alpha Pi. I disliked the idea of fraternities, but I joined out of a sense of solidarity with my Jewish classmates who were as poor as I was. There were three or four Jewish fraternities already on campus, but they were for the rich kids.

I never ran for a student government office, but during my senior year, Sidney Reagan, the student body president, appointed me to a vacancy in the University Student Assembly. I have been told that I was the first Jewish member of the assembly. Reagan was a brilliant fellow who later became a professor in the business school at Southern Methodist University. My friends and I had supported him for president of the student body. I served in the assembly for one semester only. My work and class schedules were so full that I couldn't participate in the assembly as much as I should have.

My goal was to attend law school, so I entered the university as a prelaw major. Ever since I was a youngster, I had wanted to be a defense attorney. Many of the discussions at home when I was growing up revolved around some kind of legal injustice such as the Sacco and Vanzetti trial. I also admired Clarence Darrow and other lawyers who took unpopular cases or who defended the poor. I had visions of myself as a crusading lawyer like Darrow, using the courtroom as my political battlefield.

In those days a student had to take undergraduate courses for three years before he could enter law school. Most of my fellow prelaw students majored in history or government, but I quickly gravitated toward economics. In the 1930s, economics was more political science, philosophy, sociology, and history than it is today. The field had not yet been taken over by the quantifiers, who work more with numbers than with ideas. I think that if I were in college now, I would major in political science with a specialization in public policy. Today the field of economics is so burdened with mathematics that a person has to know calculus just to get through it all. When I was studying economics, there was no delineation between micro- and macroeconomics. The monetary theories of John Maynard Keynes were new. His most important book, *The General Theory of Employment, Interest, and Money*, was published my first year of college.

I have always thought that my decision to go into economics for my prelaw course work was one of the most fortunate of my life. At the time, the university's department of economics was widely acknowledged to be one of the top programs in the nation. Years after I left the university, famed economist John Kenneth Galbraith told me that it was not only the best in the entire country in the 1930s but also the most radical. I don't know if the department was the very best, and I'm not sure it was so radical, but I can say with certainty that it was outstanding and controversial. The Texas State Legislature spent an inordinate amount of its time and energy during the 1930s and 1940s trying to purge the department of some of its most politically active and influential members.

Dr. Bob, Clarence Ayres, and E. E. Hale

I had some excellent teachers and fascinating courses, including labor economics taught by Professor Ruth Allen and business economics taught by Dr. George Ward Stocking. The most exciting single class, however, was corporate finance, which I took during my first semester at the university. How could a subject called "corporate finance" be exciting? It was taught by Dr. Robert Montgomery, one of the university's most entertaining and spellbinding lecturers. Dr. Bob (as all of his students knew him) was a tireless and vocal advocate of municipal ownership of utilities. In the 1930s in Texas, calling for government ownership of almost anything other than the military or the mail was enough to get you labeled a wild-eyed radical. Montgomery was a real showman. His classes were always full of students eager to hear his evangelistic lectures about the evils of business monopoly and the sins of the Republican Party. Montgomery's favorite target in his antimonopoly lectures was the Texas sulfur industry, which had a well-earned reputation for buying influence in the Texas Legislature.

Dr. Bob was a scourge of the Texas business establishment. He also was a primary influence in the lives of a generation of students who later became leaders of the liberal wing of the Democratic Party in Texas, including political strategist and attorney Creekmore Fath, labor lawyers Chris Dixie and Otto Mullinax, and seven-term congressman Bob Eckhardt. I can still recall one of Montgomery's lectures in which he argued for a federal tax on the

*Dr. Bob Montgomery. CN 09039, UT Student
Publications, Inc., Center for American History, The
University of Texas at Austin.*

profits of monopolies at a rate "as close as possible to 100 percent," claiming
that such a confiscatory tax would stop monopolistic practices. "Remove
monopolies and we shall have a democracy again," Montgomery declared.
"We have none today!" I also remember a letter that circulated on campus
written by a senior partner of one of Houston's most powerful corporate
law firms that called Montgomery a "scatterbrained idiot" who was "fast
giving the University of Texas an evil reputation." Independent oilman J. R.
Parten, who was on the university board of regents when I was a student,
told me many years later that he spent much of his time as a regent fighting off attempts by his wealthy friends in Houston to fire Montgomery and
several of his colleagues in the economics department.

Another economics professor, Clarence Ayres, was also a powerful influence on my intellectual development. Ayres was more esoteric than Montgomery and less of an overt political activist. His reputation as a scholar was
stronger than Montgomery's, but that didn't keep Ayres from generating almost as much controversy as his more colorful colleague. What got Dr. Ayres
in trouble in Texas were his public speeches calling for the federal and state
governments to use the income tax as a tool to redistribute wealth. That got
Ayres a lot of attention from wealthy Texans, especially those in the oil in-

dustry. Texas had no state income tax then, and it has none today. Ayres had to fight off several attempts by legislators and regents to have him dismissed as a dangerous subversive for having the temerity to demand a state income tax. Ayres didn't shape me personally in the sense that one would ordinarily think, but later, when I was a graduate student, he introduced me to a new world of economic thought.

Allen, Stocking, Montgomery, and Ayres all influenced or inspired me in different ways, but the class that proved to be my most profound intellectual challenge and that has continued to shape my thinking to this day was Comparative Economic Systems. More important to me than the subject matter was the man who taught the course, Professor Edward Everett Hale, who became my intellectual mentor. During the years I was at the university, Hale was an evolutionary Marxist who rejected violent revolution. His Marxism was not political; it was a theoretical tool with which he critiqued and interpreted the economic world. I was strongly attracted to him as an intellectual because in those days I too was an evolutionary Marxist. His class thoroughly covered the ideas of the Utopians, Marx, and the classical economists and the neoclassicists.

> **We were both enamored of Professor E. E. Hale. To this day Barney thinks he was the finest professor he had at the university. Hale did not have a doctorate, but he was a well-organized instructor and he gave us tremendous readings. We read the original stuff that Marx and Lenin wrote and things like that, which were unusual for a UT class in those years.**
> — *Fred Schmidt*

I met Professor Hale in my sophomore year, and he became my academic advisor. He and I continued to have a close teacher-student relationship until I left graduate school three years later. He meant a great deal to me. I remember that my crowning achievement for that particular period was to arrange for him to buy a watch from Zales at wholesale price. Professor Hale mentioned to me one day that he had always wanted a Hamilton railroad watch (a large pocket watch) but that he couldn't afford one. Somehow I was able to persuade Morris Zale to break one of his strictest rules, which was never sell anything at discount to anyone. Getting that watch for Professor Hale at wholesale from Morris Zale was a major achievement.

Hale was not a spellbinding lecturer like Montgomery. Ayres may have been a more seminal thinker, but he was not the teacher that Hale was. Hale was more methodical and rigid in his requirements of his students. He really made us work. In one semester we had to write eight in-depth, lengthy, analytical papers; I recall one paper was on Adam Smith and another was on labor value. His three-hour course was equivalent to anybody else's nine hours. He was demanding, but when you completed one of his courses, you knew the subject extremely well. I always resented that Hale never got the credit that was due him.

Although Ayres and Montgomery are the ones who got all the headlines, Hale did not escape attacks by the reactionaries in the Legislature. He was calm and philosophical about it, however. One year when Hale was chairman, Eric Roll, a distinguished British scholar, served as a visiting professor in the department. A legislator called and asked Hale if he could assure the Legislature that Professor Roll, a British citizen, would be willing to sign a loyalty oath to the U.S. government! "No," Hale replied, "I don't believe I could." For Hale, that was the end of that—no explanations, no excuses, no histrionics, and no sermonizing. I admired his courage. He stressed to his students the importance of standing up for our beliefs, and he taught that by his own example.

Despite the attacks from the Legislature, Hale remained a theorist who had little interest in public issues. As a Marxist he didn't think that the American political arena really offered any hope, so he was not a political activist. Hale did not do a lot of writing or public speaking, so he was not in the public eye as much as some of his colleagues, but he was a superb teacher, and he remained a Marxist in intellectual terms. He and I spent many hours in his office in Garrison Hall discussing Marxist ideology, especially Marx's materialistic interpretation of history. Hale was the most didactic person I have ever known, and I don't mean that in the negative sense of being preachy. I mean that when I engaged in a conversation with him, I always learned something meaningful. He had a zest for knowledge. He never sought to convert his students to Marxism; he was too much of an intellectual and a traditional teacher for that.

Hale's only proselytizing was for the teaching profession, which he promoted to us as the most rewarding profession of all. I still think he's right about that. Because of Hale, I decided to become an economics professor instead of a lawyer. That decision was made easier by a discussion I had with Dean Ira Hildebrand of the university's law school when I was in the middle of my junior year. The junior year was when students had to submit their applications for law school, and a preapplication requirement was an interview with Dean Hildebrand. I was surprised when the dean recommended that I not go to law school. I was even more surprised when he told me why. He explained that with so many Jews coming out of law school and, he believed, so few Texas law firms willing to hire a Jewish lawyer, it would be difficult for me to find a job after graduation. The interesting thing is that I was not offended by Hildebrand's remarks. I felt that he liked me and that his advice was not malicious. Hildebrand was a decent man, and I do not believe that he was anti-Semitic in any way, shape, or form. I should emphasize that he did not say that I would not be allowed to enter the law school—it was clear that I could. He just felt that being Jewish, I would have a difficult time in my career. One of the reasons I didn't react badly to Hildebrand's advice was that Hale had been so persuasive about my going to graduate school that by this time I was really more interested in becoming a professor. I decided to enter graduate school as an economics major.

The Progressive Democrats of Texas

Before I entered graduate school, I became involved in a liberal political student organization called the Progressive Democrats, which was sponsored by Dr. Montgomery. My membership in the Progressive Democrats, which we called P.D.'s, brought me into contact with several students with whom I would be associated in politics and in public affairs for most of my life. It was an exciting organization because of the gifted individuals who were members, and it played a major role in shaping my political outlook. Among the friends that I made as a member of the P.D.'s were Clay Cochran and Creekmore Fath. I met Clay and Creekmore in Montgomery's class, and they brought me into the P.D.'s. In the years to come, Creekmore and I would work together on several political campaigns. Clay Cochran eventually became head of the Rural Housing Project in Washington. Clay and Creekmore were two of my best friends at the university. I owe them a great deal, because I was a lonely kid that first semester, and I didn't have the time to develop the kind of friendships that most students have. Those two made a special effort to be my friends, and they helped me make other friends.

This sounds a little imperious, and I don't mean it that way, but I've always been surrounded by intellectuals because they are the people I seek out. My associates at the university were serious thinking kids. I looked with disdain on the fraternity and sorority crowd. To be honest, I don't know if we were envious because they had so much and we didn't have anything. I just had no contact with members of fraternities or sororities. We didn't have anything in common, and I couldn't afford to go to the same places that they went.

The Progressive Democrats were a group of young socialists in the British Fabian mold—really just a small intellectual group with stimulating dialogue. It was not a debating society, and it had no stated objectives, but as a group, we all were concerned with social and economic justice. Franklin D. Roosevelt was our god, and whatever he wanted, we were in favor of it. We were big supporters of the second New Deal, which featured programs that were more liberal than those of the first New Deal. We took a special interest in the labor union movement, public ownership of utilities, and economic reforms such as a progressive tax system and monopoly regulation. Senator George Norris of Nebraska was one of our pet senators because he was the father of the Tennessee Valley Authority project.

I was deeply involved in the group and at one point served as the chairman of its executive committee. There were only about thirty members, but each one was a political activist. Dr. Montgomery often invited us out to his house, where we had intense discussions about how to solve all of society's problems. We came up with a number of solutions while we were all sitting around the circle at his house; however, when the door opened, somehow the problems did not get solved.

By the time I entered the university in 1936, several former members of the Progressive Democrats had graduated and were serving as labor lawyers in different areas of the state. In some ways, they served as our role models for what we would do after we got out into the world. Among the most prominent were Otto Mullinax in Dallas and Chris Dixie and Herman Wright in Houston. They all worshiped Dr. Montgomery, who brought them back to campus occasionally to meet with us and to discuss the problems the newly created CIO (Congress of Industrial Organizations) unions were having organizing workers in Texas. This was a time of much labor unrest, especially along the Texas Gulf Coast and in San Antonio, where the pecan shellers were trying to organize, so we were eager to hear from these legal activists.

A Theater of the Absurd

The Progressive Democrats got the university into a lot of trouble with the Texas Legislature. We were aided and abetted by the student newspaper, the *Daily Texan*, which did its share of rabble-rousing with editorials attacking individual legislators. During my first semester, the Progressive Democrats gave documents to the editor of the *Daily Texan* that he used for a series of articles and editorials attacking Roy Miller, the lobbyist for the powerful sulfur companies. The *Daily Texan* reported that Miller, whose official position with the Texas Gulf Sulphur Company was public relations director, had spent $173,000 for "publicity" in Austin during a previous legislative session. That was a staggering sum of money in those days.

Because there had been little evidence of Miller's publicity efforts, some of his critics charged that he had used the money to entertain and even bribe key members of the Legislature. We learned that Miller reserved entire floors of the Stephen F. Austin and the Driskill hotels. Any legislator could have a room and charge anything he wanted on Miller's tab.

A few weeks after the *Daily Texan*'s attack on Miller, the Progressive Democrats, led by my friend Creekmore Fath, organized a free dance at Gregory Gym officially dedicated to "A Higher Tax on Sulphur." A huge crowd of students showed up. When Roy Miller heard about the event the next morning he erupted with anger, immediately blaming his nemesis Dr. Montgomery, who had earlier pinned the title of "Sulfurcrat" on Miller. The lobbyist had frequently been the target of some of Montgomery's scathing speeches. Miller struck back during a special session of the Legislature in October by persuading a state representative named Joe Caldwell to call for an investigation of rumors that communism and atheism were being taught on the campuses of the state's universities.

Representative Caldwell introduced his resolution the day after the special session opened. The wording left little doubt that Caldwell's targets were Dr. Montgomery and those of us in the Progressive Democrats club. Caldwell claimed that he had "conclusive documentary proof" that at least one professor was teaching communism and that he had "gathered about him a group of young zealots who have pledged to devote their lives to the cause." The whole thing was absurd. Dr. Montgomery was a dyed-in-the-wool New Deal capitalist. He was no communist, and he was much more conservative than my mentor, E. E. Hale, who was a real Marxist.

The special committee opened its investigation on October 13, 1936. The first to testify were Montgomery and his former students Herman Wright and Otto Mullinax. When Montgomery appeared before the committee, Caldwell demanded to know if the professor favored "private profit." Montgomery smiled and replied, "So much that I'd like to see it extended to where 120 million people could have it." The audience roared with laughter.

I was able to get away from work and school long enough to attend the Friday evening session of the legislative hearing. The proceedings made quite an impression on me. The arrogance and stupidity exhibited by some members of the investigative committee fired me up. I wrote in my diary, "Tonight I went to the Capitol where they are investigating charges of communism at the university. After hearing that, I have become inspired again. I want to become active in those organizations [that were accused of being communist affiliated]. After hearing the Legislature . . . I really do believe that a dictatorship of the proletariat is the best form of government. I wonder if I shall ever change my view."

The Legislature eventually tired of Caldwell's investigation, which failed to find anything subversive at the university. A majority voted on October 27 to disband the committee and to commend the university's faculty members for their "patience" and "fine work." It was a theater of the absurd.

But it was not the end of absurdity.

A Brush with the Dies Committee

In the summer of 1940, when I was leaving graduate school, the university's reputation for breeding radicalism attracted the attention of Martin Dies, Jr., a demagogic U.S. congressman from east Texas who was the chairman of the House Un-American Activities Committee. This witless wonder from Texas so dominated the committee that most people called it the Dies Committee. The House of Representatives created it in May 1938 to conduct hearings on subversive activity by Fascists and Nazis, as well as Communists, but the latter quickly dominated the committee's concerns. Making the committee his personal forum, the flamboyant Dies garnered national headlines by conducting sensational hearings on alleged communist activities in labor unions, the Federal Writers Project, the Federal Theatre, and the American Civil Liberties Union. He was an awful man. By the summer of 1940 Dies had ambitions for the U.S. Senate and therefore was in need of publicity in his home state.

Martin Dies came to Austin and claimed that he had acquired the secret records of the Texas Communist Party and that the records revealed the existence of a communist cell at the University of Texas. After Dies made his accusation, he sent his committee investigators Robert Stripling and Wick Fowler to Austin to conduct an investigation. They summoned students who were or had been members of the Progressive Democrats to a hotel suite to be questioned.

I was one of the students Fowler and Stripling interrogated. They asked asinine questions such as: Do you want to overthrow the government of the United States? Are you spying on the United States for a foreign power? It was ridiculous. Obviously, a real spy or violent revolutionary would never truthfully answer such questions, especially to a government investigator. They were hoping that one of us would be so naive or so stupidly brash as to say something outrageous that Dies could twist around and use in a press release as evidence that the university was full of communists.

I had friends on campus who were members of the Communist Party, but they never tried to hide that fact. There was nothing secret about their activities. It was just a different world then. The people I knew who were communists were deeply concerned about the millions of unemployed and the unequal distribution of wealth. The inequities during the Depression were horrendous. Also, there was no law against being a Communist. In fact, the party ran slates of candidates for statewide public office in Texas in several elections during the 1930s.

At a campus meeting of the Progressive Democrats I met a young lady named Ruth Koenig, who happened to be secretary of the Communist Party in Texas. She was bright and had a sincere and deep desire to help the economically exploited people of Texas. I remember going to one of the hearings that the Legislature frequently held to investigate communism at the university. Ruth was one of the people called to testify. During the hearing, one of the state senators asked her if Communists believed in free love. Ruth looked him square in the eyes and said, "Only for the comrades, Senator. Sorry."

The questions Fowler and Stripling were asking did not apply to anyone I knew. Their portrayal of communists, as intent on violently overthrowing our government and all that kind of baloney—that was so foreign to us. A communist or Marxist, from my point of reference at that time, was just someone who was concerned with having more equality for people. I use the word "equality" in terms of economic access to our society. My own father was the example that came to my mind. He had long abandoned any sympathy for Stalin's version of communism, but in his heart, he remained an evolutionary Marxist who wanted a more equitable distribution of wealth and a more humane society.

After interrogating us about communistic activities on campus, Stripling and Fowler left town. A week later, Dies charged that his investigators had uncovered two "small revolutionary groups active among Texas university students," calling the members of one group "Stalinists" and the others "Trotskyites." Obviously referring to Dr. Montgomery, Dies charged that at least one faculty member met regularly with students to discuss Marxist theory. Dies also said that his investigators had found "communist literature" in a student's dormitory room at the University of Texas. Immediately after Dies made these accusations, he dropped the subject for good and left Texas to embark on his second round of hearings on communism and the movie industry.

J. R. Parten, who was chairman of the board of regents, issued a public challenge to Dies to turn over to the university whatever evidence he had to support his accusations. Thirty-five years later, I asked Parten about the Dies report. Parten smiled and said, "I'm still waiting for it." The two investigators, both of whom were Texans, went on to wider fame. Robert Stripling won national notoriety as an investigator working for Richard Nixon in the Alger Hiss case; Wick Fowler became famous as a maker of very spicy chili.

That episode with Dies and his goons made a huge impression on me. I

learned to be leery of anyone who resorted to demagoguery. That's one reason I hated Senator Joseph McCarthy so much when he was running amok
during the 1950s, accusing half the Democratic Party of being traitors and
subversives. Today, people such as Pat Robertson, Rush Limbaugh, Ralph
Reed, Phil Gramm, and Newt Gingrich remind me of Dies and McCarthy. I
don't really see any fundamental differences between any of them. I have had
my personal experience with demagogues, and I found it very distasteful.

The CIO and a War in Spain

Two major national and international developments while I was
at the university often dominated discussion at meetings of the Progressive
Democrats. One was the formation of the Congress of Industrial Organizations (CIO) and its subsequent struggle to organize unskilled workers. The
other was the Spanish Civil War.

John L. Lewis formed the CIO in 1938 after the industrial unions allied
with his United Mine Workers had been kicked out of the American Fed-
eration of Labor. At that particular time American industrial workers — as
contrasted with the building trades, the carpenters, and the ironworkers —
were not organized to any large extent. They were underpaid severely and
had few benefits.

My friends and I in the Progressive Democrats were excited by the creation of the CIO, which we believed was going to be the mass movement for
truly democratizing our society. We were exhilarated by the possibility that
this powerful organization would stand up for all of the little people, who
would no longer have to go it alone in their struggle for a decent standard
of living. We felt a strong sense of solidarity with the CIO's rank-and-file
members. A few of us hitchhiked to Chicago to hear John L. Lewis make
his momentous speech founding the CIO. We were there for only one day.
I remember little about it except that I was excited to be there. I felt that the
CIO presented a wonderful opportunity for the future of the working class
in this country. It was an uplifting moment for me.

The dominant international issue for our group was the Spanish Civil
War. At that time, the Oxford Peace Movement was blossoming, and some
of the young people who were involved in that movement visited university campuses around the country to make speeches. I attended the program they held on our campus. Many of them had been to Spain, and they
talked about their personal experiences in the war. These speeches evoked
heated and emotional debates among the students at the University of Texas.
My group supported the Republican or Loyalist forces. We viewed General

Francisco Franco as a Fascist with the blood of innocent women and children on his hands. The knowledge that Hitler and Mussolini were providing him arms and "volunteer" soldiers from their own military was enough for us to hate him. The Republicans received support from the Soviet Union and from communist parties all over Europe as well as the United States. This is when so many of the students who were progressive politically became enamored with the Soviet Union. A lot of us at that time lost faith in the U.S. government because we didn't think that it was doing enough for the Spanish Republicans, whereas Hitler and Mussolini and the Russians were pouring everything into that fight. We all talked about joining the Abraham Lincoln Brigade, the group of American volunteers fighting for the Spanish Republicans, but only three or four actually went through with it.

The Progressive Democrats were intensely interested in state and local elections, but with one exception, my work schedule prevented me from being active in those election campaigns. The exception was Lyndon Johnson's first campaign for Congress in 1937 after Congressman James P. Buchanan died. Johnson had been head of the NYA in Texas. Because the NYA had helped me go to college in San Antonio, I felt a loyalty to Johnson, even though I did not know him personally. All of us in the Progressive Democrats campaigned for him. We went out in the neighborhoods and knocked on doors, and we worked at the campaign headquarters, addressed letters, and did other chores. I believe the students did more to elect him than anyone else. We thought Johnson was the Great White Father. We were convinced that he was going to be the real leader for liberal thought and progressive action in our country. I was an anonymous student worker during that campaign, so I had no meaningful contact with Johnson. I never knew him on a personal basis, even after he went to the Senate, because by then I was living in Indiana. After I moved back to Texas in the late 1950s, I was allied with a rival faction in the state Democratic Party. When he was president, I was so opposed to the war in Vietnam that I had no opportunity to have contact with him. Of course, after he carried the Vietnam War on like he did, I regretted many times having campaigned for him.

A Little Jewish Boy Named Bernard

Those hours I spent in the classroom with Montgomery, Hale, and my other wonderful professors were certainly the most intellectually challenging of my life. I was learning something exciting and thought-provoking every single day. The discussions at the Progressive Democrat meetings exposed me to new modes of thinking and sharpened my social and political consciousness. I soaked up as much knowledge as I could, but it took me several years to learn that knowledge and wisdom are not the same thing. I have to admit that after a few months as a university student, I fell into the same know-it-all trap into which many young scholars fall. I thought I knew everything and I was smarter than anyone who ever lived. I was not shy about letting people know just how smart I was.

One particular example of my youthful political and intellectual arrogance still stands out in my mind. When I was about twenty years old, I took a train from San Antonio to Austin. I sat behind three middle-aged, apparently substantial citizens. These men were discussing Vice President John Nance Garner, who was from Uvalde, Texas. To those of us in the Progressive Democrats, Garner was a reactionary who had opposed many of the liberal programs of the New Deal. These men, however, talked about how great he was. I was so appalled at their ignorance that I decided to educate them. I rudely interrupted and interjected myself into their conversation. "Excuse me," I said, "but I must tell you that Cactus Jack Garner is the most evil man in America." I gave them a lecture about how wrong they were about him. Despite my rude behavior, they were courteous to me.

After I gave them the benefit of my knowledge, if not my wisdom, I returned to my seat. A few minutes later, one of the gentlemen visited with me. He explained that I had been wrong, not in my point of view, but in interjecting myself in the conversation without an invitation. I had no business saying anything to those men, but in those days, I wanted everybody to know what I believed and how I thought. I'm embarrassed about that, but all of us in the Progressive Democrats carried our feelings on our sleeves in those days. We thought everything was black and white. Gray did not exist in our political spectrum, and compromise was not a word in our vocabulary. I'm certainly not proud of everything we espoused or believed in, but at least it was an honest and principled conviction.

Congressman Maury Maverick, Sr., also had to put up with a lot of guff from me during my know-it-all, true-believer days. I remember one occasion in 1937 when I was back in San Antonio for a rare weekend free from work. I was strolling on a sidewalk downtown when I saw Maury and his charming wife, Terrell, talking to D. B. Hardeman, a University of Texas student who was deeply involved in campus and state Democratic politics. Hardeman later worked on Speaker Sam Rayburn's staff. At that time I was upset with Congressman Maverick for voting to increase the military budget, so I rushed over to castigate him about his error. I was twenty-one years old. Hardeman kept a diary, which is now in his papers in the LBJ Library in Austin, and he recorded this incident: "October 23, 1937: . . . a little Jewish boy named Bernard R—— of San Antonio came up to gush over Maury.

Maury Maverick, Sr., with President Franklin D. Roosevelt in San Antonio in 1936. CN 00336, Maverick (Maury, Sr.) Photograph Collection, Center for American History, The University of Texas at Austin.

He asked Maury why he voted for military expenditures. 'So you're one of those liberals who wants me to be so liberal that I'll get beat, huh?' Maury snapped back. 'A liberal is good just as long as he can do something and no longer.' [Maverick] spoke of the impossibility of getting liberals to agree on anything."

Sixty years later, I have to acknowledge the truth in Maury's response to a brash university student; nothing is ever advanced by kamikaze liberalism (or conservatism), and it is impossible to get unanimity from any group of hard-core liberals. There is also a lot of gray to just about every complex issue. That is a truth I have learned the hard way.

A Greedy Capitalist

My university friends and I were a prejudiced group of people. Naturally, we looked on the business students at the university as complete reactionaries. I had a personal taste of our collective self-righteousness. Several of my friends in the Progressive Democrats criticized me for working in the capitalistic world of Zales Jewelry. One bought a ring at Zales and didn't pay his bill. When Zales sent him a letter threatening to repossess his ring, he called me and said, in a voice full of bitterness, "You and Morris Zale and everyone who works for him are greedy capitalist exploiters."

> **When Barney first started working at Zales, he worked in what they called the boiler room, which is a telephone room for calling customers who owed money to the company. If they didn't come forward with the money, he'd have to go over to their house and try to get it. It was a lousy job he had.** — *Fred Schmidt*

The job at Zales wasn't easy, and it had a lot of bad moments, especially when I had to go to our customers' homes to collect late payments. The worst was when I tried to repossess a ring from a guy named Kenneth Robertson, who had failed to make any payments. When I went to his apartment and announced that I was there to repossess his ring, Robertson punched me in the eye and I fell back. The blow shattered my glasses and cut my eye. I ran away from the apartment, scared to death that I was going to lose not only my job but also the sight in my eye. It took several stitches to close the cut, but I suffered no permanent damage.

By the time I graduated from the university, I was being pulled in two different directions. I had learned so much about business and felt so prepared that I seriously thought about starting a career with Zales. Morris urged me to do so. My dream, however, was to be a professor of economics, and to do that I had to go to graduate school. I knew that it would be difficult ever to return to school if I pursued a career with Zales or any other business, so I decided to go with my dream. I enrolled in graduate school as an economics major.

Veblen and an Unfinished Thesis

Of course, going to graduate school didn't improve my financial situation. I had not been able to save any money, and I was still trying to support my sister. I earned some money as Professor Hale's grader, but not enough. I had no choice but to continue working at a job outside the university. Unfortunately, my situation at Zales was not good. Morris didn't look with favor on my decision to continue my schooling. He felt that it showed a lack of commitment to the business. I got the impression that I didn't have much of a future with Zales. Another problem was my relationship with my cousin Sol, who was my boss at the store. Working for Sol for three years had been a miserable experience. He had treated me like I was a parasite,

Garrison Hall on the UT campus during the mid-1930s. CN 10818, Prints and Photographs Collection, Center for American History, The University of Texas at Austin.

and he made fun of my desire to get a college degree. Sol also didn't like my political ideas or my opinions about current events, which I was always more than willing to express to him. I was beginning to despair when luck intervened. Aunt Fania's husband, Sam Kruger, opened a jewelry store in Austin and offered me a job. I was happy to accept.

Going to graduate school was just as natural for me as eating. I loved every moment of it. Although I was a graduate student for a little more than one year only, that was the period of my life when I absorbed the most as a reader and thinker. That year was deeply satisfying for me. As Hale's grader, I was given a little office in Garrison Hall, and it became my home. I taught Hale's classes whenever he was out of town. He was such an outstanding mediator that he frequently was asked to serve as an outside arbitrator in labor disputes. Those few months constituted the only time in my life when I was able — even if only partially — to live out my dream to be a professor.

Graduate school gave me much more exposure to Professor Clarence Ayres, who introduced me to the ideas of John Dewey and guided me through an in-depth study of the writings of Thorstein Veblen. My high school teacher Olga Vogel had introduced me to Veblen's theories, but it was Ayres who really delineated his thinking for me. It was my intense study of Dewey and Veblen that finally freed me from Marx. I found Dewey's approach to pragmatism and empiricism extremely attractive. Veblen proposed that economics cannot be studied as a closed system but rather must be treated as an aspect of a culture whose customs and habits constitute institutions that are rapidly changing. It was that idea that made him the founder of the so-called institutionalist school of thought. I became an institutionalist in my worldview, and it was then that I really began to think independently.

Incidentally, most of the students in the Progressive Democrats were also influenced by Veblen, and most of us still adhere to his theories. As institutionalists we came to understand that the people who are part of an institution are more concerned with self-preservation than the purpose for which the institution was founded. Understanding that reality is the key to understanding why governments and large organizations behave the way they do.

Before this shift in my thinking toward Veblen and Dewey, I had decided to write my master's thesis on Marx's theory of surplus value, which is the major theme of his master work, *Das Kapital.* Marx assumed that the value of any product equaled the total amount of labor that went into its production. His theory of surplus value argued that the difference between the wages paid to the worker to produce an article and the price received by the owner, if it was a profit, represented surplus value. Surplus value, therefore, was the amount that the capitalist robbed from the worker.

I completed all of my course hours and researched and drafted most of my thesis, but as I neared the end I realized that I had undergone an intellectual metamorphosis. I was thoroughly disillusioned with Marx's ideas. It was now clear to me that Marx's theory of history — that economic forces were the sole determinant of historical change — was wrong. I was beginning to understand that change could result from individual decisions or actions — often irrational or counterintuitive in nature — that had nothing to do with larger economic forces as Marx understood them.

It was my work at Zales, however, that changed my thinking about Marx's theory of surplus value. Because of what I knew about Morris Zale's role in creating his company, I realized that Marx had not recognized the value that entrepreneurship, as well as other factors, added to a product. The most profound change in my mind stemmed from the realization that the fundamental Marxist tenet, that the end justifies the means, was more destructive than any correction that could be made within a social system. These realizations took all of the spirit out of my work, destroying my motivation. As a result, I found it exceedingly difficult to finish the thesis.

While I struggled with the thesis, my sister, Idel, decided to enroll in graduate school at Columbia University. I knew that unless I worked full time to help her pay the bills, she would not be able to go to New York. I decided to drop out of school for a year to help her and to give myself some time to think about what I could do with a thesis that no longer interested me. Starting a new thesis from scratch was not an attractive option.

Professor Hale was disappointed by my decision, but he understood my situation. He was a great man and one of the most salutary influences on my life, and he continued to be a guiding light of intelligence and vision at the university for another quarter of a century. He died in 1975. When I think of Hale I am reminded of the old Talmudic saying, that if you have saved one soul you have saved the world. I've always had a personal feeling that this is my debt to him.

When I dropped out of the university in 1940 without my graduate degree, I thought it would be for one year only. After that, I would reenter school, finish my degree, and become a professor. I could not have imagined then, of course, that my next formal association with the University of Texas would be as a member of its board of regents and that it would not happen until fifty years had passed.

3 ▶ A Blind Date and the Rainey Crusade

I really didn't know what I was going to do when I left graduate school in 1940. With the Nazi war machine smashing through western
Europe and the Japanese laying waste to large regions of China, I don't think
many of us made long-range plans in those days. At least the job at my uncle's
jewelry store gave me a little financial security. I thought about applying for a
teaching position in the public schools, but I soon realized that I was making
more money at the jewelry store than I could make as a public schoolteacher.
My dream of being a professor had not died, I just did nothing to make it
happen.

This situation continued for a few months until a man I knew casually
invited me to be his partner in a jewelry store in San Antonio. Although he
would put in all of the start-up money, he would allow me to acquire 50 percent of the ownership. I could purchase my half with my share of the profits.
I was only in my early twenties, but working for Morris Zale had made me
a more knowledgeable businessman than a lot of guys older than me. My
prospective partner knew this.

He asked me to go to San Antonio to see the store. I knew that I couldn't
get the time off, so I had a coworker tell Sam Kruger that I was sick and
unable to work. I wasn't comfortable with this little white lie, but I didn't
see that I had any other choice. I thought this was my opportunity to have
my own business. When I went to San Antonio, I asked Papa to go with us
to check out the store, which was near Fort Sam Houston. My prospective
partner believed the store could attract a lot of business from soldiers and
their families. When we arrived, Papa noticed a big sign on the front win-
dow that said "Loans." When Papa asked him what that meant, he said that
the jewelry store would also have a pawnshop. Papa's face turned beet red.
He looked at him and said, "Listen, no son of mine is ever going to work
in a pawnshop." That was the end of that. It also was the end of my job at

Sam Kruger in the mid-1930s. CN 10756, Rapoport (Bernard)
Photograph Collection, Center for American History, The University of
Texas at Austin.

Kruger's jewelry store. My uncle fired me when he found out that I had lied about being sick, and he was right to do that.

Suddenly unemployed, I was forced to move in with my parents in San Antonio. I collected payment from the occupants of some rent houses Papa had acquired. He paid me only $5 a week because I was getting free room and board at home. It was not a happy situation, as I noted in my diary: "Worked for Daddy in the office. He and I get along worse each day. I hate working for him. He's so damn hard. Oh, God how I wish I had an understanding father—if he were only like Mother."

Papa was a tough taskmaster. He was so cynical about life that it made it difficult for him to embrace people, including his own family. I think that any person who has been in a prison camp loses much of his or her humanity. They had treated him like an animal in that prison camp. Papa was insensitive so far as I was concerned, and it was difficult for me to work with him. I could have worked twenty hours a day and it would not have been good enough. At the end of the week, when it was time for him to pay me, he acted as though I was on charity and he was giving me money I hadn't earned.

> **Our father was pretty stormy and very stern. He was a tough dad in many ways.** *—Idel McLanathan*

Wichita Falls

After about three or four months working in that stressful and unpleasant situation, I received an invitation from Max Kruger, Sam Kruger's nephew, to be the credit manager of his jewelry store in Wichita Falls. The offer was totally unexpected. I thought the incident that had resulted in my dismissal from the Austin store had ended the possibility of future employment at any of my uncle's stores. Max was willing to forgive me. He and I had been together in the Austin store, and he was well aware of how hard I had worked there. I really didn't have to think twice before I accepted Max's offer. I left San Antonio and my parents' house as fast as I could.

The move to Wichita Falls was not hard because the dusty town on the Red River was like a second home to me. My grandmother had spent her later years there living with my aunt Fania and uncle Sam Kruger. As a child, I traveled with Mama to Wichita Falls nearly every year to visit them. I have vivid memories of Sam and Fania's house on Buchanan Street because it was the nicest house I had ever been in when I was a child.

The job in Wichita Falls paid $150 a month. I rented a room from Max's brother Ted and his wife, Virginia, who lived on Dayton Street. Ted also worked in Kruger's store in Wichita Falls. In those days I could live on $50 a month, so I had extra money to help support my sister at Columbia University. I came from a family that always had one pocket, and I kept up the tradition. That is the influence of our mother on our lives.

> My brother has done wonderful things for me that I would
> not know about until much later. After our mother died, I was
> sorting through papers, and I found a letter from him to her.
> It was only then that I learned that he stayed out of college
> for one year to pay my tuition. He sent money to Mother for
> my tuition. I did not know at the time that he was doing that.
> —*Idel McLanathan*

After I had worked in Wichita Falls for a few weeks, I became depressed because I realized for the first time that I was not going to return to the university to get my doctorate and I was not going to be a professor. I had no other goals, and it made me terribly unhappy. I wrote Mama a letter that indicates my feelings: "I know that you're worried about me, but don't be. Of course, I realize that I cannot kid you. You know that I'm not happy. I would probably be a little happier in Austin, but it is the absence of a goal toward which I might struggle that is the root of my unhappiness. I must find it myself. I do know that it is in the field of education, but I cannot bring myself to working and going to school again. It's just too hard of a struggle."

The time I was in Wichita Falls was the most sterile period in my life. There are some wonderful people living in Wichita Falls, but the place is cursed with some of the worst weather imaginable — dusty and hot in summer, icy and cold in winter. I remember that awful red dust that seemed always to be in the air or on the furniture, clothes, and bed sheets. There was little to do for entertainment. Thank God that I was able to read plenty of books. There has never been a period of my life, no matter how sterile, that I did not read voraciously. But I didn't think about my long-term goals or objectives. My life was boring. When I wasn't selling jewelry at Kruger's, I was in my room reading or listening to the radio to hear the latest news about the war in Europe. In terms of my career, I was going nowhere.

Audre

Thankfully, the boredom ended in late January 1942 when I met a beautiful young woman named Audre Newman. Like so many other things in life that turn out to be fundamental, meeting Audre was a serendipitous situation. Occasionally I had coffee at a café with a man from Waco named Benjamin L. Art, who was working for his brother at another jewelry store in Wichita Falls. One day I mentioned that I was taking some time off to go to San Antonio to visit my parents. Ben, who was about forty years older than me, knew that I was living in Wichita Falls by myself and that I was lonely. He suggested that when my bus stopped in Waco I should get off to meet Audre Newman, the attractive daughter of his fiancée Josephine Newman. Audre had been a student at the University of Texas during the fall of 1941, but she had transferred to Baylor University. I thought that was an interesting idea, so Ben called Audre and she agreed to a blind date.

When I met Audre a few days later in Waco, I was knocked over by her beauty. Audre was born in Chicago, but she had lived in Waco ever since she was three years old. Her father was a physician in Chicago, but her mother and father had divorced. She was reared primarily by her mother, who was a member of the Goodman family, a distinguished family with deep roots in Waco and the central Texas area. Audre's uncles were Aubrey Goodman, a highly respected physician and civic leader in Waco, and Harold Goodman, a prominent businessman. Audre suggested that we go out to a popular dance place called Arnold's. I don't dance, but I was ready to go anywhere with her.

> The truth is that Bernard and I didn't get along very well on that date. I wore mascara, and he did not like it and told me so. I was eighteen and wanted to have a good time. I was in no mood to put up with this guy telling me I shouldn't wear mascara, and then he wouldn't dance, which was a real bore to me. To be honest, it was not a fun evening. I was very happy to get home. —*Audre Rapoport*

Although that first date didn't go as well as I would have liked, I was hooked. The next morning I sent Audre some flowers and asked her to go out to breakfast. I was surprised when she accepted my invitation. We got along better at breakfast than we did the night before. I have always been a good salesman, and I am always impatient to do the things that I want to do, so I wasted no time in this matter. After breakfast, I asked Audre to marry me, and she said yes.

> Understandably, Mother was a bit concerned when I told her that we were engaged. Everybody liked Bernard—that was not the problem. Mother just thought this was happening way too fast. My uncle Aubrey came over to the house and advised Bernard to go back home, because he was a nice boy who could do much better than me. He told Bernard that I was very spoiled, that I had no idea what I was doing, and that I was a lot of trouble. —*Audre Rapoport*

Audre's mother was not happy about our sudden engagement. I really had to do my best selling job to persuade her to allow Audre to accompany me to San Antonio to meet Mama. She finally decided that if Audre did go to San Antonio she would have more time to think about how impulsive she had been and she might change her mind and end the engagement.

> How he persuaded my mother to do that I will never know, because I had hardly ever crossed the street by myself. He did get Mother to talk to his mother on the telephone before I went, just to assure my mother that it was all on the up and up. Anyway, Mother realized that she had made a mistake almost as soon as our bus left Waco. When we arrived in San Antonio, Mother called and told me to come home. It was too late for that, however. I liked Bernard's parents, and we decided to go ahead with the marriage. —*Audre Rapoport*

Audre and I set our marriage date in February. She returned to Waco after spending the night at my parents' home, and I returned to Wichita Falls. I saw Audre only one more time before we got married, and that was when she and her mother went to Wichita Falls to find an apartment for us. We had the wedding in Waco on February 15, 1942, and then we went back to Wichita Falls to live in a tiny garage apartment. For our honeymoon, we took the bus to Mineral Wells and stayed at the Baker Hotel, which in those days was a popular resort with a hot springs.

We moved around a lot in Wichita Falls because Audre couldn't find an apartment that she liked. Nice apartments were hard to find during the war because Wichita Falls had a big Army Air Corps base, which provided a lot of competition for places to live.

> I would find a new apartment while he was at work and then move everything we owned—which was very little—by myself without telling him. When he got off work he would learn that he lived someplace else. That didn't bother him because he didn't really care where he lived. He just didn't get involved in those kinds of matters—he never has. —*Audre Rapoport*

> My brother wrote me the news about his marriage. When I found out it was Audre Newman I knew who he was talking about. I remembered that I had seen Audre at a party at the University of Texas. I just thought she was sheer glamour. —*Idel McLanathan*

They say brief courtships don't work out, but Audre and I have been married for more than fifty-five years.

Another Job at Zales

After Audre and I were married, I left Kruger's Jewelry for a job at the Zales store in Wichita Falls. I quit my job at Kruger's because of a personality conflict I had with Max's wife, Sara. Max told me that my conflict with Sara was making it uncomfortable for him at home. He suggested that it would be better if I left, so I did. Looking back, I have to admit that I was a hardheaded kid in those days. I did not make much of an effort to get along with her. I've often wondered, since Max and I were such close friends, if I didn't make a contest out of his affection for Sara and myself. That may have been the underlying cause of the conflict. I think it is important for people to recognize a weakness within themselves and to understand and deal with it. In life one is often in a contest vying for someone else's affections, and when that happens, one always ends up a loser for being so ego-oriented.

I was glad to be back with Zales because it was obvious that Morris Zale and his brother-in-law and partner, Ben Lipshy, were on their way to creating a giant organization. By this time they had twelve stores in three states. They eventually built the most successful jewelry company this country has ever known. As I said earlier, Morris had a tremendous influence on me. He taught me just about everything I needed to know about marketing and sales. Morris also was one of the most honorable businessmen I have ever known. He taught me the importance of having high standards. He also taught me that a business must be treated like a child: one does whatever one wants with the profits of the business, but one must never mistreat the business itself. An owner can give away the profits but never cut-rate the product.

Morris gave me a personal lesson about not discounting the product. In those days Zales would buy a diamond ring for maybe $10 wholesale and then mark it up for a retail price of $49.50. That ring would be sold on terms of $1 down and $1 a week. One day, when Morris happened to be working in the office at the Wichita Falls store, one of my customers offered to buy a $49.50 ring for $40 cash—no layaway, no weekly payments, just a simple cash deal. I took it, thinking that getting the cash right away was worth losing $9.50. I rang it up on the cash register. After the customer left the store, Morris came out of the back office and gave me a lecture.

"Let me tell you," Morris said, "Zales is going to be a big business some day. I want it to be the kind of business where my daughter Gloria can walk into any one of my stores and buy that ring at the same price that anyone else can."

Morris was a zealot about treating all customers the same. I knew that the ring had cost Morris $10, so I thought that he would still be making a $30 profit if the ring sold for $40. I didn't understand, however, that when he determined profit, he had to subtract payments in default and the cost of overhead such as advertising, insurance, taxes, rent, and personnel. That meant that his profit was much less than I had realized. It was a fundamental lesson, but it was one that I had to learn.

As a Zales credit manager, I also learned some lessons about human nature that have helped me throughout my business career. I learned that people are people: some are good, and some are bad, and it is not always easy to predict how different individuals will act when it comes to meeting their financial obligations. I sold jewelry on credit to many people on whose integrity I would have bet my life but who skipped out and didn't pay. I gave credit reluctantly to several people who I feared were total deadbeats but who paid back every cent on time. I was lucky to gain that kind of experience early in my business career.

Morris Zale moved his headquarters from Wichita Falls to Dallas in 1946, when the company began a period of phenomenal expansion. I had a lot of contact with Morris until his death in 1995. He was proud of my success because he felt that he had contributed to it, and he had. I owe him a lot.

The truth is they weren't very nice to Bernard at Zales. I didn't like the way they treated Bernard, ever. They didn't appreciate him. He worked twenty hours a day, and no one there ever said a kind word to him. —*Audre Rapoport*

Not long after Audre and I were married, I received a summons from the Wichita Falls draft board to take my physical exam for the Army. At the end of the exam, the doctor said that I had passed every test with flying colors and that I was fit for military duty. As I walked away, the doctor noticed my limp and asked me to come back. He measured my right leg and discovered that it was slightly more than one and a quarter inch shorter than the left leg. "Well, the Army can't use you," he said. "We can't afford to build you special shoes. You're 4-F."

That 4-F classification kept me out of the war. I did not welcome the decision. Don't get me wrong, I wasn't gung ho to jump into a situation where I could get killed. I don't think of myself as being brave in a physical way, but being Jewish and aware of the tragic situation for the Jews of Europe, I was ready to go in an emotional sense. I had played with pacifism when I was at the university, but Germany's invasion of Poland changed my view. A number of my parents' relatives were killed in eastern Europe. My mother's aunt and uncle were burned alive, although I would not know that until after the war. I understood what the war was about—I wanted to defeat Nazism—but I was physically unable to contribute to the war.

Art's Jewelers

Early in 1943 Ben Art married Audre's mother, and she moved to Wichita Falls. Audre and her mother, however, preferred to live in Waco, and they were eager for me to go into business for myself. They talked me into opening a jewelry store in Waco with Ben.

> **Mother was the person who urged us to operate our own jewelry store. It was really her idea; she was the instigator. Mother decided that it would be great if we got Ben and Bernard together in a business because they were both good salesmen. She had two little rent houses in Waco that she mortgaged to provide us with the seed money to get started. I thought it was a wonderful idea.** —*Audre Rapoport*

I was only twenty-six, but Ben felt that I could bring a lot of energy and enthusiasm to the business. I jumped at the opportunity. When I gave notice to Morris Zale, he asked me to stay with his company. I had been successful as a credit manager, and Morris believed that I had a bright future. Quite candidly, if I had stayed with Zales I probably would have accumulated more money than I did in the insurance business. Morris had an excellent employee profit-sharing program, and he was generous about his employees' owning stock in his company. He made lots of millionaires. I had an excellent opportunity with Zales, but I had really had all that I could stand of Wichita Falls.

> **I think it is Audre who took him, more than perhaps anyone else, into a business career. They started out dirt poor, but I think she wanted more than that and kind of pushed him a little bit.** —*Hiram Friedsam, family friend*

So we all moved back to Waco in 1944, and Ben and I started this little business that we called Art's Jewelers. It was on Austin Avenue, which was one of the main streets in Waco at the time.

The Rainey Affair

Wichita Falls was such a sterile period for me. I was never involved in the civic affairs of that community. Soon after I moved to Waco, Frank Baldwin, the editor of the local newspaper, befriended me. In my view, Frank was one of the greatest newspaper editors of all time in Texas. He pushed me to get involved in community affairs in my new hometown. I wrote letters to the editor, and Baldwin published them. He introduced me to a wonderful woman named Gussie Oscar who had a public program in Waco called "Town Hall." Gussie asked me to introduce some of the speakers when they came to town, which raised my visibility in Waco. I began to feel a part of a community for the first time in my life.

My increasing involvement in Waco's civic affairs was one of the factors that led to my first really deep involvement in a political campaign. That campaign was Homer Price Rainey's bid in the summer of 1946 to become governor of Texas. The Rainey crusade profoundly shaped my political worldview for many years to come.

I had not participated in any political campaigns in Texas after I left the university. As an intellectual of liberal persuasion, I was interested in politics and I always followed the campaigns closely, but I was not an active participant. I had never even been to a precinct convention before 1946. That is par for intellectuals, who too often want to sit on a pedestal and tell everybody how to do it. We want people to listen, but we're not eager to move ourselves. The Texas gubernatorial campaign in 1946 was different, however. For the first time in memory, we had an intellectual running for governor, and he was not an ordinary intellectual; he was the former president of the University of Texas whose dismissal by a board of regents filled with political reactionaries had been a cause célèbre in Texas during the 1940s.

Born and raised in a northeast Texas farming community, Homer Rainey attended Austin College in Sherman. After earning his doctorate from the University of Chicago, Rainey taught briefly at the University of Oregon and served as president of Franklin College in Indiana for four years. At the age of thirty-five, Rainey became president of Bucknell University in Pennsylvania. After a distinguished tenure at Bucknell, Rainey was appointed director of the American Youth Commission in Washington, where the quality of his leadership attracted national attention. A rising star in the educational world, Rainey had other attributes that should have made him especially attractive to his fellow Texans. He was an ordained Baptist minister, a family man with two daughters, and a former athlete who had played professional baseball. News of his appointment as university president in 1939 was greeted with widespread approval in Texas.

Homer Price Rainey, ca. 1940. CN 07250, Prints and Photographs Collection, Center for American History, The University of Texas at Austin.

I was in graduate school when the university staged an impressive inaugural ceremony to install Rainey as president. My friends and I in the Progressive Democrats were excited about his appointment. It was well known that when he was in Washington Rainey had worked on a project with Eleanor Roosevelt and that he held liberal pro–New Deal political views. We expected Rainey to usher in a new progressive era at the university, but it was not to be.

Not long after Rainey's installation as president, Governor W. Lee "Pass the Biscuits Pappy" O'Daniel appointed a bunch of ultraconservative know-nothings to the board of regents. After O'Daniel was elected to the U.S. Senate in 1941, his successor, Coke Stevenson, packed the board with other reactionaries. Extreme anti–New Dealers, these men were against everything Homer Rainey wanted to do. To be more accurate, they were against the twentieth century. Four of these regents stood out as fine examples of narrow-mindedness, parochialism, and prejudice: Wichita Falls businessman Orville Bullington, Kerrville rancher Scott Schreiner, south Texas attorney and corporate lobbyist D. Frank Strickland, and Houston independent oil-man Dan Harrison. My friends and I referred to them as the Bullington crowd.

These gentlemen believed that the university was crawling with politically subversive New Dealers, moral perverts, and other undesirables who advocated such dangerous ideas as labor unionism, civil rights for black people, fair labor standards and antitrust laws, and corporate and personal income taxes. They had no intention of allowing the state's dominant institution of higher education to be run by people who threatened the political, social, and economic status quo. Their mission was to muzzle Rainey and his faculty supporters and to prevent the university from generating or providing the inspiration for economic, political, and social reform in Texas.

In the summer of 1942 the Bullington crowd initiated a series of confrontations with Rainey and actions against the university faculty that ultimately led to Rainey's dismissal. I was in Wichita Falls during that time, but I paid close attention to the disturbing attacks on my beloved university, especially because my former teachers in the economics department bore the brunt of them. At a meeting of the regents in June 1942, Strickland told Rainey to fire E. E. Hale, Bob Montgomery, and Clarence Ayres. Rainey was able to protect his economics professors because of the tenure rule. Temporarily defeated, the Bullington crowd later fired four instructors in the economics department who weren't protected by tenure. This action was taken over President Rainey's heated objections.

Other confrontations with Rainey quickly followed. Bullington and his allies passed a regents' rule stating that the faculty could not attend professional meetings on state time and at state expense because of the dangers of mixing with subversives and perverts from out-of-state universities. Confrontation followed confrontation, as the president and the regents clashed over a variety of issues, including a highly publicized squabble that resulted in the removal of the acclaimed novel *USA* by John Dos Passos from a list of recommended readings in the English department. Bullington charged that the book was obscene and subversive.

In January 1943, frustrated that he couldn't fire Montgomery, Ayres, and Hale, Strickland tried to destroy the tenure rule. Rainey warned that the removal of tenure would destroy the university, because it would not be able to recruit good faculty members from other universities with sound tenure rules. Strickland responded that Rainey shouldn't worry; he was certain they could find good patriotic Texans to teach at the university who were from smaller Texas schools that had no tenure. With help from a faction of moderate regents, Rainey was able to postpone the vote on tenure.

By October 1944 Rainey had reached the limits of his patience. Before an assembly of 400 of the university's faculty and staff, Rainey listed sixteen points on which he and the regents had differed during the previous months. They included the attack on tenure and attempts to fire tenured professors, the dismissal of the instructors in the economics department, an effort to stifle social science research and to intimidate the faculty, and frequent accusations by regents of subversive activity on campus. His basic charge against the regents, however, was that they wanted to destroy academic freedom and to impose a type of political control at the university. Looking back on it, it should not have been a shock to any of us when the board of regents fired Rainey a few days later, but it was as if an earthquake had occurred. Naively, many of us thought reason would prevail and Rainey would survive; it didn't and he didn't.

Rainey's firing made newspaper headlines and dominated radio news programs throughout the state on November 2. I was stunned and outraged when I heard the news on the radio early that morning. As far as I was concerned, Rainey's firing was a terrible injustice.

Rainey's many supporters on the campus reacted swiftly. The faculty passed by an overwhelming majority a resolution demanding Rainey's reinstatement. Five thousand people marched down Congress Avenue in Austin to protest Rainey's dismissal. A major effort to force the board of regents to reinstate Rainey ultimately failed. It was not a high point in the history of the university.

> It was just so unfair and ridiculous what the university's regents had done to Rainey. If you lived in Texas when this happened and you had any conscience at all, you had to be outraged. —*Audre Rapoport*

> I met Bernie at a Young Democrats meeting in Austin in 1944 while I was on leave from the military. I was twenty-one and he not much older. The purpose of that meeting was to protest the dismissal of Homer Rainey as president of the University of Texas. We went around quoting Thomas Jefferson, determined to avenge what we saw as an assault on academic freedom. In the confident idealism of youth, Bernie and I vowed to make things better for our generation and the ones to follow. —*Jim Wright, former Texas congressman*

The Rainey Campaign

Almost as soon as the board officially refused to reinstate Rainey as president, in January 1945, rumors spread through Texas that he would run for governor in the Democratic primary in 1946. In the spring and summer of 1945, former University of Texas students upset by Rainey's

*University students march in protest against Dr. Rainey's firing, November 1944.
CN 10803, Prints and Photographs Collection, Center for American History, The
University of Texas at Austin.*

firing joined with liberal political activists to organize "Rainey for Governor" clubs in several counties. By this time, Audre and I were living in Waco and we helped to organize the local club. Rainey finally declared his candidacy over a statewide radio network on May 23. I remember how excited Audre and I were by his announcement speech. Promising a crusade to "unshackle Texas from the powerful economic forces which today control our politics, our industrial life, and threaten our education," Rainey declared that his opponents would be the "people who fear any change or progress; people who now enjoy special privileges; people who fear they will have to help foot the bill for better schools, better roads, better hospitals, and a better welfare program." It was a soul-stirring speech.

At the time of Rainey's announcement, Audre and I were thinking about having a baby. After we heard that speech over the radio, we decided to wait. Audre and I agreed to postpone having a child because we wanted to do whatever we possibly could to help get this wonderful man elected governor. I remember telling Audre that the whole future of Texas depended on that campaign. I really believed that.

I went to Austin a few days later and offered my services in Waco. Rainey's campaign manager was former *Daily Texan* editor D. B. Hardeman, the man who had documented in his diary my argument with Congressman Maverick in San Antonio back when I was a student at the university. Boyd Sinclair, another former editor of the *Daily Texan,* was Rainey's press officer. D.B. asked me if I would manage central Texas. I agreed, even though I knew nothing about running a campaign organization. I especially didn't know anything about how much money it took.

When I returned to Waco, Audre and I were faced with the challenge of opening and running a campaign office without start-up money. We had worked twenty hours a day, six days a week, in our jewelry store, and by the time Rainey announced for governor, we had saved about $2,000 in cash. That was all the money we had. We were so committed to the Rainey cause that we used our entire savings to open up the campaign office in the old Roosevelt Hotel in Waco. Then I borrowed another $2,000 and put it in the campaign. It's funny to realize now, but when I could least afford it was when I was the most committed politically.

> **Bernard didn't know anything about political fund-raising. I often spent our grocery money to buy stamps for the campaign office.** —*Audre Rapoport*

> **In those days during the Rainey campaign, neither Bernard nor I could have made change for a fifty, maybe not a twenty-dollar bill.** —*Jim Wright*

Fourteen people eventually announced as candidates for governor, but only Dr. Rainey and four others were seen as major candidates. On the extreme right was Lieutenant Governor John Lee Smith, whose supporters included the university regents who had fired Rainey. Also among the major candidates were former railroad commissioner Jerry Sadler and Attorney General Grover Sellers, both of whom were more moderate than Smith but still far to the right of Rainey. The candidate who concerned me the most, however, was Beauford Jester, a member of the Texas Railroad Commission who could count on major financial support from the oil industry. We were optimistic about Rainey's chances, however, because we believed that the four major candidates would splinter the conservative vote, while Rainey would attract a solid bloc vote from Roosevelt loyalists.

In the campaign Rainey adopted the economic ideas advocated by my former professors Bob Montgomery and Clarence Ayres. He insisted that great wealth in Texas was going untaxed while the basic needs of people were not being met. He called for higher taxes on oil, sulfur, lumber, cigarettes, and liquor to provide money for improved health services and education, pay raises for teachers, pensions for the elderly, and farm-to-market roads for farmers. A key part of Rainey's plan to make state government more responsive to the people was his call for the abolition of the poll tax. Initiated in 1902 to discourage people from voting for the Populist Party, the poll tax was used in the late 1940s to keep African Americans and Mexican Americans as well as poor whites from voting.

Rainey's campaign was a full-blown populist attack on the Texas economic and political power establishment. In his campaign speeches Rainey stressed that out-of-state companies owned or controlled at least 75 percent of the state's developed resources of crude oil and natural gas and that about 96 percent of the utilities in Texas were controlled by out-of-state interests. Focusing on Dr. Montgomery's favorite target, Rainey also charged that a small group of wealthy Wall Street investors controlled almost 100 percent of the state's sulfur production. Rainey said that something was desperately wrong when 70 percent of the state's residents had incomes below the federal poverty line, despite the fact that Texas had a world monopoly on sulfur and over half of the nation's oil reserves. "Why are we so poor?" Rainey asked. "Because we don't own our own resources and the profits go elsewhere. We are Wall Street's richest colony." That was an accurate critique of the state's economic reality at the time. Because of Rainey's willingness to expose such unpleasant facts, his campaign became a crusade. There is no other way to describe it. People are more cynical today, but that was a time when most of us really believed that we could make a difference in government and that it was within our power to change things. Audre and I definitely felt that way.

> We did feel that the world would come to an end if Dr. Rainey didn't win. We were young, and we believed it was so important, and it was important. Dr. Rainey's election would have changed Texas for the better. —*Audre Rapoport*

Audre managed the county campaign office, while I traveled around central Texas. Every single night I was out campaigning somewhere. I was away from the store for several weeks. I gave speeches for Rainey in little towns scattered around Waco, such as Mart and Marlin and Lorena and Bruceville. I got people to pay their poll taxes and urged them to vote.

> I ran the Rainey campaign office, but I also walked door to door in the terrible heat of summer and handed out literature. I had a full-time job during that campaign. I loved it. —*Audre Rapoport*

We brought Dr. Rainey to Waco and surrounding towns maybe four or five times during the campaign. We also raised money at courthouse rallies. We had as many as 2,000 people at a political rally out on the lawn in front of the McLennan County courthouse. We passed the hat and picked up $2,000 or $3,000, which was a significant amount for a campaign that had an extremely hard time raising money.

Nearly all of the big money people were supporting Rainey's opponents, especially Smith and Jester. One exception, however, was independent oil-man J. R. Parten of Houston, who as a university regent had played the leading role in recruiting and hiring Rainey as university president. J.R. became *the* angel for Homer Rainey in 1946. He was Rainey's primary support. It is hard for me to imagine how that campaign could have happened without him. Parten personally contributed or raised nearly half of Rainey's campaign money. The remainder largely came from small donations ranging from $1 to $25.

What the Rainey campaign lacked financially, it made up in human resources, especially with its women volunteers led by Marion Storm, Lillian Collier, Minnie Fisher Cunningham, and other members of the Women's Committee for Educational Freedom. Rainey also enjoyed the help of a large number of student volunteers, who performed most of the organizational work at the county level. We all came together in the Rainey campaign; it really was an existential experience.

The gubernatorial campaign of 1946 deserves a place on any short list of the dirtiest campaigns ever conducted in the Lone Star state. I have been directly involved in more political campaigns than I can count since then, and I can say without any hesitation that none has been blemished so thoroughly by blatant demagoguery (although a couple of the campaigns against Ralph Yarborough were close runners-up). As always, these demagogic tactics were used by defenders of the status quo as an effective smoke screen to obscure the real issues. The problems were real, and they were numerous. They included an inadequate public school system (except for high-income areas), a shameful lack of public health and welfare services, the continuation of Jim Crow segregation laws, a feudalistic farm labor system exploiting Mexican Americans, a civil code that treated women as children, an extractive economy not unlike those of the old European colonial systems, election laws structured in such a way as to disenfranchise a large segment of the population, a legal and business environment utterly hostile to the idea of collective bargaining for workers, and a regressive and inequitable system of taxation.

Of Rainey's four major opponents, the most demagogic were John Lee Smith and Grover Sellers. Both men seemed to get special pleasure out of the trumped-up issue of Rainey's alleged sponsorship of immorality while president of the university. The evidence at hand was *The Big Money,* one of the books in the Dos Passos trilogy *USA,* which Regent Bullington had cited as a reason for his vote for Rainey's dismissal. Although Rainey had no part in the English department's decision to use *The Big Money* on a recommended reading list, Smith and Sellers charged that he was responsible for creating an atmosphere on campus that allowed faculty members to expose young and innocent students to such "filth." Rainey's opponents reprinted passages from *The Big Money* and circulated them among the state's clergy as proof of the former president's personal "depravity."

Sellers took the prize for theatrics, however. He typically ended his campaign speeches with a request for the "little ladies" to leave, so that he could present his evidence about *USA* to the men. After the women departed, Sellers put on a pair of white gloves to protect his hands from contamination by the "filth" in the book. He then read aloud "perverted" passages from the "degenerate" book. At the conclusion of the reading, Sellers would declare dramatically, "This is the sort of filth your daughters were required to read at Texas University when Dr. Homer P. Rainey was president." The *USA* stories were tied so closely to Rainey's name that it was common for people to think that he was the author. I later read that when Rainey was riding in a taxi in Dallas one day during the campaign, the cab driver — not knowing his identity — asked him if he had ever read "that dirty book that Homer Rainey" had written.

Initially, Jerry Sadler's campaign focused on his east Texas brand of southern populism, but as his poll ratings dropped, Sadler began to appeal to racial prejudice. He charged that Rainey had encouraged racial integration of the university. Grover Sellers and John Lee Smith also engaged in race baiting. In his speeches Sellers frequently repeated the charge that if Rainey became governor he would "herd white and Negro children into the same schools." Smith charged that if Rainey won the election, he would move into the governor's mansion and hang pictures of "some kinky headed ward heeler of the CIO" on its walls.

The accusation Rainey's opponents made most frequently, however, was that he was a Communist or a Communist dupe. John Lee Smith charged that Rainey had filled the university faculty with Communists who were busy indoctrinating naive young Texan children. These allegations weren't limited to Rainey. Some of the people who worked for his opponents spread rumors that many of Rainey's supporters were Communists. I learned that their work included spreading gossip around Waco that the FBI had a big file on me and that I was a Communist. My guess is that the rumor was the result of my being questioned by the investigators from the Dies committee.

The rumor never affected me personally, but I'm sure it hurt my effectiveness as a Rainey campaigner with some people.

Rainey fought back. During a speech in Austin, he noted that "desperate and frightened men, on the verge of being defeated at the polls, always yell Communism." Rainey argued that FDR had been called a communist whenever he tried to help the people. He stated that Texas desperately needed better schools, more rural roads, more hospitals, and improved public health programs. It was not communistic, he argued, to pay for these improvements by making corporations that were growing fat and wealthy exploiting the state's natural resources pay their fair share of taxes.

Despite those and other efforts to counteract his opponents' smear campaign, Rainey's standings in the opinion polls fell while Jester's ascended. Smith, Sellers, and Sadler threw mud at Rainey, while Beauford Jester played the role of statesman, free to conduct a more moderate campaign aimed at getting his name before the voters and presenting him as a responsible choice between extremists on the right and left. Jester was able to announce near the end of the campaign that he was the only candidate with clean hands. That tactic paid off. With each passing week, he gained in the polls at the expense of everyone else.

In the late 1940s, Waco was the heart and strength of populist thinking. In most cities, the newspapers opposed Rainey, in some cases virulently, but the newspaper in Waco was magnificent. The editor, Frank Baldwin, felt the same about Rainey as I did. He had courage and an awesome sense of outrage at improprieties, so far as malevolent politicians were concerned. Baldwin even let me write his newspaper's stories on Rainey. I took the stories to him, and he didn't let his editors touch them. You would have thought I owned the paper! We had everything going for us in Waco. It was with some pride that Audre predicted to Rainey headquarters the night before the election that we would carry McLennan County. The prediction proved accurate.

As we had anticipated, no candidate won enough votes in the July 27 primary to win the nomination. Beauford Jester won the most votes, with 38 percent of the total. Placing second, Homer Rainey won a spot in the runoff against Jester, but he received only a disappointing 25 percent of the vote.

The runoff campaign was even more bitter and dirty than the regular campaign. We all worked our hearts out, but the odds were just too formidable. Beauford Jester overwhelmed Homer Rainey by a vote of 701,000 to 355,000, winning every large city and all but seven counties. The day before the election, I went to the radio station and broadcast a plea for everyone to vote. In my heart, I knew we were beaten. It gave me an awful feeling, sort of like believing in God and then suddenly realizing that there isn't one after all. I lost hope that our society would ever be better.

The Jester campaign had pulled off an amazing feat. It had convinced a majority of voters that an ordained Baptist minister was an atheist. Red scare tactics also took their toll on Rainey's campaign, making the Texas primary a preview for the use of such tactics in the fall's general election campaigns throughout the country. In November a young war veteran by the name of Richard M. Nixon won election as a Republican congressman from California by red-baiting his liberal Democratic opponent, Jerry Voorhis. The election results in Texas also reflected a fundamental change in the national political environment. The New Deal era was over in Washington as well as in Texas. The general election in November resulted in a sweeping victory for the Republican Party, which took control of both houses of Congress for the first time in more than two decades.

Although Jester and the newly elected lieutenant governor, Allan Shivers, won election as Democrats, they had campaigned against the national Democratic Party and the Roosevelt legacy. The Democratic Party in Texas was now firmly under the control of conservatives who identified with the national Republican Party and who ran for office as Democrats only because Texas was still a one-party state.

That defeat was a terrible blow. I remember Rainey's as the most idealistic campaign ever conducted in the state of Texas. All of Rainey's opponents talked about honor, but in my view, they were a group of men without virtue. Anyone who reads the history of that campaign has to reach the same conclusion. It was one of the most tragic campaigns in the history of Texas, and we've had some bad ones.

That campaign divided people and left a bitter legacy in the political environment that took thirty years to subside. Rainey's dismissal as university president and the subsequent Rainey campaign for governor were defining episodes for me and other Texas Democrats who remained loyal to the Roosevelt legacy and the national party. Split away from the conservatives who opposed the national party and its more liberal agenda (which included support for civil rights, labor unionism, and the welfare state), the Rainey Democrats became the opposition party within the party in Texas.

I became disillusioned with my fellow Texans as a result of Rainey's defeat. I felt that if people were so stupid that they would prefer a Beauford Jester to a man the caliber of Homer Rainey, then they deserved whatever bad happened as a result. We had tried to show Texas the light, and it had opted for darkness. Many of the people who worked hard for Rainey felt the same way. I believe that individuals can make a difference, and I sincerely believe that Homer Rainey could have taken Texas down a different and better path. He possessed all the qualities needed to be an outstanding governor. Texas suffered as a result of his defeat. During the ten to fifteen years after the election of 1946, we had no meaningful leadership in higher education in this wealthy state. Our brighter students went off to colleges like Oberlin or Harvard or Yale. Not until Harry Ransom became president of the University of Texas did we have any real leadership, in terms of quality and broad vision.

I stayed in touch with Dr. Rainey until his death in 1985, at the age of eighty-nine. He served as president of Stephens College in Missouri, and then he spent his last years as a professor at the University of Colorado in Boulder. We corresponded often, and I never lost contact with him.

Homer Price Rainey Hall

Five decades after Rainey's defeat, I became chairman of the University of Texas Board of Regents. Among the most satisfying things that I did during my time as chairman was to shepherd a resolution through the board renaming the university's music building the Homer Price Rainey Hall. Members of the university's class of 1946 who were preparing for their fiftieth class reunion came up with the idea. I was delighted to be in a position to see that it happened. UT-Austin president Robert Berdahl and UT System chancellor William H. Cunningham also agreed that such an action was long overdue, as did my colleagues on the board of regents. The dedication ceremony, which was held in the recital hall of the music building on April 25, 1996, was a deeply moving event for me. Among the special guests in the auditorium were several members of Dr. Rainey's extended family, including his daughter, Helen Rainey Parolla, who gave a lovely speech about her father. I was deeply touched by Helen's willingness to forgive the university for the wrong that had been done to her father.

It was my honor to give the keynote speech at the Rainey Hall dedication. The occasion was an opportunity to remind ourselves that Rainey had sacrificed his presidency, with all of the prestige and perquisites that the position provides, because he was unwilling to sacrifice his legitimacy as an educator. Years after his dismissal, Rainey wrote that he had reasoned that others before him had made "sacrifices . . . to establish our system of free schools in the first place" and that he had been "called upon to defend and maintain what they had passed on to us." I urged the audience always to remember that Rainey's experience was an example of what can happen when teaching and research are made to conform to the prejudices and narrow purposes of the economically dominant elements in our society.

"Public institutions belong not to the few," I declared, "but to the many, the multitudes, and the masses in society wanting and deserving the opportunity to receive a good education." This is a belief that I hold most strongly. In order for a university to be able to take its place among the great institutions of democracy and enlightenment, it must be free. It must be a place where freedom of thought, freedom of research and investigation, and freedom of expression are nurtured, promoted, and—whenever the need arises—defended. Intellectual freedom is the light that pushes back the darkness on the plane of existence. Education cannot exist without it.

"Let us dedicate this building . . . as a monument to a fighter for independence," I declared. "Let us reach a high note of freedom in the life of this institution, rising from this place in clarion call to everyone who wishes for the education of our people. From this hallowed hall the poetry of justice, the song of freedom, and the light of truth shall rise."

Rest in peace, Dr. Rainey.

4 ▶ *An Insurance Entrepreneur*

The ugliness of the campaign against Homer Rainey and his overwhelming defeat in the election drained me spiritually and emotionally. I truly believed that I was fighting for virtue, and when I saw it so brutally and decisively thwarted, I withdrew from active political involvement for several years. The Rainey crusade taught me the bitter lesson that truth and virtue don't always win out in politics. I was thoroughly disillusioned with the political system in Texas at that point. I put everything into the Rainey campaign, and when we lost, I assumed the attitude that nothing I could do personally in politics would ever make a difference.

The three or four years following the Rainey campaign were unhappy ones for me. I was deeply disillusioned about politics, I was in debt, and my business struggled. Audre and I had spent all of our savings, and we had borrowed money to keep the campaign office open. For about two months, I had spent more than half of my time working for Rainey. Our jewelry business suffered as a result. There were several days when we had to close the store because Audre was running the campaign office and I was out in the county trying to attract votes for Rainey. This cost us income that we could not afford to lose. As a result, Audre and I were deeply in debt. That debt scared me. It seemed so overwhelming.

> We ended up with a personal debt of $3,000 because of the campaign. That was a fortune. We borrowed it from a bank, and it was in our names. Why the bank loaned us the money is beyond my understanding. We had an income of only $65 a week. —*Audre Rapoport*

With the business not doing well, I knew I was going to have a hard time paying off that debt. I was terrified by the thought of defaulting on the loan and ruining my good name. I was at the point of despair when an angel came to my rescue. My angel was Jack Kultgen, a Ford car dealer in Waco who was one of the city's outstanding civic leaders. He had supported Rainey for governor, and we became friends during the campaign. When Jack learned that I was in financial difficulty, he stepped forward and paid off my loan. He was a wonderful man. To show our gratitude, Audre and I have always bought our cars from Jack's Ford dealership. He is dead now, but you will always find two Kultgen Fords in our garage.

I have to admit that another reason for my unhappiness in those days was that I never really liked the jewelry business. I also was disappointed that I had not pursued my dream to be a professor. I was young and idealistic in many ways. I believed that I would never be happy as a businessman. I had the attitude that business was evil, that it was an immoral and predatory pursuit of money. When I was a student at the university, I would have been repelled at the thought of taking any kind of business course. To my way of thinking then, business college was where the reactionaries went to school. As I've said, Thorstein Veblen's *Theory of the Leisure Class,* which articulated his ideas about conspicuous consumption and pecuniary emulation, had a great impact on my thinking. In the jewelry business I was not only catering to those who were guilty of conspicuous consumption, but I was also encouraging it for my own profit. I was plagued by guilt feelings the entire time that I owned that jewelry store. That was the do-gooder instinct in me. To be honest, I can't help but wonder whether I would have felt differently about it if the store had been making a lot of money.

> **Bernard didn't like the jewelry business because he didn't like to have to wait for customers to come in. It was too passive for him. He wanted to go directly to the customers, and that wasn't the way it worked. But I loved it. I thought it was great fun.** — *Audre Rapoport*

Thankfully, this wasn't a totally bleak period for Audre and me. Early in 1947 Audre learned that she was pregnant, and we spent most of the rest of the year eagerly anticipating the arrival of our baby. Our son, Ronnie, was born on October 25, 1947, at 12:14 P.M. I can remember the time of birth to the minute, because it was the most wonderful thing that had ever happened to me. When I saw my son for the first time, my first thought was that Audre deserved international recognition because she had produced the world's greatest child. I teased all of my good Baptist friends in Waco with the news that our son was going to upset all of Christianity, because he was really the Messiah. As you can tell, I was and still am a very proud father.

Audre and I scraped by as best we could for a couple of years, but I was unable to squeeze much of a profit out of the jewelry store. We were always strapped for cash. The addition of a third member to the family stretched resources even thinner. This period in my life was almost as bad as the time in Wichita Falls, because I really didn't know what I was going to do. I felt lost. I finally decided to get out of the jewelry business.

> **We didn't make a success of it. We couldn't get merchandise during the war. I just don't think it was good timing.**
> —*Audre Rapoport*

At the beginning of 1949 Ben Art and Audre and I closed the store, auctioned our inventory, and paid off our debt. The auction went so well that I decided to try my hand at the jewelry auction business. I conducted a few auctions in small towns in east Texas and southern Oklahoma. We made some money, but my heart really wasn't in it. I also soon realized that there was no stability in that kind of life. I felt like a vagabond.

> **Mother loaned us some money to buy the store inventories. Mother was always there for us when we needed money.**
> —*Audre Rapoport*

At the beginning of the summer of 1949 Audre and I were forced to take a desperate step. We moved back to San Antonio, and I took another job with Papa. At 32 years old, I was back at home and once again depending on my father for a living. It seemed like I was on a fast track to nowhere.

> **I didn't mind going to San Antonio. I didn't feel like Bernard was a failure. In those days, we didn't know anyone who had any money. It was a different world then. People weren't as affluent. Also, we were young, and that makes a big difference in how you view the world and your own circumstances. I was never worried. I knew Bernard would always figure out something.** —*Audre Rapoport*

A First Taste of the Insurance Business

By 1949 Papa had moved up in the world. He wasn't wealthy by any standard, but he was bringing in enough money to be comfortable. Papa had prospered as the general agent for the Texas Life Insurance Company,

and he had an office downtown. In addition, Papa had started a house construction and remodeling business. It was nickel-and-dime stuff. He built
tiny frame houses in San Antonio's West Side barrio with no inside plumbing for $300 or $400 and sold them for $700 or $800. In most cases, he
financed the purchases himself. The buyer would give him $15 or $20 down,
and the monthly payments would be a few bucks a month. This additional
income made it possible for my parents to move into a larger house at 1337
West Woodlawn, just down the street from where I had grown up.

I returned to the job I had abandoned when I worked for Papa nine years
earlier: collecting rent and mortgage payments for his houses. Audre and
I moved into a little place on West Huisache and tried to make a go of it. I
worked with Papa for about a year, with the same result as the last time. I
couldn't do anything right as far as he was concerned. We argued constantly
about everything.

> It didn't work out. You couldn't be in business with David
> Rapoport. We didn't realize this before we moved down there.
> It was impossible. — *Audre Rapoport*

After a few weeks of this misery, I was desperate to find a way out. One day
I happened to pick up one of Papa's insurance sales brochures, and I saw a
life insurance savings plan that interested me. As I read through the details
of the policy, I thought of different ways that the policy could be presented
to a prospective customer. It excited me because it seemed that I might be
able to sell this policy. Papa was dubious about my potential as an insurance salesman, but he had no objection to my giving it a try, so I went out
and made a sale almost immediately. I made additional sales very quickly.
Soon I was selling so many policies that I attracted the attention of Audre's
uncle, Harold Goodman, who was a major stockholder and executive of a
company in Houston called Pioneer American Insurance. At Goodman's
suggestion, Bob Schulman, the executive vice president of Pioneer American, offered me a sales job. I was delighted to accept the offer because it gave
me the opportunity to get away from my father.

It's funny, but in my early thirties I had never thought about going into
insurance. Quite candidly, the insurance business had been repugnant to
me. My idea of an insurance salesman was a man who knocked on doors
asking for 25 cents. I thought of it in terms of industrial insurance. The idea
of being a salesman was equally abhorrent to me.

I received no training when I joined Pioneer American's San Antonio
agency in the fall of 1949. In those days insurance salesmen just learned by

doing. My lack of training didn't deter me. Using San Antonio as my base, I traveled to small towns throughout south Texas. I walked up one side of the street in a neighborhood and down the other selling policies.

Pioneer American was a full-line life insurance company. My favorite policy was similar to the savings plan I had sold for Papa. With memories of the Depression still fresh, I had phenomenal success selling people on the wisdom of putting money away for a rainy day. My sales presentation took about five minutes. The client only had to save about a dollar a week and then pay a $13 premium every three months. I made six or seven sales a day like that. When I sold a policy for $13, I made about $10. Each time the customer paid a premium, I got a certain percentage of that for the balance of the first year. Each year thereafter I got a much smaller percentage. As a result, I had no idea how much money I was earning because I was only drawing my earnings for each initial sale. When I left Pioneer in March 1951, however, the company sent me a residual check for $25,000. I had led the entire company in sales without knowing it. I was stunned. I had never earned more than $5,000 in any one year in my life.

I then realized, really for the first time, that I had a talent for selling. I guess I've always been a good salesman, but I refused to recognize that talent in myself. I never perceived myself as a salesman until I went with Pioneer American and started selling insurance. I was so good that within a few months they promoted me to general agent for the Waco area. At the end of 1949 Audre and I moved back to Waco, and I opened my general agency office.

Even after I opened my insurance office, I still harbored the faint hope in my heart that after I made some money, I would go back to the university, earn my doctoral degree, and become a professor. In my head, however, I knew that was not to be. I was thirty-three years old with a wife and baby. As a husband and father, my responsibilities were too important for me even to think about resuming my academic career.

> When he first went into the insurance business, I remember him saying he was going to stay in it for eight years, and at that time he would have accumulated enough money that he could go back and get his Ph.D. and get into academics. That was his desire at that time. He got more and more successful, so he never did let go. But that was his goal when he started out.
> — *Vera Friedsam, family friend*

I opened my Pioneer American Insurance Company agency in the old Service Mutual Building in Waco. This was the first time I had ever had a business or an office entirely my own. A general agent is really in business for himself. My agency consisted of myself and a nice guy named Herb Brenner, who later became American Income's vice president in charge of claims. In Waco I operated the same way I had in San Antonio, concentrating on little towns, with most of my clients being mom-and-pop businesses. I actually began to enjoy selling insurance, and I liked the feeling that being in business for myself gave me. I also was making some money, which was a big help to my family.

I learned a great deal about myself those few months when I had my general insurance agency. This sounds egotistical, but I discovered that I had a talent for the business and that I had the potential to build a big company. The realization broke me out of my shell. I used to think that if I ever made $200 a month in my life, it would be fantastic; now, for the first time, I had thoughts about really making a lot of money.

A critical reason for my success was my unbridled enthusiasm for the product I was selling. I learned that sincere enthusiasm is contagious. If one conveys an authentic excitement about whatever it is that one is selling, most people will have an instinctive attraction to that product. I don't know whether a person has to be born with an enthusiastic and gregarious personality or whether it can be developed, but it is essential for selling.

The second thing I learned was the importance of treating customers well and giving them honest and continuing service. Too many salespeople think that they are intelligent and the customer is stupid. Even if they get the customer to sign the application, and they collect the first month's premium, they never get around to understanding that unless the prospect keeps the policy, the salesperson hasn't earned anything. That type of salesperson makes the quick kill for the initial commission and then moves on to the next fast buck. The old customers are left to themselves. I learned the importance of maintaining my customer base more quickly than most insurance men do. The key to making money as a salesperson in the insurance business is to have a large base of clients who keep their policies for a long period of time. I believe in getting rich sure rather than getting rich quick. That has always been an important part of my philosophy, and it's something I learned that first year as a general agent.

I also received a valuable lesson from a kind old gentleman named Mr. Judd, whose office was across the hall from mine. My only employee, Herb Brenner, often arrived at the office before me. He would wait out in the hall until I arrived and unlocked the office. Mr. Judd called me into his office one day and asked if I would mind if he gave me some advice. He said that he could tell that I was a nice young man who was trying hard to build a business. "I've noticed that your employee is always here before you arrive for work," he said. "That's not very good leadership. You need to lead by example. You should be at work before your employees, and you should leave after they do." That was a valuable lesson in discipline for me, and I have followed it ever since.

The Rebirth of American Income Insurance Company

In March 1951 Audre's uncle Harold Goodman was so impressed by what I was doing with my agency that he asked me to meet with him in Indianapolis, Indiana, to discuss the possibility of our going into business together. Harold was the major stockholder in a small company in Indianapolis called American Standard, and he had recently become president of another small company, called American Income Insurance, which sold hospitalization insurance.

Harold was one of the great salesmen of all time. He started in business in Waco at the age of eighteen, selling accident insurance policies to cotton gin workers. By the time he was in his early twenties, he and two other men started a business in Dallas called Reserve Life Insurance Company. After several years, they decided to end their partnership. One of their companies was American Standard. Harold and his partners decided to draw straws to determine how they would divide their holdings. Whoever pulled the short straw took the company in Indiana. Harold got the short straw, and his former partners took the company in Dallas. Harold subsequently developed his American Standard into a mail-order business selling insurance to physicians. The company was modestly successful at first, but it eventually stagnated. Harold decided to convert the company into an agency with a sales force. The first people he recruited to manage the conversion didn't work out. That's when he called me.

At first, I wasn't that interested in Harold's invitation because my agency was prospering. But Harold was so insistent that it really made me curious. He even paid my train fare to Indiana. When we met in his office in Indianapolis, Harold told me that he had decided to develop American Income, which had been chartered in Indiana in 1924, into a bigger and more aggressive company. His plan was to reinsure American Income through American Standard and create a new mutual reserve company. American Income at that time operated only in Indiana. Harold explained that under Indiana law, he could start a mutual insurance company for a minimum of $25,000 in legal reserve. A stock company required $300,000 reserve.

Harold proposed that I move to Indianapolis and run the company, and he would borrow the $25,000 needed for the reserve. He would give me 20-

percent ownership of the company, and he would own the rest. He would assume the title of president; I would be the executive vice president. It took me about twenty seconds to accept Harold's offer. I realized that Harold was giving me an opportunity to build my own company and that his terms were more than generous.

> **Harold gave Bernard the opportunity because he knew how competent he was. He had always been impressed with Bernard. In addition, Harold wasn't about to live in Indianapolis to run that company. He had turned his company, American Standard, over to his secretary, Vera Allen. It was a mail-order business, and he wanted to stop that.**
> —*Audre Rapoport*

I stayed in Indianapolis for two or three days and then took the train back to Texas. On the way back, I worried about Audre's reaction, because I knew that she would be extremely reluctant to move away from Waco. When I told her about the agreement I had made with her uncle, she became very upset. "I'm not going," she said. "I hate that damned place. I'm not leaving Waco." We fought and argued for several days about it. Quite candidly, this developed into a major crisis for our marriage. To me, the new company in Indiana seemed to be our golden opportunity, but Audre did not want to move to the Midwest for any reason. She eventually agreed to go, but she was never happy in Indiana.

> **I didn't mind going to Indianapolis as long as I didn't have to live there for more than a year or two. We were supposed to get the company started and then move it to Texas. It was with that understanding that I finally agreed to move.**
> —*Audre Rapoport*

I closed our business with Pioneer American, and we moved to Indianapolis in May 1951. That is the month that we officially started American Income Insurance Company.

Frank McKinney

Harold and I borrowed the $25,000 that we needed for the company's reserve from Frank McKinney, who then had a small bank called the Fidelity Bank and Trust Company in Indianapolis. Frank McKinney and

I developed a strong and warm friendship, and he quickly became an important person in my life. Frank was the first really rich person I ever knew. Some people thought he had a cold personality, but he was warm to me. Actually, he had a winning humility. Even when he became rich and famous, Frank never showed the hubris that taints so many who rise from the depths.

The son of a poor Irish-American family, Frank McKinney's life epitomized the American dream. He quit high school at the age of fourteen to take a job as a messenger boy at Fidelity Bank. Sixteen years later he was the bank president. He was a fascinating guy who had a wide range of interests. For a few years after World War II, Frank, movie star Bing Crosby, and their partners owned the Pittsburgh Pirates baseball team. Frank loved politics, and he was devoted to the Democratic Party. A few months after Frank loaned us the $25,000 to start the company, President Harry Truman appointed him chairman of the National Democratic Party. Truman needed someone to help restore the credibility of the party bureaucracy after a series of scandals. The former chairman, William Boyle, had made a pretty big mess of things. Frank took the job because he knew that 1952 would be a tough year for the Democrats, and he wanted to do whatever he could to help the party keep the White House. Frank was so dedicated and selfless that he declined the $35,000 annual salary that Boyle had been paid. Although the Republicans won the presidency and the Congress in the 1952 election, it certainly wasn't Frank's fault. No one has ever worked harder as party chairman.

Anyway, Frank McKinney was a significant influence on my life. He had a strong confidence in me that made an important contribution to my development as a businessman. Frank was one of the first models that I had as a businessman. He showed me that building a business and being politically involved weren't mutually exclusive activities. Frank played a critically supportive role in the development and success of American Income Life Insurance Company almost until his death in 1974. A year after we borrowed that initial $25,000, we borrowed another $25,000 without paying a penny on the principal of the first loan. We kept borrowing money from him to support our expanding operations. At the end of three or four years, we owed him $200,000 to $300,000. Eventually, our debt totaled millions of dollars. During that course of time, I never paid a penny toward the principal or the interest on that debt. We never planned it that way, but McKinney basically financed the company.

Long after American Income had become a successful company McKinney told me a story that revealed how much confidence he had in my abilities. In 1953 Indiana state bank examiners conducted a routine audit of McKinney's bank loans. One of the examiners went to McKinney and reported that the Rapoport loan looked a little questionable.

"The collateral doesn't seem heavy enough for the amount that he's borrowed," the examiner said.

McKinney answered, "Well, I'll tell you this. This Rapoport is the finest young executive in the country, and he is building a great company." That impressive statement satisfied the examiner.

About two years later my debt to McKinney's bank had grown to $500,000. During another review, the examiner went to McKinney and said, "Mr. McKinney, I'm concerned about the size of this loan to Mr. Rapoport." McKinney gave him the same story about what a good executive I was and how well the company was doing. The examiner was concerned, but he let it go.

About one year later, the same state examiner came back to McKinney's bank and discovered that I owed $1 million. Exasperated, the examiner said, "Mr. McKinney, don't worry, I'm not going to ask you about this Rapoport loan. I just want you to answer one question. Is Mr. Rapoport in good health?"

> **In 1951 Bernie told me he was getting ready to make a lot of money. He had just borrowed $25,000 to buy an interest in a fledgling life insurance company. At one point during the early days, his banker called to complain that the company account was overdrawn by $30,000. "Why are you complaining to me?" Rapoport asked. "Don't you know that if I had $30,000, I'd already have put it in the bank?"** *—Jim Wright*

McKinney was not the only person in those early days who had confidence in me. A few days after Audre and I arrived in Indianapolis in May 1951, Harold Goodman came to me and said, "Bernard, it's obvious to me that you are a bright young man. You are now in total charge of this company. Go build it. I'm going to Europe tomorrow and then back to Waco, and I will not return to Indiana for at least six months." I was stunned and a little scared, but I was also excited. I realized that he was giving me the opportunity to do something significant and that only my own skill and talent would limit me. I was now free to test those limits.

> **Harold sort of dumped the company in Bernard's lap and he and his wife went to Europe. He thought Bernard was fabulous. He just trusted him completely.** *—Audre Rapoport*

Looking back on Harold's decision, I am awed by the risk that he took. I am also embarrassed by the attitude I assumed when he turned me loose. I was so determined to stand or fall entirely on my own, I never asked Harold for advice or help, even when I was in desperate need of it. That approach was indulging in pure foolishness. I could have saved a pile of money and pain if I had gone to Harold for advice in those early days. Only a fool thinks he or she can build anything of value without help from others. Whenever Morris Zale was introduced as the person who had built Zales into the leading jewelry company in the world, he was always quick to correct that statement. "I couldn't have built Zales by myself," he would point out. "Even if I could have," he would add, "why would I have wanted to? That would not have been interesting or fun." That is a truth I have never forgotten.

Judge Joseph G. Wood was another person who was a major help to me during the company's founding years. As our lawyer in Indiana, Wood handled the legal issues related to getting our business sanctioned by the state. Joe was one of those attorneys who really love the law. He was a Lincoln-like figure, a marvelous man. In the early 1950s, one of our employees stole some money from the company. When the insurance investigator came to check it out, he told Joe that we had not exercised diligent oversight in supervising the staff and that his insurance company might not pay us for our losses. Joe stared at him for a minute and then said, "Listen, Rapoport is so damn busy building this business that he doesn't have time to look over everybody's shoulder every day. You better pay him!" They did. Joe later became commissioner of insurance for the state of Indiana. His son later served as our attorney in Indiana.

Learning How to Manage a Company

When Harold Goodman left the company in my hands, he already had four or five people working in the office, which was fortunate for me, because I knew absolutely nothing about underwriting or claims or any of the other technical aspects of the insurance business. All I had ever done was sell insurance. I had no clue about how to run an insurance company. That first office staff included James R. Johnston, a highly intelligent man who became our company secretary and general office manager. Jim is a religious person and one of the most honorable men that I have ever met. He did not know how to take me at first. I was aggressive and brash, and it caused some problems between us in the very early days, but when Jim and I took time to talk about something other than insurance, he realized how interested I was in philosophy and ethical issues. That created an entirely different and positive relationship between us. We developed a close friendship.

My personal secretary was Vera Allen, who stayed with me for many years. She had been with Harold Goodman about seventeen years before he moved her over to the new American Income in 1951. She was with me until her retirement in 1975. If there were a list of the all-time great secretaries, Vera's name would have to be at the head of it. She had a bright mind and outstanding judgment. She taught me a lot about life. I used to be terrible about not carrying any cash, and occasionally I would borrow a dollar or two from her. Finally, one day she came into my office and pointed out that I had borrowed $5 and not paid her back. "Five dollars doesn't mean much to you," she said, "but it means a lot to me." I realized then that I had been insensitive. That taught me a lesson that I have never forgotten.

I spent much of that first month acting like I knew what I was doing, but I really didn't. A few days after I had settled into my office, Mary Jo Abigt (who became head of our policy owner service and was with the company many years) came to me with a problem. "Mr. Rapoport," she said, "a very difficult insurance claim has just arrived in the mail. It doesn't look right to us. What do you think we ought to do about it?"

I looked at the claim. I don't recall what it was about, but I do remember that it was a complete mystery to me. I decided to act as though I was testing her competence. "Well, Mary Jo," I asked, "what do you think we ought to do with it?" She told me how she thought we ought to handle it.

"You know," I responded, "I think you're exactly right." Her way of handling it must have been the correct way, because I never heard anything else about it.

I was supposed to be the boss, but it was just a big bluff. Learning to run a business involves a lot of self-education. I slowly realized that to be an effective manager I had to rely on the people around me; I couldn't be too proud to ask for help. I learned during those first few months that it was important to understand what it was that I didn't know and to go to the right person to find out the answer. I couldn't let my ego get in the way. Once I understood that rule, I really had no problems with my staff. If we ran into a problem that no one had handled before, we all just pulled together and worked it out.

> Bernard really didn't know what he was doing. It wasn't easy. It was a whole new job. He had never tried to build a company from scratch, much less manage one. —*Audre Rapoport*

A major problem that confronted me as the chief executive of the company was that I didn't understand budgeting. I didn't know how to control expenses, except that I obviously knew I couldn't spend more money than

I took in. We didn't even have a budget that first year; I just ran the company instinctively. One significant but complex issue that I didn't comprehend the first two or three years was our reserve. Let's say that my insurance company takes in $5 million in premiums one year while paying out only $1 million in claims. The remaining $4 million has to go into a reserve because it belongs to the policy owners, not to the company. The company is just holding it in a reserve. I really didn't understand that the first year we had the insurance company.

Luckily, our treasurer William R. Frank was exceedingly penurious, which was good for me. Bill had what I call a balance-sheet view of business. He sat on my enthusiasm all the time, keeping me from jumping into risky financial waters. Bill became my right-hand man, even though we argued constantly. His willingness to disagree with me openly was his strength and primary value to me. I don't like people who are always agreeing with me. I believe that I can stand a great deal of dissension from my advisors without losing my cool. Throughout the years, nearly all of my executives have been ultraconservative in their business orientation. I am the optimist in the company, and every time I want to do something, I bounce it against these conservatives. If I can't outreason them, then I don't do it. That is the kind of balance companies must have to be successful.

We started out with one salesperson and soon had about three hundred, including myself. I was a working president. I personally sold a policy in every one of the ninety-two counties in Indiana. The sheer force of my determination is what carried us through the first six years of the company's existence. I had the will, the enthusiasm, and the willingness to work sixteen hours a day. I was in the office from eight o'clock in the morning until four-thirty in the afternoon. Then I recruited personnel, took them out in the field, and trained them until eleven or twelve o'clock at night. I have personally field-trained hundreds of agents in my career. The first office I opened was in Fort Wayne, about a hundred miles from Indianapolis. Many times I left the office at four-thirty in the afternoon and drove to Fort Wayne, worked in the field with an agent for three or four hours, drove back to Indianapolis by midnight, and was in the office the next morning at eight o'clock.

> **Bernard was gone from home most of the time. He would leave the house at 6 A.M. and often not return until 2 A.M. Ronnie would ask, "When is Daddy going to come visit us again?"**
> —*Audre Rapoport*

It was that routine that caused Audre's uncle Aubrey Goodman in April 1954 to write me a letter with some advice: "Dear Bernard: It was a pleasure being with you [in Indianapolis], but I want to give you a few words of advice. You are working entirely too hard . . . you are too tense and your mind is wandering and you are doing too damn much. I know that you are a very smart person in some respects, but in other ways, you are very dumb! If it takes a little longer to get things up to where you want them, that's all just as good; I'm sure Harold would want it that way."

We had a lot of agents, but the quality of our business was poor. A company today couldn't exist with the low persistence rate we had. By that I mean the high lapse ratio of our policies. One reason we survived was our low overhead—costs were so much less then than they are today. We also survived because we specialized in health and hospitalization insurance. Life insurance is by far the more profitable business in the long run, and that's what builds the assets of an insurance company and gives the company its stability and its strength. But in the 1950s small companies like ours were much better off working on the health and hospitalization side of the business than in life insurance. In those days, the majority of the American people had no hospitalization insurance. Blue Cross and Blue Shield had not taken hold to the extent that they did later. The federal Medicare and Medicaid programs didn't exist.

We developed a simple, straightforward strategy to take advantage of the opportunities in the hospital insurance field. We set up a boiler room: about ten or twelve telephone operators who selected prospective customers from the telephone directory. Our boiler-room people called these prospects on the telephone to set up appointments for our salespeople to meet with them. The phone staff used a written sales presentation that we called a pitch to get the appointments. The pitch was simply that we had a low-cost hospital plan, which is about all one had to say in those days to get the prospect's attention. I would say that the average person to whom we sold medical insurance in those days was not an informed customer. Most were low-salaried, unsophisticated buyers. After the telephone pitch, the agents would go to the prospect's house and make our official presentation, which was aimed at the prospect's emotions. Our sales representatives painted a frightening picture of the prospect or the prospect's spouse or child in the hospital and an enormous hospital bill hanging over him. The point was to make the prospect realize that he was totally unprotected. We wanted the prospect to be so worried about being in the hospital and saddled with such a crushing medical debt that he would buy a policy before the sales representative walked out of the house.

Perhaps we should not have appealed to emotion or fear to make a sale, but the fact is that those people did need health insurance. It wasn't a luxury. It was a necessity. Sometimes it takes a scare tactic to make a person aware of a critical need. It is unethical to use that approach to sell jewelry or any other nonessential commodity, but in this case, I don't believe there is an ethical issue. I have been deeply concerned with the question of business ethics all my life, especially the ethics of selling in a free enterprise economy, which is obviously predatory in basis. Concerns about these ethical issues are the most important considerations that any business can or should incorporate into its operating culture.

I have to admit that we sold policies in the early days that I wouldn't sell today. Nevertheless, I sincerely believe that we gave our medical insurance customers good value for their premiums. A large percentage of that original business remained on the books for many years. We just kept their policies on the books, even though they were unprofitable. We made good money on those policies during the early years, but as people get older, obviously their incidence of hospitalization rises. What was rather a modest value in those days became a marvelous bargain. We couldn't possibly sell insurance at those equivalent prices today.

Despite my inexperience, the company took in about $95,000 worth of premium income the first year. It was a good start, but I knew we could do much better. The main point was that we had survived the first year. The truth is that starting out we had no definitive plans except to build a large company, and to that we were totally committed. That commitment, however, was not a substitute for a solid background in the insurance business. I certainly would not say that I was a very good businessman in the early 1950s. I ran a hodgepodge operation. But in our case, commitment was supported by enthusiasm, hard work, and sheer will power that hid many of our deficiencies. A company could not do that today and survive. I don't even think you could start an insurance company today; the costs are too high.

I told Harold Goodman at the end of that first year that if we ever got the company to where we were taking in $1 million a year in premiums, we would never have to work again. Two years later, when we reached that million-dollar mark, I told Harold that if we got the company to where we were taking in about $2 million, we would have it made, and he agreed. Then in 1954, we took in $2 million. I realized then that I was capable of building a really big company.

> Bernard built something out of nothing. That's basically what happened. He had enough energy to take twenty or thirty people and literally drive them all by himself. There were some incredibly helpful external things that happened, but what built a primarily accident and health company — with peddlers going down the street, with no lead system, knocking on doors

and selling their stuff—was Bernard Rapoport's sheer force of will. *— Charles Cooper, former president, American Income Life Insurance Company*

American Income Becomes a Stock Company (1954)

As our premium income climbed toward $2 million, Harold Goodman and I decided to make American Income a stock company. To do that, Harold and I formed an entirely new company called American Income *Life* Insurance Company (AILICO), with $200,000 in capital and $100,000 in surplus. In September 1954 this new company reinsured the policies of our old mutual company. The stock ownership percentage remained roughly the same as in the original deal, with Harold Goodman having about 80 percent while I had about 20 percent. We sold 30,000 shares of the remaining stock at $20 per share. That stock offering brought in $600,000, which was what we used to build the company. Frank McKinney bought a large chunk of the new shares. I watched in amazement as Frank sat at his desk and wrote a personal check for $15,000 to buy his stock. I had never seen anyone write a check for that much.

Three months after we converted into a stock company, Harold decided to merge his American Standard Company with American Income. American Standard sold insurance to physicians by direct mail. It didn't amount to much. I don't think they had more than $400,000 worth of premiums, but the merger did add to our rapid growth during those last four months of 1954.

Growing beyond Indiana

I believed almost from the beginning that eventually AILICO would be a national company, but I had no particular plan or strategy to make that happen. At first, my only goal was survival. By 1954, however, we were receiving 6,000 insurance policy applications a month in Indiana, which was an astounding number of applications for a company our size. It was about that time that I began to look for opportunities in other states.

Kentucky was the obvious first choice. We had brought to Indiana several agents from an industrial company in Kentucky, which gave us some expertise in that state's market, and I knew of several other good agents still in Kentucky who wanted to work for us there. Having an effective sales force already on the ground, I thought Kentucky offered an excellent opportunity. The Indiana company could not apply for a license to do business in Kentucky because we had not yet converted from a mutual company into a stock company, so we formed a stock company in Louisville, Kentucky, with $125,000 in capital and $75,000 in surplus debentures (financial obligations to investors that are secondary to the interests of policy owners). The Kentucky insurance commissioner ruled that we could use a surplus debenture to count for our reserve. We used debentures for tax reasons. Investors get their money back as a simple repayment of a debt rather than as a dividend, which is taxed twice.

A year later, however, a newly elected Kentucky state insurance commissioner ruled that the debentures could not be counted as a company asset. That ruling put us into an untenable position. We lacked the borrowing power to handle the financing of both the Kentucky company and the Indiana company if something went wrong and we found ourselves in a tight financial spot. Fearing that our company in Kentucky might drain resources from our Indiana company and cause us to lose both, I decided to sell off the Kentucky company. Fortunately, our Kentucky agents had sold enough insurance policies to make the company attractive enough to sell to Wabash Life of Indiana in 1955.

Kentucky taught me to pay close attention to the political situation in the states in which we operate. If I had been more aware of the political situation, I would have developed a personal relationship with the new commissioner and made my case about why our company needed to use the debentures for reserve, hoping to prevent the change in policy. My failure to do that cost us the Kentucky company. That was a political and business mistake I worked hard not to repeat.

Despite our experience in Kentucky, I continued to look for opportunities in other states. In 1956 I concluded after careful study that Ohio was the best state in the country for our kind of insurance operation. Ohio has more large cities than any other state, yet it is relatively small in size. I could see that a central office in Columbus would put us within easy driving distance of all the major population centers, such as Cincinnati, Akron, Dayton, and Cleveland.

It was difficult in the mid-1950s for an insurance company to get a license to do business in Ohio. The chief insurance examiner in the state, Glenn Waugh, was the toughest in the nation. My friends in the business laughed at me when I told them we wanted to operate in Ohio. They predicted that Waugh would throw me out of his office and that it would all be a waste of my time and resources. I was warned that it would take two or three years to complete the applications and to jump through all of the hoops Waugh had set up just to find out in the end that he was turning us down.

Ohio was too critical to our future for me to be that easily scared off. Determined to make the breakthrough and eager to do it in a period of months, not years, I made an appointment to see the formidable Mr. Waugh. When I was ushered into his office at the state insurance commission headquarters in Columbus, I dispensed with the standard preliminary small talk and went directly to the point. "Mr. Waugh," I declared, "I want to bring my insurance company into the state of Ohio." I handed him the AILICO financial statement.

Waugh glanced at my document and frowned. "That's not much of a statement," he said as he pushed it back at me. "Forget it, I'll never let you in."

That was the reaction I had expected, so I screwed up my courage and declared, "Yes, you are going to let us in."

Waugh jumped up from his chair with a scowl on his face. "Didn't anybody tell you how tough I am?"

"Yes, sir, they did," I replied, "but I know that you'll let my company into Ohio because I'm going to do everything you tell me to do, and you won't have a good reason to keep us out."

"Oh, is that so?" Waugh said. He then pulled a thick stack of documents out of his desk drawer. "Well, you have to fill out all of these papers before we can even begin to talk about it."

This was about eleven o'clock in the morning. I took the application papers and raced to catch the next plane for Indianapolis. My staff and I worked all night filling out the application. The next morning I took the six-thirty plane from Indianapolis to Columbus, and by eight-thirty I was waiting in his office.

"What in the hell are you doing back here?" Waugh asked.

"You told me to fill out these papers," I replied. "Here they are. I told you I'm going to do everything you wanted."

"Well, that's just the start," Waugh said. "Now you have to get these things done."

He handed me a list of about twelve things I had to do. I rushed back to Indianapolis, and my staff and I worked until about eleven o'clock that night. I jumped back on the six-thirty plane to Columbus the next morning and walked into Waugh's office at eight-thirty. When I handed Waugh the material from his list, he just looked at me, shook his head, and declared, "Rapoport, I can see right now that you're going to drive me crazy."

During the next two months I made about fifteen trips to Waugh's office. As I had promised, I did everything he asked, and I did it quickly. We met all of the legal requirements, and our reputation in Indiana was impeccable. I finally just wore him down. It took us two months to get a license in Ohio. I doubt that anyone had ever gotten permission to operate in that state in less than three years. My work in Ohio is an example of what I mean when I say that a person has to have the will and the energy to get things done. That is what I always stress to the people who are associated with my company. That's what Tolstoy meant in *War and Peace* when he talked about that unknown "x," that spirit that enables people to do things that just aren't reasonable to others.

Getting into Ohio in 1956 was a watershed in AILICO's history. Ohio soon became the most profitable state in the company's operations, giving us the financial means and the administrative momentum to expand into other states. We also jumped an enormous psychological hurdle when we entered the Buckeye state. It allowed us to cast off our pushcart peddler mentality and showed us that American Income could be a national company.

A state license to engage in the insurance business is a valuable asset, so we decided to accumulate as many as possible. We took a buckshot approach and sent our statement to every state insurance commission. I can't take credit for having a particular plan. If a state agreed to let us in, we went in. There was no geographical pattern, it just depended on which state opened up first. We made a drive to get into all the states, but I wanted all the big states, especially Pennsylvania and Illinois. With the exception of California, the time it took to get approvals varied from thirty days to three years. It took us ten years to get into California, but its insurance commission is one of the toughest in the country. The California commission requires insurance companies to have a much larger reserve than that required in other states, which was a real problem for us because our reserve was so small. When we finally made it into California, however, it quickly became our best market.

My most important job after we received permission to enter a state was to recruit a state general agent. The success of our business was determined essentially by the quality of our sales management in each state. If the general agent in a particular state was good, we did well, so that person couldn't be recruited in a haphazard fashion. That is why I personally recruited the general agents. Many people thought that I should have delegated that duty to others, but I have always believed that recruiting personnel is one of my strengths as a businessman.

During this period of major expansion, I was on the road constantly. I went wherever I thought I could find good candidates for the job of general agent. In those early days, I acquired a reputation as a talent raider who grabbed bright young agents from other companies. Being the romantic that I am, I thought of myself as a liberator, because I gave my general agents larger commissions than they could ordinarily receive from their former companies.

By the end of 1956 American Income was operating in thirteen states, including Ohio, Pennsylvania, Michigan, Florida, and Texas, and we were on the verge of entering several other states. We had 300 sales personnel in the field operating out of ninety-six general agencies. During the previous two years our assets had doubled, our net reserve had tripled, our capital and surplus had more than doubled, and we had about $15 million of insurance in force, a 50-percent increase from 1954.

It was an exciting and deeply satisfying time for the business side of my life. Unfortunately, the private side of my life was not in such good shape.

Return to Waco

Audre moved back to Waco in 1956. She simply decided that she was not going to live in Indianapolis any longer. Audre disliked Indianapolis, but that wasn't the only reason she left. She did not want to live that far away from her mother. They were extremely close.

> I was not happy in Indianapolis at all. Ronnie was sick frequently with colds and asthma; he went through the measles and chicken pox. It was freezing outside most of the time. When I went to the store, I had to drive on ice and snow. When B *was* at home, he wasn't real happy. He was under a lot of pressure, and he was tense and stressed out. It wasn't a real happy time. I finally had to move back to Waco. Actually, I stayed three years longer than I had agreed to. —*Audre Rapoport*

This was a crisis period for me. I refused to move, so Audre and Ronnie left Indianapolis and we separated. I hate to admit this, but initially I chose my business over my family. I moved into an apartment in Indianapolis. That lasted five or six months. Audre and I nearly split up because of her move back to Waco. The reason we did not get divorced was our child, Ronnie. I could not stand the thought of being without a family, so I went to Waco and told Audre that I would commute between Waco and our company office in Indianapolis. By then, American Income was operating in Texas, with the state office in Waco, but the company's management offices were in Indianapolis, and that's where I had to be. I began a tiring routine in which I spent each week in Indiana and then flew back to Waco for the weekends.

After commuting for nearly two years, I realized that the physical and mental toll was too heavy. I decided to explore the possibility of moving our home offices from Indianapolis to Waco. When I proposed the move to Harold Goodman, he had no objection so long as it did not affect our Indiana charter. I went to the Indiana insurance commissioner and explained my predicament. He assured me that having our headquarters in Waco would not affect our charter. So we made the move in March 1958. To this day the main office is in Waco, but the company continues to be chartered in Indiana.

After I transferred our offices to Waco in 1958, AILICO's growth continued at a steady but unspectacular pace for the next five or six years. During that period, I began to wean the company away from the accident and health business. Income from our accident and health policies made it possible to build enough profit into the company to withstand a drain on surplus and allow us to get into life insurance more deeply. By the early 1960s our life insurance, which was a more profitable product, was exceeding our accident and health income.

The RIC Fight

In April 1960 Harold Goodman decided to resign as chairman of the board and to sell his share of the company. Eager for retirement, Harold wanted to be free of any business responsibilities. He made this decision with my blessing and gratitude. Harold was the man who had put up the money to make the company possible, and he was entitled to have his years of peace. During all the time that Harold and I were in business together, he never interfered with my management of the company. He was supportive of everything I did. Harold always said that he was a high school dropout, but he was one of the wisest men I have ever known.

> **Harold was very bright and well read. He never gave Bernard any problems with the business. He never second-guessed Bernard, or if Bernard made a mistake he never gave him a hard time about his mistake.** —*Audre Rapoport*

Harold sold his stock for a profit of about $2 million to the Reinsurance Investment Corporation (RIC), a holding company that also controlled Loyal American Life Insurance Company of Mobile, Alabama, and Hamilton Life Insurance Company of New York. In turn, Ladenburg, Thalmann, and Company, a substantial Wall Street investment banking house, controlled RIC. With the purchase of Harold's stock, RIC owned 46 percent of American Income, plus it acquired a voting proxy on my stock, which gave it control of another 20 percent. When RIC took control of American Income, one of Ladenburg, Thalmann's senior partners, Otto Marx, Jr., replaced Harold Goodman as chairman of American Income. I retained my job as president.

The purchase of Goodman's stock entitled RIC to select eight of the fifteen members of American Income's board of directors. RIC chose seven of its own people and then asked Frank McKinney to remain on the board as the eighth director. RIC recognized the value of having the former head of the Democratic National Committee serve as one of the company's directors. Keeping Frank on the board, however, turned out to be a major tactical mistake for RIC, because it gave my allies and me a one-vote majority. Frank respected my judgment, and he admired the way I had built American Income, so whenever RIC asked for the board to approve some action that I opposed, Frank sided with me and my allies on the board. At every board meeting, the vote was eight to seven in our favor. That resulted in acrimonious board meetings, but it also made it possible for me to retain control of the company.

The basic reason for contention was that the seven RIC directors had no interest in building the company; they saw American Income only as a way to make a fast buck. In those days, there were a lot of fly-by-night investment companies, and RIC was one of them. All they were interested in was financial manipulation. They wanted the stock to go up as quickly as possible so they could sell out and make a quick dollar, the kind of behavior that eventually produced more stringent regulation by the Securities and Exchange Commission (SEC). The ringleader among RIC's seven directors was an investor by the name of Richard Weininger. He and the other RIC directors wanted to milk American Income, and they wanted to do things that were improper. They decided to value all of our life insurance policies (term insurance, whole life insurance, and even group insurance) at the same price, a scheme that created fictional assets. The number of policies they listed was correct, but the stated value was not the real value. For example, a $100,000 group insurance policy has about one-twentieth the profit value of a $100,000 whole life insurance policy. They were inflating the value of the company stock artificially so they could sell it for a quick profit and get out. That was their only interest. They had no pride of ownership in the company. I refused to cooperate with them in this scam.

There were some nefarious characters associated with RIC, particularly a four-flusher named Philip J. Goldberg, RIC's vice chairman. The management at Ladenburg, Thalmann was enthralled with Goldberg because he wrote a lot of big-dollar insurance policies rather quickly. I kept telling them that the only thing that counts in the insurance business is premium income. You can write millions of dollars' worth of life insurance, but what's important is how much money it actually brings into the company through persistent and long-term payment of premium. No one at Ladenburg, Thalmann wanted to listen, however. Goldberg tried to run roughshod over me, and we fought constantly. This was a guy who bragged about having spies on his payroll who reported inside information to him about the various companies in which he had financial interests. He refused to accept the idea that one could have a different opinion from his and still be a friend. Anyone who disagreed with him about anything was his adversary, and if someone who disagreed with him wasn't Jewish, that person was also an anti-Semite.

Weininger soon became frustrated by his inability to get a majority of the votes at American Income board meetings, so at a specially called meeting of the board in the late spring of 1962, he demanded that the board be expanded. The motion was rejected. After that defeat, Weininger asked me to consider various means by which 100,000 shares of American Income could be issued to RIC for services. He told me that he fully expected to take control of American Income's board of directors at the next annual stockholder's meeting in 1963. It was then that I knew that RIC and I were headed for a full-fledged fight.

> **Our house was like Grand Central Station during the RIC fight. All of these people were in and out and hanging around the house. It was a madhouse, and there was a lot of tension. It was a mess. Mr. Goldberg was not a very nice guy. I don't know how we survived.** — *Audre Rapoport*

A way out soon developed, however. Harry Lake, the managing partner of Ladenburg, Thalmann, asked me to join them in taking complete control over RIC. In return, Ladenburg, Thalmann would spin off American Income and return control of the company to me. I readily accepted his invitation. After the fight began, however, Lake called and said that the effort was getting too messy. They had lost control of the situation, so they were pulling back. At this point, it really wasn't clear just who was in control of RIC. I was stunned. I had agreed to support them, and now they were abandoning me. That did not make any difference to them. They would leave me at the mercy of Weininger and his group.

That's when I decided that I had to get AILICO away from RIC. I met with Harry Lake and other executives at Ladenburg, Thalmann and told them that I wanted to purchase 30,000 shares of AILICO stock from RIC at $20 a share and have the remaining stock spun off to the 7,000 or 8,000 other shareholders, which would diffuse RIC's ownership. This would give me approximately 25 percent of American Income and put me in control. They indicated that my proposal would be accepted, but a few months later

Weininger managed to block the deal. When I realized that I was getting the runaround, I decided to use my talent as a counterbalance to their capital. I informed Ladenburg, Thalmann that unless they agreed to my purchase I would resign from the company, walk out of my office, and take my salespeople with me. I would just close down the company. I gave them a deadline of just a few hours to make up their minds.

> Bernard hired and trained all of the company's agents. He was on the road all the time meeting with the agents. The personal bond between him and the agents during this period was such that he could easily have taken the agents with him. There's no question about it. — *Charles Cooper*

The thing that saved us was that I had the talent to build, the others did not, and they knew it. My talent was bankable. That allowed me to stay in the fight without any significant assets. Ladenburg, Thalmann knew that if I left, the company's stock value would plunge, so Harry Lake called me back before the deadline and said he would do it. This was good news, but it meant that I had to raise $1.5 million quickly, which was an awful lot of money in the early 1960s.

I persuaded the banks to give me most of the money, but I came up $300,000 short. I began to scour the world, so to speak, to find that last chunk of money. I went to New York with my lawyer Pat Beard, but we had no luck at all. Pat and I had met in 1955 when he was a partner in the law firm of Beard, Kultgen, and Nokes. George Nokes, whom I had met through Jim Wright, was our lawyer from that firm. When George decided to leave the firm in 1958, I decided to stay with Pat Beard. He soon became my closest business associate and one of my best friends. Pat has been my attorney for nearly four decades now, and he became a member of American Income's board of directors. He's not really the kind of guy you want as a business partner, but when you are in trouble he is the best person you could ever have on your side. We fight like cats and dogs and we get separated sometimes, but we never get divorced. Pat has a tremendous capacity for loyalty, and he's always there when I need him. He was my guiding light during the RIC fight.

I was ready to give up after we had exhausted every possible source in New York searching for that $300,000. Pat and I shared a hotel room in New York because we had to watch every penny we had. Just as I was going to bed, I told Pat that it was all over; we had lost the company. The next morning Pat said, "You son of a bitch, you went right to sleep as soon as your head hit the pillow. I couldn't sleep at all."

I said, "Pat, everything's perfect. I got some rest. We are going to beat those bastards."

As cocky as I was, I really had no idea what to do. I just had this odd feeling that we would prevail somehow. I called Audre and told her that we had failed to raise the money we needed. Her mother was there, and she got on the telephone. She urged me to come home and try to raise the money from our friends in Waco. Audre agreed with her mother.

"Audre," I replied, "there's not three hundred thousand dollars in all of Waco."

"There just has to be," Audre insisted. "Come home and try."

> If it hadn't been for Mother, we wouldn't have survived. Mother got on the telephone and said, "Bernard, come back to Waco. This is where people know you. I know you can get twelve people to give twenty-five thousand dollars." That struck a chord with Bernard. Mother also loaned us money to help. In fact, she loaned us all she had. Mother didn't have a lot of money, but she accumulated some over the years and played the stock market. —*Audre Rapoport*

I had no other choice, so I went home, and a remarkable thing happened. I called twenty-one people in Waco and asked them if they would buy $15,000 worth of stock each, and twenty people agreed to do it. I raised the money in just one day. The people in Waco are good people, and if you have a solid reputation, they will go along with you. Those wonderful folks saved my life. That put me back in control of American Income. We got rid of those RIC people, and we replaced them with directors who were interested in making the company grow and who understood that it was a long-term process.

The RIC fight was the roughest and most traumatic event in my business career; the day that I gave up in New York was the low point. It didn't take me long, however, to get fired up again. With the help of a new base of customers—the hardworking members of our nation's labor unions—we soon had American Income back on track.

5 ▶ *A Liberal Trichotomist*

My return to Texas in 1956 eventually led me back into the political wars that I had abandoned with such disillusionment after the Homer Rainey debacle ten years before. Actually, my political alienation lasted only three or four years. The main reason for my political inaction in the decade following Rainey's defeat was my need to make a living. In those years Audre and I struggled financially, and my work to build American Income left me little time for anything else. In addition, my move to Indiana in 1951 took me away from the political scene in Texas, and I was reluctant to become politically active in a newly adopted home state where I had much to learn. I remained deeply interested in national politics, but only as a distant observer.

During the 1948 presidential race, for example, I paid close attention to the campaign of former vice president Henry Wallace, who was running on a third-party ticket against President Harry Truman and the Republican candidate, New York governor Thomas A. Dewey. In those days I remained (mistakenly, as I look back on it) sympathetic with the Soviet Union. I thought that we could make deals with Joseph Stalin that would help humanity and preserve the peace. Henry Wallace ran on an anti–Cold War platform that appealed to feelings I had developed as a youngster years before, on those Sunday afternoons in San Antonio when I listened to my Marxist father plead for the "workers of the world to unite." I had rejected Marxism as an economic system, but I still admired the socialist experiment in the Soviet Union. I had a less than critical view of the actions of a nation that had played such a crucial role in crushing Hitler's Germany. It seemed to me that Wallace and his Progressive Party offered an appealing alternative to the confrontational foreign policy of the Truman administration. I also felt that Truman's domestic policy was too conservative. Wallace advocated reforms that echoed the liberal spirit of the Homer Rainey campaign in Texas, and many of Rainey's supporters favored Wallace.

So I was set to cast my ballot for Wallace, but a funny thing happened as I entered the voting booth. I discovered that I could not turn against the national Democratic Party. I was torn between my emotional commitment to Wallace, who I knew could not win, and my pragmatic realization that we had better elect Truman rather than Thomas Dewey. I voted for Truman, and I suspect that many other Wallace sympathizers finally made the same decision.

I came out of my political lethargy in 1952 when Frank McKinney, the man who loaned me the money to start American Income, invited me to Chicago as his guest to observe some of the sessions of the Democratic Party's national convention. As chairman of the national Democratic Party, McKinney played an active role in the convention, which was held in the huge international amphitheater at the Chicago Stockyards.

Frank gave me tickets to get into the amphitheater as a spectator. I wasn't a delegate, and I played no role in the political action there, but I was excited about seeing my first national convention. It was a fascinating show. I remember the pride I felt as a Texan seeing the legendary Sam Rayburn, Speaker of the House of Representatives, preside over the convention.

Adding to the thrill of the event, of course, was the struggle for the nomination. In those days, state primaries did not decide the parties' presidential candidates. With Truman refusing to run for another term, no one had the nomination locked up. Senator Estes Kefauver of Tennessee led the pack, but he was far short of having enough votes to win. Not until the third ballot, which occurred late on Friday night, July 25, did the convention finally swing over to Illinois governor Adlai Stevenson. I was in the audience when Truman escorted Stevenson to the rostrum after his nomination. It was a dramatic moment. Floodlights illuminated the two men as they walked arm in arm up to the rostrum.

It's a good thing I didn't have a lot of money in 1952 when Adlai Stevenson made his acceptance speech at the convention, because I would have given it all to him that night. Stevenson made as great a speech as I ever heard in my life. After that speech, I would have bet my life that Stevenson was going to win the election. I'm a frustrated professor, and Stevenson's academic demeanor really attracted me. Of course, that very demeanor turned out to be one of his liabilities. He was attacked for being an egghead, but that was why I was for him. I thought that Stevenson was who we needed in the White House.

Frank McKinney, however, was not enamored with Stevenson. When President Truman made him party chairman, Frank had agreed to serve only until the end of the 1952 campaign. When Stevenson won the nomination, he dismissed Frank and replaced him with Stephen Mitchell, one of

Stevenson's lawyer friends from Chicago. Mitchell had practically no political campaign experience. Stevenson's action deeply insulted Frank, and it outraged Truman, who took it as a personal snub. I was bothered by the way Stevenson treated Frank, but I remained a Stevenson supporter. At that time Audre and I still did not have much money, but we gave a little bit, something like $100, which was a huge contribution for us.

When Stevenson ran against Eisenhower in 1956, my economic situation had improved to the point that I could afford a $250 contribution, but that was the extent of my personal involvement in the campaign. The 1960 presidential race between John F. Kennedy and Richard Nixon was really the first time that I made a sizable financial donation to a national political campaign. I think I gave Kennedy a couple of thousand dollars. To be honest, my donation in 1960 was motivated more by my dislike of Richard Nixon than by any attraction I had to Kennedy. I saw Nixon as an absolutely scurrilous person. Nixon's involvement in a campaign always made me enthusiastic for the other candidate.

Ralph Yarborough

During the first couple of years after Audre and I moved back to Waco, I was commuting to Indianapolis every week to run the company. I didn't have the time to be active politically. In 1958, however, my twelve-year hiatus from Texas politics ended with my involvement in the election campaign of Ralph W. Yarborough, who was seeking election to his first full term in the U.S. Senate.

I had never had a close personal relationship with any elected official until I got involved in Yarborough's campaign. He was also the first U.S. senator that I ever knew. It was my relationship with Ralph that brought me into the political big leagues. I first knew about Ralph Yarborough when he ran an unsuccessful race for Texas attorney general in 1938. He had been a protégé of Texas governor Jimmy Allred, the hero of the University of Texas Progressive Democrats when I was a student. I kept up with Ralph's political career even when I was in Indiana. When he ran for governor in 1952 and 1954, I sent him a little money. Ralph was defeated each time, but I continued to hope that an elected office would one day be his. He was a genuine and sincere advocate for the people.

It wasn't until late in 1957, after his first election to the U.S. Senate in April of that same year (to fill the vacancy left by Price Daniel's election as governor), that Yarborough and I established a relationship. My childhood friend Fred Schmidt and Austin attorney Creekmore Fath, my former university classmate and fellow Progressive Democrat, brought Ralph and me together, and they lured me into the campaign. Somehow I scraped together a $200 contribution, and I raised money in the central Texas area for Yarborough.

That's when I discovered that I was a pretty good fund-raiser. I made personal visits and telephone calls to potential donors, and I gave them a pitch about how we needed their help to buy Yarborough television and radio time. I had some success and persuaded a few people to make $1,000 donations, which in those days was a hefty contribution. I learned that the more I asked people to give to a politician, the more they enjoyed giving. The interesting thing about all of the Yarborough campaigns was that between elections he never heard from the people who gave him his biggest contributions. Now, I'm not talking about vested interest groups. I'm talking about the people who I knew gave Ralph the most money. He never heard from them until the next time he ran.

> **B was indispensable to Ralph Yarborough. I doubt that Yarborough had one other supporter in the insurance industry in all of Texas.** — *Charles Terrell, insurance executive*

Ralph Yarborough was a native of the little town of Chandler in east Texas. His small-town and Baptist church background was very different from mine, but Ralph well understood the social and intellectual narrowness that can stem from that kind of background. Ralph Yarborough was not restricted by his upbringing; he was a man of the world. Ralph did some fine things when he was in the Senate, especially for military veterans. I liked his efforts to preserve the Big Thicket in east Texas, and I admired and strongly favored all of the social legislation he introduced and got passed. Ralph was a good friend of the labor movement. He worked overtime as a member of the Senate Labor and Public Welfare Committee to help working-class men and women of this country get a decent economic break. I am a trichotomist. By that I mean, when I'm in business, I'm a predator and, I hope, a civilized one; when I'm charitable, I'm philanthropic; but when I'm in politics, I'm idealistic. It was my idealism that brought me to Ralph Webster Yarborough. I was attracted to him because of his absolute integrity and his unshakable commitment to liberal political values.

One of the things the general public did not know about Ralph was that he had a deep love for books and for learning. He had a fabulous personal library stuffed with thousands of rare or scarce volumes. He wasn't the kind of collector who just likes to possess important and attractive books; he was a voracious reader who could give a brief synopsis of every volume on his double-stacked shelves. Ralph's lovely home in a quiet neighborhood in

Ralph Yarborough. CN 10804, Lee (Russell) Photograph Collection, Center for American History, The University of Texas at Austin.

west Austin was overflowing with his book collection. He had a special interest in the history of this nation, especially nineteenth-century Texas and the Civil War. I have had professors of history tell me that Ralph was as knowledgeable about the history of his native state as any specialist with a formal doctorate in the subject. Ralph could talk for hours about Sam Houston, and I wouldn't have been surprised if he could recite the names of every family who settled in Stephen F. Austin's colony.

Yarborough's love of books and history brought him into contact with some of the leading figures of Texas letters, such as historian Walter Prescott Webb, folklorist J. Frank Dobie, and naturalist Roy Bedichek. Dobie, who died in 1964, was a particularly good friend. On various occasions Ralph delivered a wonderful speech on his relationship with Dobie. It was when I heard Ralph give his Dobie talk at a dinner in 1968 that I really began to appreciate what a humanist he was. I was so taken by the speech that I persuaded Ralph to let me get it published. One reason for my interest was that I also admired Frank Dobie. He visited Audre and me at our home in Waco right after Homer Rainey's defeat in 1946. Aware that Audre and I were in financial trouble because of the campaign, Dobie told us to remember that "being poor of spirit was far more degrading than being poor financially." I have never forgotten that, so as a public service, American Income purchased several thousand copies of Yarborough's published speech, titled

"Frank Dobie: Man and Friend," and distributed it to more than 2,000 college libraries in the United States.

Happily, Ralph won reelection to the Senate in 1958. That was the beginning of a close relationship between the two of us that lasted until his death more than thirty-five years later. In Texas politics during the 1960s, my basic goal was to keep Ralph in the Senate. I served as his campaign finance director in his successful reelection campaign in 1964.

I believe congressional work suited Ralph in many ways (he was an outstanding senator), but his lifelong dream was to be governor of Texas. After losing to Allan Shivers in 1952 and 1954, Ralph came within an eyelash of moving into the Governor's Mansion in 1956 when he lost to Price Daniel by a few thousand votes. Although he served in the Senate for nearly fourteen years, down deep inside, he never quite gave up his dream of being governor. Every two years during the 1960s, the press would report rumors that Senator Yarborough was contemplating a bid for the governor's office, and it was true, the governor's office was never out of Ralph's mind. I always strongly discouraged him from running, however. I feared that if Ralph was elected governor, his successor in the Senate would be an antilabor conservative who would oppose the Great Society and support the Vietnam War. It seemed to me in those tumultuous years of national upheaval and international confrontation that we needed Ralph in Washington more than in Austin. Thankfully, that's where Ralph stayed.

A Full Entry into Texas Politics

As I have said, the race between John F. Kennedy and Richard Nixon in 1960 was the first time that I was able to make a sizable financial contribution to a presidential campaign. I also raised money for the Kennedy-Johnson ticket in Texas. Kennedy carried Texas, but the vote was much closer than we had expected. We spent several uneasy hours the night of the election when it became clear that despite Senator Johnson's presence on the ticket, the Democrats were not going to win the state easily. It was a big relief when we finally knew the next morning that Kennedy had been elected president and that Richard Nixon would have to find a new job.

Kennedy's victory, of course, meant that Lyndon Johnson would be giving up his seat in the U.S. Senate. The special election that was held in the spring of 1961 to fill that vacant seat was a painful event for me. I was forced to choose between two of my favorite people in politics: Fort Worth congressman Jim Wright and former San Antonio state representative Maury Maverick, Jr., the son of the late New Deal congressman who had been so important to my family.

Jim Wright had been a close friend of Audre's and mine since 1944, when we met during the Rainey affair. After his election to Congress in 1954, Jim became one of the rising young stars on the Texas political horizon. He was a gifted orator and speechwriter, and he had been an outstanding member of the House of Representatives. Jim had been carried away by the exciting new spirit that John F. Kennedy's election to the presidency had swept into Washington. He longed to have an active role in the New Frontier. Realizing that a seat in the Senate would give him more opportunity to play that role, Jim jumped into the race to succeed Lyndon Johnson.

Hoping that he could scare off potential candidates by entering the race first, Jim was astounded when seventy other Texans soon announced that they too were candidates. Most of those candidates were unknowns who never mounted a serious campaign. The major candidates included John Tower, the Republican college professor who had waged a spirited challenge to Lyndon Johnson in the 1960 election; William "Dollar Bill" Blakely, a conservative Dallas oilman who was serving as the interim senator; San Antonio legislator and future congressman Henry B. Gonzalez; and Maury Maverick, Jr.

I had planned to support Jim Wright until my old high school buddy Fred Schmidt came along. Fred had moved back to Texas as an official with the oil and chemical workers union. Not long after his return, Fred became head of the Texas AFL-CIO. Fred Schmidt was always a problem for me because he was going to be the minister and I was going to be the communist. I talked him out of being a minister, and he became more radical than I did. I have always had the guilty feeling that he's the clean one and I'm the wayward child. Fred told me that Jim Wright had angered the AFL-CIO because he had voted the wrong way on some important antilabor legislation and they wanted to teach him a lesson. He pleaded with me not to endorse or support Jim's candidacy.

> I remember inviting Barney down to Austin to meet with Maury Maverick to get him involved in the campaign. Now this was a very touchy thing, because Henry Gonzalez ran in that campaign, and Henry also went to Jefferson High School. He was a year ahead of Barney and me. But labor did not support Henry or Jim Wright. We induced Maury to run, and Henry of course took umbrage at that. —*Fred Schmidt*

I now faced a major personal dilemma. Jim Wright and I have been close friends always, but no one has been closer to me than Fred Schmidt. I tried to persuade Fred not to oppose Jim, but I got nowhere. Fred made my dilemma even more difficult when he explained that he and his labor union colleagues had persuaded Maury Maverick, Jr., to run. I did not know Maury well then, but Maury's father had been an authentic hero to my family, and he had been kind to me when I was at the university. I did know of Maury's progressive record as a member of the Texas Legislature in the early 1950s and his courageous opposition to the anticommunist hysteria of the era. Papa was strongly in favor of Maury Junior's candidacy, and he joined Fred Schmidt in urging me to support him. I knew that either Jim Wright or Maury would make an outstanding senator, but I really had no choice. I had to go with Maverick. I can tell you, that created problems for me at home because my wife adores Jim Wright and he is one of my son's political heroes. They remained steadfast in their support of Jim, while I sided with Maury.

> **When Maury and his assistants visited during the campaign, Ronnie and I marched through the living room carrying signs that declared "Be Right with Wright!" I'd known Jim for many years, and I love him. I had nothing against Maury, but Jim is an outstanding person, and I felt strongly about supporting him. I know the unions were supporting Maury, but I couldn't have cared less.** —*Audre Rapoport*

I was able to raise some money for Maury. One of the benefits that I got from that campaign was getting to know him better. Maury Maverick, Jr., is the spiritual conscience of Texas. He is one of the really wonderful people in the world. During the Vietnam War he defended protesters and conscientious objectors on a pro bono basis, and he caught hell from the war hawks for it. Wherever there was a progressive cause, Texans could find Maury Maverick, Jr., before just about anyone else. Former *Texas Observer* editor Willie Morris once noted that when Maury gets fired up about some issue, he runs his friends to the asylum and his enemies up over the wall. That is an accurate description of Maury. For many years now, Maury has been a columnist for the *San Antonio Express News.* He has a large following, the majority of whom undoubtedly disagree with most of what he has to say. I can guarantee that Maury keeps things stirred up in San Antonio with that column. He is one of the last of a breed. Texas and the nation really need many more like him.

That 1961 special Senate election put the liberals of Texas in a difficult situation. In the past, we rarely had one good person in a race, and now we had three outstanding candidates in Gonzalez, Maverick, and Wright. I considered Jim to be a liberal despite labor's opposition. Henry Gonzalez was a good friend of mine and I liked him very much, but I felt strongly that he should not have entered that race. For many years, liberals in Texas had a death wish; we just didn't want to win. We should have had only one candidate in 1961, and that should have been either Maverick or Wright. Gonzalez really didn't have a chance. Egos just got in the way. All three wanted to be the senator, and as a result, none of them went to the Senate. The three liberal candidates split the vote to such an extent that Blakely, an extreme conservative, made the runoff against John Tower. Jim Wright came in a close third. Maverick came in behind Wright and just ahead of Gonzalez.

Blakely was really a Republican in Democrat clothing, so I went fishing on the day of the runoff. A lot of us did. We did not want to vote Republican, so we did not vote. Tower defeated Blakely in the runoff. If Wright, Maverick, and Gonzalez had sat down before the campaign and drawn straws or something to see which one would get to run, we would have had a liberal senator in Texas, and John Tower would never have been heard from again.

In the late 1950s V. O. Key and C. Vann Woodward, two important students of Southern political history, argued that as long as Texas and other southern states had a one-party political system, the reactionaries would always control the states' politics. Paying heed to that argument, we liberals decided to form a rebuilding committee to help Republicans win elections so that they could have Republican primaries. The conservatives in both parties could vote in the Republican primary, which would leave the Democratic primary for the liberals. Then in the general election there would be a face-off between true Democrats and Republicans. That was the concept behind our strategy. Three of our young liberal firebrands at the time, Dave Shapiro, Bill Hamilton, and Chuck Caldwell, pushed the idea, did the work, and took the heat for it. I think the long-term result has been positive, even though today the Texas Democratic Party is moribund at the state level. Ultimately, this state will have a real two-party system, and that is far healthier for democracy than the former situation.

The Turman and Spears Campaigns

I remained deeply involved in the Texas political scene after that special Senate election in 1961. There were a number of candidates that I supported and helped to finance during the 1960s, but I was not involved in the management of their campaigns. My participation was not significant enough to leave many memories after all these years.

Two campaigns, however, were memorable. Both were unsuccessful. One was Jimmy Turman's 1962 race for lieutenant governor, the first campaign since Homer Rainey's in which my involvement went beyond raising money. The other was in 1966, when Franklin Spears ran for attorney general, the first political campaign in which I took an official statewide position as finance chairman. It also was memorable for introducing me to three men who were profound influences on my life.

By 1962 my insurance company had started doing business with the labor unions, so I was working closely with the political arm of the Texas labor movement. Labor's candidate for lieutenant governor was Jimmy Turman, who, at thirty-four years old, was Speaker of the Texas House of Representatives. Jimmy was not exactly a fire-breathing labor union man. He supported the state's so-called right-to-work laws, which the unions obviously hated. Jimmy, however, was a moderate and much more enlightened than his conservative opponents. He was strongly in favor of higher salaries for public schoolteachers, and we knew that he would give a fair hearing to other legislation important to the labor movement.

I was very active in Jimmy Turman's race, raising most of the money for him. Although Jimmy made it into a runoff with Preston Smith, the state senator from Lubbock, he ran a really dumb campaign. A few days before the runoff, some of the senators who were supporting Smith accused Turman of having sailed on a yacht on Chesapeake Bay as the guest of an alleged loan-shark lobbyist. The accusations were silly, but Turman ran away and hid. He easily could have handled the situation in a diplomatic way, but he didn't, and it cost him the lieutenant governorship.

In 1966 I was state finance chairman in the Franklin Spears campaign for attorney general. Franklin, the state senator from San Antonio, was thirty-four when he entered the race. He had earned a reputation as a strong liberal, especially on civil rights issues, while serving in the Texas Legislature in the late 1950s and early 1960s. Franklin's voting record as a legislator was decidedly prolabor, so he had the full support of the unions.

The Spears campaign was fun because it was one of the few campaigns in which I worked as a strategist as well as a fund-raiser. Franklin's main opponent was the Texas secretary of state, Crawford Martin, the candidate of Governor John B. Connally's conservative faction in the Democratic Party. Martin's campaign strategy was to beat Franklin over the head with his labor record. The conservative business establishment in Texas poured a huge amount of money into Martin's campaign. It seemed as though I couldn't turn the corner on a street anywhere in Texas without seeing a Crawford Martin billboard. We did not have the money to keep up, which was not a new situation for liberal candidates in Texas. In the primary, Franklin got enough votes to force Martin into a runoff. We couldn't overcome Martin's lead, however, and he won by a decisive margin.

Three Extraordinary Men

The Spears campaign was not a total loss because it gave me the opportunity to meet three extraordinary men with whom I forged close friendships that would last the rest of their lives: John Henry Faulk, Frederick Palmer Weber, and J. R. Parten. Each man, in his own distinctive way, influenced my life significantly.

I met John Henry Faulk when I was trying to raise money for Franklin Spears. I was not having much success in Texas, so Ronnie Dugger, publisher of *The Texas Observer* and a Spears supporter, urged me to go to New York City to meet political humorist and civil liberties activist John Henry Faulk, a native Texan residing in Manhattan at the time. John Henry was well connected with many of the wealthy liberals in New York, so Dugger thought he might be able to persuade some of those friends to contribute to the Spears campaign.

I knew John Henry Faulk by reputation as a talented political satirist. I also knew that he had been blacklisted as an entertainer during the red scare of the 1950s. That was a horrendous time in our country, when demagogues such as Republican senator Joe McCarthy spread fear across the country with their unsubstantiated accusations that Communists had infiltrated the federal government and many of the nation's institutions, including the entertainment industry.

All of us who were involved in liberal and progressive movements, and especially people with my kind of family background, were frightened by what went on during the red scare. Nobody was beyond the reach of extreme anticommunists, who were obsessed with the fear that commie subversives had penetrated every level of society. I had close friends who remained in a state of quiet panic throughout the red scare. The red hunters personally didn't frighten me, but I was fearful in a larger sense. I knew that while the red scare raged, legitimate protest about social and economic conditions in this country was effectively silenced. The fear generated by the red scare in the 1950s has left an imprint on our country from which we are still recovering.

Thankfully, by the time I met John Henry Faulk in March 1966, the red scare was a bad memory. John Henry, however, was struggling to make a living despite having cleared his name in his successful lawsuit against the blacklisters. I had read *Fear on Trial,* Faulk's classic book about his epic fight against the blacklisting racket. Outraged by what had happened to

John Henry Faulk. Unnumbered, Faulk (John Henry)
Photograph Collection, Center for American History,
The University of Texas at Austin.

John Henry, the jury in his trial (*Faulk* v. *Aware, Inc.*) gave him $3.5 mil-
lion in damages, the largest libel award in U.S. legal history at that time.
Although the appeals court agreed with the jury's verdict, it reduced the
award to $500,000. After paying his legal expenses, John Henry saw little
of the award money. He also failed to find a job with his former employer,
CBS, or with any other network. John Henry's lawsuit had embarrassed the
television industry by exposing its cowardly acquiescence in the blacklisting system. As a result, John Henry found himself to be persona non grata
so far as the network executives were concerned.

John Henry and I became friends almost immediately. We connected
on nearly every level. In particular, he and I shared a deep commitment
to the labor movement and to the liberal wing of the Democratic Party. A

graduate of the University of Texas, John Henry had supported and worked for Homer Rainey during the 1946 Texas gubernatorial campaign. We also shared a sense of outrage against injustice and a passion for civil liberties. John Henry was intensely hostile to anyone or anything that even hinted at anti-Semitism. He was well versed in Jewish culture, and he actively supported the creation of Israel. During World War II John Henry had served as a Red Cross field director in Cairo, Egypt, and he had made frequent trips to Tel Aviv and Jerusalem. He told me that he became so devoted to the movement to create a Jewish homeland that he secured a leave of absence from his post in Cairo and moved to Tel Aviv, where he lived for several months. He lived for a brief time at the Givat Brenner kibbutz. That experience inspired in John Henry a sincere enthusiasm for Israel and its people.

During our first visit, I could see that John Henry was a talented storyteller and political humorist in the tradition of Mark Twain and Will Rogers, but in a Texas style. I couldn't help him restart his career in broadcasting, but I knew that American Income could make good use of his talent as an after-dinner speaker and convention lecturer. I was delighted when he accepted my offer to speak at a company banquet later that summer. John Henry's speech was such a success that I used his services on a fairly regular basis over the next several years, not only for my company but also for a variety of good causes in which we both believed. John Henry and his wife, Liz, became two of the dearest friends that Audre and I have ever had. When their son, John Henry "Johan" Faulk III, was born in 1969, they asked our son, Ronnie, to be his godfather.

During that first visit, John Henry told me about his close friend and political soulmate F. Palmer Weber. One of the most respected brokers in New York, Weber managed Troster, Singer, and Company, at that time one of the largest over-the-counter trading houses on Wall Street. John Henry was certain that Weber and I would find much in common. Weber came from my kind of background. He was an old-time radical who had worked in the trenches of the labor movement. He had managed Henry Wallace's Progressive Party campaign in the South in 1948. Weber also was a scholar who had earned a Ph.D. from the University of Virginia, where he taught for a number of years. I was intrigued by the image of this liberal political and labor movement activist who was also an intellectual and a pragmatic, successful businessman. He seemed to be a potential political ally as well as a man with whom I would enjoy doing business.

Palmer Weber was out of town at the time, so I asked John Henry to show him my insurance company's annual statements. I was as eager to have his evaluation of my business as I was to have his help in raising money for Spears. Palmer and I finally met when I returned to New York a few weeks later. It was love at first sight. He told me that my company seemed interesting and that I was an exciting personality who had much to offer as a national leader for progressive causes. I was forty-nine years old, and I had never thought of myself that way. Palmer actually changed my perception of myself. It was because of him that I realized, really for the first time, that I had the capacity to be a leader. Palmer became my political mentor.

Palmer believed that I could be a force for the promotion of liberal concepts in America. He recognized that I'm articulate and that if I have a platform I can be effective. He introduced me to the top people on Wall Street. When his associates got to know me, they invited me to make speeches to all kinds of groups, from the Rotary Club to liberal political gatherings throughout the country. During the war in Vietnam, he arranged for me to go to universities and talk against the war. I became nationally known as a result.

Palmer and I also did a lot of business together. I eventually asked him to manage American Income's investments as well as my personal finances. He was a financial genius, an old-time commie who could beat the capitalists at their own game. Palmer was one of the most magnificent human beings I have ever known. He was gruff and rough and beholden to no one, yet he was wonderfully generous, sensitive, and loyal. He was one of the five or six most important people in my life. From the day I met him in 1966 until his death more than twenty years later, Palmer and I talked almost every day on the telephone. I have kept a framed photograph of him on my desk ever since his death.

> Palmer Weber was my very best friend, and he was my mother's very best friend. Mother and I were in love with him. Palmer introduced Bernard to a lot of political people who became important to him. He was an unbelievable human being. He was sweet, considerate, bright, warm, and attractive.
> —*Audre Rapoport*

During our first meeting, John Henry Faulk had also urged me to meet J. R. Parten, an independent oilman and rancher from Madisonville, Texas, who, like Palmer Weber, defied conventional political stereotypes. Parten was a wealthy Texas businessman with conservative economic views who remained to the end of his life a vocal advocate for liberal social principles. His quiet, formal, and reserved manner did not fit the flamboyant stereotype of the Texas oilman and rancher. A former Army major who nearly chose the military as his career, Parten opposed the Vietnam War and denounced the nuclear arms race. He was a Texan with deep rural roots, yet he was a fervent internationalist who supported the United Nations and advocated a harmonious relationship with the Soviet Union.

Although I had never met Parten, I certainly knew about him. He had been a highly visible member of the University of Texas board of regents when I was a student. My friends in the Progressive Democrats considered him to be the most intellectually and politically enlightened of the regents. We knew that he had protected members of the economics faculty, including Bob Montgomery and Clarence Ayres, when state legislators had called for their dismissal. Parten was also known to be a close advisor to another one of our heroes, Governor Jimmy Allred. He was only in his early forties when he served as a university regent, but he was already one of the most esteemed citizens in Texas. I would have gone through the concrete if he had said something to me when I was a student. I had never met anybody of that stature.

As chairman of the board of regents in 1939, Parten had recruited Homer Rainey to be president of the university, and he had led the protest against Rainey's dismissal in 1944. In 1950 Parten was one of a small group of influential business leaders who helped Dr. Robert Hutchins create the Fund for the Republic and, several years after that, the Center for the Study of Democratic Institutions. Parten was a vigorous critic of Senator Joe McCarthy and the House Un-American Activities Committee during the red scare in the 1950s. That's why he was one of the driving forces behind the Fund for the Republic, an organization that served to educate Americans about threats to their civil liberties.

John Henry Faulk introduced me to J.R. in early January 1967. Parten invited Audre and me to visit him and his wife, Patsy, at their house in Madisonville, so we drove down from Waco and had lunch with them. By this time J.R. was reputed to be one of the richest men in Texas. I had never met anyone with that kind of money. I was also in awe of his achievements as a political and educational leader. I learned during that first meeting that he had built an oil refinery in Minnesota that people said could not be built. He had been associated with some of the major oil enterprises in the country and had established a hugely successful sulfur company in Mexico. Despite all the success he had enjoyed in his business and the money he accumulated, Parten remained committed to the First Amendment, and he was dedicated to the protection and extension of civil liberties to all Americans. We became friends and political allies.

For a period covering more than two decades, J.R. and I worked together on more projects than I can recall. Many of those projects were small. For example, when John Henry Faulk sued the FBI because it refused to release his personal file, J.R. and I split the costs of hiring his lawyer. I don't know how many times that type of thing happened, but it was often. John Henry Faulk was usually the person who pointed us in the right direction.

Hutchins and the Center

In 1971 J.R. recruited me to serve on the board of the Center for the Study of Democratic Institutions, which was one of the most intellectually exciting experiences I have had outside graduate school. The center, established in 1959 in Santa Barbara, California, was the brainchild of the legendary Robert Maynard Hutchins, the former president of the University of Chicago. The center's official mission, in Hutchins's words, was to investigate the question of how "a free society may be maintained under the strikingly new political, economic, social, and technological conditions of the second half of the twentieth century." Hutchins once said that the center's "prejudice is democracy; its operating procedure, the dialogue." By the time I became a board member, the center had attracted much attention nationally with highly publicized convocations and research projects, had a membership list in excess of 100,000, and published an official journal (*The Center Magazine*) and a series of book-length studies called *Occasional Papers*.

Being on the center's board was a heady experience for me. It gave me an opportunity to meet and deliberate with a variety of leading intellectuals, political activists, and public policymakers. For example, two of the individuals elected to the board with me were former U.S. attorney general Ramsey Clark and movie star and political activist Paul Newman. Through the center I also was able to meet Arkansas senator J. William Fulbright, Supreme Court justice William O. Douglas, two-time Pulitzer prizewinning journalist Harry Ashmore, the coauthors of the best-selling novel *Fail-Safe* Eugene Burdick and Harvey Wheeler, Nobel prizewinning nuclear physicist Isidor Rabi, former New Deal brain trusters Adolf A. Berle and Rexford G. Tugwell, diplomat and author George F. Kennan, Civil War historian Bruce Catton, Admiral Hyman Rickover, and former Episcopal bishop James A. Pike.

Of course, the real star at the center was Bob Hutchins. I have never met anyone as intellectually impressive as Hutchins. He had become president of the University of Chicago in 1929 at the tender age of thirty. Prior to his move to Chicago, Hutchins had been the child dean of Yale Law School, where he transformed Yale into a center of experimentation in legal education. At Chicago, Hutchins was the boy wonder of higher education and the storm center of American academic life. His attempts to reorganize the University of Chicago and to reform its curriculum, as well as his calls for fundamental changes in American higher education, attracted controversial attention in educational circles and in the national press. Hutchins opposed the view that education should be centered on the concept of usefulness. A major influence on my own thinking was his belief that the most effective way to produce a truly educated person was through an emphasis on the liberal arts.

At six feet three inches tall, Hutchins was a striking figure. Articulate, handsome, and cultured, Hutchins scorned pettiness, small talk, and pretension, yet his intellectual arrogance and magisterial personal style was softened by his self-deprecating wit and his masterful use of the ironic. When Hutchins started talking, I knew I was in the company of a rare individual.

Serving on the center's board also gave me the chance to work in a formal capacity with J. R. Parten. By the time I came on the scene, J.R. had become the center's largest financial contributor. Although they weren't intimate friends, Hutchins and Parten respected and admired each other, and Parten took deep pride in the center's growth and accomplishments.

My work with the center and the senior fellows who served as its resident scholars gave me new ways of looking at educational, environmental, and other public policy issues. One of the most profound sentences I have ever heard was spoken at a seminar by a senior fellow, John Wilkinson. Quoting Decimus Juvenal, Wilkinson said that "there is a continual dying of possible futures, and two mistakes are common: to be unaware of them while they are, so to speak, alive, and to be unaware of their death when they have been killed off by lack of discovery." That thought, which has stayed with me ever since, was typical of the type of exposure to compelling ideas that one could get at the center.

Unfortunately, the center fell on hard times during the mid-1970s, a victim of petty factionalism among its staff and a prolonged financial crisis that created disharmony on the board. The coup de grace, however, was a serious dispute that resulted from Hutchins's retirement in 1974 and his replacement as president by Malcolm Moos, former president of the University of Minnesota. Confronting a severe budget deficit, Moos tried to reorganize and change the center to such an extent that Hutchins intervened and orchestrated Moos's dismissal. That episode led to J.R.'s resignation from the board and the end of his friendship with Hutchins. I felt that J.R. misunderstood and overreacted to the situation. The whole controversy was a tragedy, more because of the personal animosities that resulted among lifetime friends than for any other reason.

The center was so much the creature of Bob Hutchins that it couldn't survive his death in 1977, although for a few years it did limp along in a different form as a unit of the University of California at Santa Barbara. I am proud of my association with Bob Hutchins and the center. I believe that the center's dialogues, conferences, and convocations brought meaningful public attention to the issues of racism, poverty, civil liberties, public education, militarism, and the threat of nuclear war. The center made a number of contributions to the civic good, especially in the fields of civil liberties and civil rights. Its sponsorship of a series of international convocations inspired by Pope John's encyclical *Pacem in Terris* enriched and raised the level of public discourse during the Cold War.

Funding Liberals

I don't know how many millions of dollars J.R. and I raised together for politicians like Ralph Yarborough, Hubert Humphrey, Eugene McCarthy, Edward Kennedy, George McGovern, Frank Church, and Alan Cranston. We cohosted fund-raising luncheons in Houston, where J.R.'s oil company had its offices. Being the salesman, I was always the pitchman at those luncheons. J.R. was austere and always sat in the corner. People came to him.

> J. R. Parten was reserved, distant, and dignified. He seemed very Old World to me, like an English gentleman. Rapoport, however, is openly passionate and driven by these deep ethical emotions about the human race. Their common characteristic was political and moral passion. It was interesting to see how differently it was manifested in each. — *Ronnie Dugger*

Those fund-raisers gave me an insight into J.R. One of the reasons he shied away from the limelight was his desire to be known for his character and the quality of his mind and his commitment to the values he held dear. He did not want to be looked on as the wealthy oilman that he was. He was as influential as any person that ever lived in this state, yet he was shy when it came to publicity. He was not well known at all, but he was known among that inner circle of people who understood what made things move in the state of Texas and in this nation. He was a most unusual man.

J.R. was in the oil business, and he usually supported those people who advocated his point of view, especially with respect to the oil business. I didn't agree with his laissez-faire approach to oil industry regulation, but he didn't agree with my views on the insurance industry either. He didn't believe in insurance, and he didn't want to be involved in the insurance business. He never had any interest in my business, and I had no interest in his. That's probably one reason that we were such close personal friends.

Having forged close affiliations with Palmer Weber and J. R. Parten, I felt for the first time that I was a player in the larger world of liberal politics.

> Bernard Rapoport has been on the progressive side of every important fight in Texas for over forty years, raising money for our great senator Ralph Yarborough and for every other progressive candidate who's come along. He has been a man the small progressive community in this state could count on.
> —*Molly Ivins, author and columnist,* Texas Observer

In Texas, the political fund-raising partnership that I had with Parten during the late 1960s and throughout the 1970s was supplemented by significant monetary support from Walter Hall, a feisty small-town populist banker. I first got to know Hall and his wife, Helen, in the spring of 1968. Walter was a graduate of Rice University whose political views had been shaped by progressive Texas governor Jimmy Allred. He was the president and major stockholder of Citizens State Bank of Dickinson, a little town near NASA's Manned Spacecraft Center.

My relationship with Walter was not nearly as personal as my relationship with J. R. Parten. Walter Hall was the kind of man who would scare you off if you didn't really know him. He had a short attention span, and he was not as dialectically inclined as Parten was. When Walter didn't want to discuss something, he would cut you off short. As a result, he was much more difficult to work with than J.R. He didn't have the generosity of giving that I experienced with J.R., but Walter was a real populist as well as someone who liked to make money, a real bottom-line man. He ran his bank to make money, not just to have something to do. J.R. was no different in that respect. When it comes to character and integrity, Walter didn't take a back seat to anybody in the world. He was a good man.

J.R., Walter, and I did not agree on every issue. Hall was a hawk on Vietnam, and J.R. would never support anyone he thought was hostile to the oil business. But whenever liberal candidates wanted to run for office in Texas, they usually went to the three of us for money. We generally supported the same candidates, we were solidly behind Ralph Yarborough, and we were unanimous in support of *The Texas Observer* as a much-needed voice for the liberal cause. The three of us pulled the *Observer* out of the financial fires more than once. During the Yarborough campaigns, whenever we needed money, I would call J.R. and Walter and they would get it for us, usually out of their own pockets. What made J. R. Parten and Walter Hall great was that they knew when to be outraged. And when they were outraged, you knew it.

Don Yarborough for Governor

The first political campaign in which the three of us worked closely as a fund-raising team was the Texas gubernatorial race in 1968. Our candidate was Don Yarborough, a brilliant Houston attorney who was making his third bid for governor. Although they shared last names, Don was not related to Senator Ralph Yarborough. Don had first run for governor in 1962, when he opposed Price Daniel, who was seeking his fourth term. I gave Don a small contribution in 1962, but I did nothing else for him that year. I didn't view Don as a truly liberal candidate because the labor movement was not that enthusiastic about him. At that time, I supported only those candidates who received a full endorsement from the labor unions.

Had Don been a little smarter, he would have been governor of Texas in 1962. He was in a runoff with John B. Connally, who was seeking his first elected office. Connally had tons of money at his disposal as well as the support of Lyndon Johnson's organization. Nevertheless, Don lost to Connally by only 26,000 votes. He didn't court the labor leadership that year, and it cost him the election. Had labor gone all out, Don Yarborough would have been governor of Texas, and we would have never heard of John Connally again. With my fund-raising ability, I believe I could have raised enough money for him to win that election.

Don Yarborough ran against Connally in 1964, but that was a hopeless effort. Having been seriously wounded in the Kennedy shooting in Dallas in 1963, Connally was riding a strong sympathy wave. On top of that, labor again withheld its support because of President Johnson's desire to avoid political warfare in his home state in a presidential election year. Johnson had to carry Texas in 1964, and he needed a unified state Democratic Party. He also opposed any strong challenges to Ralph Yarborough by the conservative faction.

In 1968 Don Yarborough decided to run for governor once again. This time, however, he had labor's support, and with Connally's decision not to run for a fourth term, there was no incumbent candidate. I was much more interested in Don as a candidate this time. For one thing, we had become better acquainted on a personal level and I really liked him. His liberalism also became much more evident after his defeat in 1964.

I agreed to be Don's finance chairman. Actually, I was his major fund-raiser. I pulled Walter Hall and J. R. Parten on board. With our enthusiasm and the desire to have a winner, we brought in more money for Don Yarborough than any liberal candidate for governor in Texas had ever raised.

I also agreed to help Don in other ways. In January 1968, a few days before Don made a formal announcement of his candidacy, I hired him as a consultant for American Income for a term of one year. Don was not in the best shape financially. Our retainer gave him some additional income to help pay personal bills while he was in the campaign. We gave him a real job. Don helped promote American Income's labor-union business, usually by making public appearances on our behalf at union events.

That 1968 gubernatorial primary race was an unusual one for me because I was much more involved on the operational side of the campaign than I am normally. I raised money, wrote a few speeches, and participated in the shaping of strategy. I persuaded Don to endorse a proposal for a high-speed passenger train line between Houston and Dallas, a governor's office on Mexican-American affairs, and significant tax credits for businesses and industries that located in depressed rural areas. I was so optimistic about his prospects for election that I even proposed a governor's shadow cabinet to be established after his inauguration. Jimmy Allred had such an advisory group when he was governor in the 1930s.

The 1968 Texas Democratic primary was held on May 4, 1968. A few days before the election, our polls indicated that Don was leading the field of ten candidates, which included Lieutenant Governor Preston Smith, former attorney general Waggoner Carr, and Uvalde rancher and banker Dolph Briscoe. Despite our lead, we knew that Don could not win enough votes to avoid a runoff, so we started planning for the second campaign even before the first one was over.

When the votes were counted on May 4, Don led the pack as expected, but his lead was not as large as we had hoped. He received about 24 percent of the vote, and Preston Smith was close behind with nearly 22 percent. It was clear to me that we had a real problem because the other leading conservative candidates Carr, Briscoe, and Locke together polled roughly 45 percent. We still believed we had a good shot at winning. Don's energy was limitless, and his enthusiasm for politics was something to behold. He campaigned with evangelistic fervor, often speaking in a mesmerizing singsong pattern similar to the old Protestant revival preachers. Preston Smith, on the other hand, was a dull and uninspiring candidate who hid behind his radio and television ads.

Nevertheless, by the last week of the campaign for the runoff, I knew we were in trouble and that Preston Smith was far ahead. When the votes came in on election day, Don actually did much better than we had feared, but he still lost. It was not a good year for politically progressive candidates. Smith beat him 55 percent to 45 percent.

That 1968 campaign was Don Yarborough's political swan song. Twenty-two years would pass before the liberal wing of the Texas Democratic party would have another candidate it could support with enthusiasm who had a solid chance to become governor. That candidate would be Ann Richards.

6 ▶ *Insuring Labor*

American Income and I were known throughout the insurance industry for our close ties to the labor movement. As the largest writer of supplemental insurance for union members in the United States, American Income worked with the entire spectrum of labor: the AFL-CIO, the United Auto Workers, the Teamsters, and the United Mine Workers. Our labor union business was what set American Income apart from other insurance companies; it was that relationship that made the company such a success.

We formed our relationship with labor in the early 1960s, after Harold Goodman sold his interest in the company and while we were part of RIC. We had worked with the Teamsters in Indiana in the 1950s, but that experience had not been a happy one, so we avoided labor for nearly a decade.

> **The union leaders that Barney dealt with in Indiana weren't idealistic people. They were on the take, and I'm sure that some of them were absolutely corrupt. If you wanted a favor from them, you had to buy that favor.** — *Fred Schmidt*

I wish that I could say that American Income's entry into the labor market was the result of some brilliant flash of insight on my part. The truth is that it was a serendipitous happening. After Fred Schmidt persuaded me to support Maury Maverick, Jr., during the U.S. Senate race in 1961, he came to Waco and asked me to contribute a sizable amount of money to the campaign. The amount he needed was well beyond what I could donate personally, so I asked him if the campaign laws would allow my company to make the contribution. He advised me that it was legal to use company money for political education and for voter registration. The laws have changed since then, of course, and businesses can no longer do that. When I wondered out loud how I could justify a political contribution from a business standpoint,

Fred, who was the head of the Texas AFL-CIO, said, "Why don't you get the company to do more business with union members? That's who you're the most comfortable with anyway; their philosophy is the closest to yours of any other group that you could do business with."

> Barney was disillusioned with labor when I suggested that he do his business with them. I was a labor organizer myself in those years, and he was telling me, "You are all full of these ideals and you're going to change the world. That's bullshit. That's not going to happen. You ought to see the kind of labor people we've got in Indiana, because they aren't of that stripe. They are business unionists instead of social unionists, and I would identify myself as a social unionist." I told him that the labor union movement was pretty complex and that he should not assume that everyone was like the Teamsters.
> — Fred Schmidt

I had not thought about targeting labor union members until Fred suggested it. The timing could not have been better. A few weeks before my meeting with Fred, I had become aware of the need to develop a new general sales marketing strategy for American Income. When we started the company in 1951, we marketed most of our policies through mass mailing, which generated lots of leads. That method eventually lost effectiveness as everyone started doing it. The lead return went down from about 10 percent to about 0.5 percent, which made it unprofitable to use the mail. Then we came up with a gimmick approach. We mailed cards to prospective clients with a promise that if they returned the card to us, we would send them some little gift, such as a box of Band-Aids. That strategy worked for a short time, but it also played out. We tried some other gimmicks, but by 1961 I could see that we had a potentially serious problem. We were not giving our sales force the leads they needed. I decided to formulate a completely different marketing approach.

After my discussion with Fred Schmidt, I realized that although there were a couple of thousand insurance companies in the country, there were only ten really big ones. A couple of thousand little minnows were floating around emulating ten whales. It suddenly occurred to me that the minnows—and American Income was a minnow—had better not swim where the whales feed. It seemed to me that our future would be determined by our ability to find a special niche, some part of the insurance business where we would not have to swim with or emulate the whales of our industry. Serving the labor market appeared to be the obvious way for us to create that niche.

I think it was a niche that most other insurance people didn't care about. It was one they probably hadn't thought could be organized into a success story. During those years, most insurance people wouldn't even talk to the unions, much less cater to them. Whatever put that light on in his head, it was a real good light, because he really has had a virtual monopoly on that part of the business. — *Charles Terrell, insurance executive*

I could see that a labor union focus would provide a ready-made marketing scheme for our agents. Most insurance company agents spend 99 percent of their time prospecting and 1 or 2 percent of their time selling. The key to success is increasing the amount of selling time by constantly feeding leads to the agents. I realized that if we forged close links with the unions, especially at the local level, the union membership rolls would provide an automatic source of leads. Our agents would not have to do a lot of prospecting; they could spend most of their time selling.

Here's a guy who built an insurance company as cleverly and uniquely as anyone I've ever seen. Obviously, he's one hell of a salesman. But he decided to zero in on a special market. He wanted to sell to labor unions. Not health and accident, which is the big-dollar insurance that the unions handle themselves, but he wanted to sell supplemental life insurance to the individual members of the union. — *Ben Barnes, former lieutenant governor of Texas*

I was confident that I could establish a relationship with the labor movement that could not be duplicated by anyone else in my business. With my family background, educational training, and political worldview, I knew that I could relate well to the labor leadership. Most of my close friends while I was a student at the university were either in the labor movement or teaching in universities. I was the only one that went into the business world. I had friends in the labor movement all over the country. I have an ingrained empathy for the labor movement that has been shaped by a lifetime of experience. With all that in mind, I decided to move as much of our business effort as possible into the selling of supplementary insurance to union members.

I think that if you know his history it's not surprising that he would be concerned about labor. You know, he came out of a labor-oriented background. The University of Texas economics department, when he went through it, had a strong labor orientation. He's always been active in the liberal wing of the Democratic Party in Texas, and he had friends like Fred Schmidt who were labor leaders. — *Ray Marshall, former U.S. secretary of labor*

It took us a few years to develop our relationship with the unions. Our first business was mostly in the AFL-CIO building trades in Texas. We began our efforts in Houston because two-thirds of all the union members in Texas are on the Gulf coast. We eventually duplicated our Texas operation in nearly every one of the forty-eight states in which we were licensed.

We enjoyed some success with the unions in those early years, but our labor business did not take off until 1964, as a result of a new friendship I established with Hank Brown, the leader of the Texas AFL-CIO. Actually, my friendship with Hank was an unexpected development. Before 1964 I resented and disliked Hank Brown. He had opposed and overwhelmingly defeated Fred Schmidt as president of the Texas AFL-CIO in 1961. It was Fred Schmidt all the way with me, and I was angered by his defeat. I'm pragmatic, and I've made many compromises for business reasons. I'm proud of that. But when it came to Fred Schmidt, I was totally supportive, and I would have given him any amount of money to help him get reelected. Hank Brown knew that, so we were not friends.

> I really didn't like Rapoport because he had supported Fred Schmidt against me in the election for the presidency of the Texas AFL-CIO, but he and I really got to know one another very well when he became the finance chairman for Ralph Yarborough in the 1964 campaign. As president of the state labor conference of the AFL-CIO, I was raising money and politicking day and night to help the senator get reelected. That's when I found out that Rapoport was a pretty decent guy.
> — *Hank Brown*

When Ralph Yarborough faced reelection to the U.S. Senate in 1964, he had the total support of labor in Texas. As head of the state AFL-CIO, Hank Brown realized that he would have to work with me to get Yarborough reelected. Hank met with me and Audre in our house at Waco. Because of my feelings about Fred Schmidt's defeat, I was not eager to talk to Hank, but I was willing to do it for Yarborough. When Hank came in, he sat on the edge of the chair, and it was obvious that he was uncomfortable. He made inappropriate remarks, such as "You're a fat cat, and I don't like to be in the presence of fat cats," and that kind of thing. But after a while he began to relax, and we were able to have a good talk.

Hank Brown, Hubert H. Humphrey, and Ralph Yarborough.
CN 10753, Rapoport (Bernard) Photograph Collection, Center
for American History, The University of Texas at Austin.

Actually, what broke the ice was a problem we were having with our toilet. Audre considers herself a part-time plumber. There was something wrong with our commode, so she thought she would take advantage of having this labor union guy in our house and get him to help her fix this problem. She and Hank went into one of our bathrooms and beat around on the plumbing for several minutes. Hank's a faker when it comes plumbing. He couldn't put a washer in a faucet. He and Audre lost the battle with the toilet, but they had fun trying. By the time Hank left the house, we had developed a wonderful relationship. We soon became close personal friends.

> **During that first meeting, I could tell that Rapoport wanted a good relationship with the unions. Partly he had a selfish reason—that he wanted to sell them insurance—but also that's where his feelings are, and have been for many years. So, we just worked through politics, and about ninety percent of the time we were with the same candidate.** *—Hank Brown*

Over the years, Hank Brown has pulled me into more political fights than I can count. One fight that stands out in my mind occurred in August 1969, when the Texas State Legislature was meeting in a special session. The Texas

Senate passed a sales tax on groceries early on a Sunday morning. It looked like the House would pass the tax quickly on Monday or Tuesday. Governor Preston Smith had already announced that he would sign the bill. All sales taxes are regressive, but a tax on food is about as regressive as it gets. The burden falls most heavily on those who can least afford it.

Hank called me late that Sunday and pleaded with me to cancel my Monday schedule and meet him in Austin the next morning. "When you come," Hank said, "bring twenty-five thousand dollars with you. We need to buy time on television to tell the people that they're fixin' to be engaged with the corporations of Texas in a sexual intercourse act and the people are gonna be on the receiving end." How else could I respond to a statement like that? I went to Austin with a $25,000 check in my hand. I met Hank and John Henry Faulk and senators Barbara Jordan, Oscar Mauzy, Charlie Wilson, and Joe Bernal at the KTBC television studio. I paid the advertising bill, and the senators and John Henry Faulk went on the air to attack the food tax. The next day, several thousand people marched on the Capitol building to protest the tax. Finally realizing that this food tax was not going to go down with the voters, the House failed to pass it. Fortunately, Hank was never shy about imposing on me.

A Union Label Company

Hank Brown enlarged my vision of what was possible for American Income to accomplish with the labor movement. Hank is the person who persuaded me to organize a union for American Income's home office workers. I realized that we couldn't be half in and half out in our labor business. We needed either to get in totally or to get out. If we were going to advertise ourselves and our policies as union friendly, then we needed to demonstrate that orientation in tangible ways. Having American Income's home office staff in a union was as tangible an indication of our support for the labor movement as we could make.

I asked the Office and Professional Employees International Union (OPEIU) to organize the home office in June 1966. American Income then became a company where the person who processed the policy at the office was a union member. We were the only company that could make that statement to our customers.

> Barney organizing the office employees was consistent with his own thinking about the place of unions in our society, but it was also good business. — *Fred Schmidt*

After our home office workers organized, I received invitations to speak to all of the state AFL-CIO conventions. We hired a number of former labor leaders, including Hank Brown. In 1972 I invited Hank to be our guest at American Income's annual convention at Lake Tahoe. At that meeting Hank saw the way the company worked, and he liked our people. When he decided soon after that to retire from his post at the Texas AFL-CIO, he accepted my offer to be our vice president in charge of labor relations. Hank served as our goodwill ambassador to the union movement.

> I was fifty years old, and I thought it was time to move on to other things. The labor movement is a great place to have a wonderful time and to do what you love to do, but if you're an honest man, you're not going to make a lot of money at it. I also was getting weary of kissing the back sides of the politicians in Austin. That's primarily what my job was. I was the lobbyist for the labor movement in Texas. My job was to try to pass legislation for the workers, and in Texas that's a tough job. I decided I really needed to think about a retirement fund, and the only place I knew in Texas where you could be associated with a private company and still work with unions was with Bernard. — *Hank Brown*

Hank Brown is one of the most impressive orators in the American labor movement. His speaking style was typical of the old-time fire and brimstone labor agitators. Those guys came out of the Depression, and they are all hard-ribbed Democrats. We sent Hank all over the country to make speeches to all of the AFL-CIO conventions. At the time Hank joined the company, we had serious problems with three or four of our general state agents. I knew Hank was tough and smart enough to confront some of those people, so I asked him to serve also as my troubleshooter out in the field.

> The company just had an outright crook in Florida. He was stealing from the people. He was selling policies under false pretenses. They had a terrible man in Louisiana. His idea of hospitality was to bring in some prostitutes to the AFL-CIO convention to entertain what he thought were the delegates. Well, there may have been a time, way back there, when that was a regular thing, but today the labor movement is a family affair. People bring their wives and their children to the conventions. American Income also had some characters on the West Coast that certainly left a great deal to be desired in their

> shoddy manner of doing business. That's the job I worked
> the hardest on after I joined his company. We got rid of those
> people in Louisiana, Florida, in California, and a few other
> places. — *Hank Brown*

Hank, who had a national reputation as a union leader, played a key role in making American Income synonymous with labor. He performed magnificently. A few months after he joined the company, Hank formed a committee of the salesmen to work with a committee of the office workers to bring about a national labor contract to cover all American Income workers. That contract made the company a union shop. Anyone who worked for American Income Life automatically, on the sixtieth day of employment, became a member of the Office and Professional Employees International Union.

> I recall one lawyer saying to Bernard that if he created a union
> shop, it would get him some lawsuits. I told Bernard that it'll
> also make you rich. When the unions find out that you had
> been sued because you insisted on running a union company,
> it'll just double your business. Rapoport, being the kind of
> guy he is, said, "Put the union shop in," and that's what we
> did. — *Hank Brown*

We had salespeople in our different state agencies who were making bundles of money off the union market but who were fundamentally opposed to unions and who protested loudly against our becoming a union shop. They were hypocrites, happy to take money from union members despite being antiunion personally. I removed the phonies out of our operation when we proceeded with full unionization.

> Some of the general agents put together a committee to let
> Rapoport know that this union activity was carrying things to
> an extreme. All they wanted the union for was to sell insur-
> ance. They didn't really want the union to be of any benefit
> to their people. When the general agents' committee met with
> Rapoport to tell him that, he just notified them that if they
> could not go along with the program, they were no longer
> general agents of his. Several of them backpedaled pretty fast,
> but some of them left the company. That convinced me that
> Rapoport was really sincere in what he was about, and while
> he's not infallible, he basically wants to do the right thing.
> — *Hank Brown*

In October 1973 the AFL-CIO granted us an official designation as a Union Label company, which made American Income one of only two insurance companies in the United States with that status. The other company is Union Labor Life Insurance of New York, which is union owned and concentrates on large group policies. That designation allowed us to advertise in trade-union publications and to have an exhibit at the annual AFL-CIO Trades and Industry Show. American Income is a fully organized company, and everybody in the company is a member of the union, including me. Labor viewed the organizing of our workers as an act of good faith toward the movement.

Reorienting the company toward the labor market required other changes in the way we operated. A company that is targeted for a market is not run the same way as a company that is mass-marketing. Let me be candid about it. In a mass-market business, if there's a doubt about whether a claim is legitimate, the benefit of the doubt goes to the company. Once the company targets a particular market, however, the benefit of any doubt has to go to the customer. Our focus on labor unions necessitated a total change in our claim handling philosophy. We had to bring in new claim personnel, people who had come out of the unions and could communicate with union people. We hired Herb Brenner, who had a union background, to oversee the claims department. We had lots of meetings with our home staff about how to deal with union members and how to write to them. Everybody in the company had to learn union semantics.

It was more difficult to reorient our sales force than the home office, because most of the sales force had no experience in dealing with labor unions. We produced audio training tapes for the agents to teach them the history of unionism. We let them know that unions are not the ogres that the right-wing press and the Republican Party portray them as. Every agent had to listen to those training tapes. We made it clear to the agent that he or she was privileged to serve a special market. Because the company nurtured this market, a new agent could come in and after only ten days of training start earning good money right away.

By the early 1970s our relationship with the labor leadership had become extremely close. I always say that we're not related, in that the bonds of friendship are a little thinner than those of family, but we're darn good friends. One of the things that Hank Brown and I did to get us even closer to the union leadership was to create an American Income National Labor Advisory Board. Nearly every member of the board was a president or past president of a major labor union. We were careful to make it clear that membership did not mean that the labor leader was endorsing American Income or its products. That statement appeared prominently on every publication associated with the board. By serving on the board, the labor leader was recognizing that American Income was a fully organized, Union Label company and that our primary market was union membership. The only obligation of a board member was to advise American Income about how the company could better serve its union clients.

Throughout the years we had many outstanding labor leaders on the advisory board, including John J. Sweeney, the head of the AFL-CIO; Morton Bahr, president of the Communications Workers of America; Howard Coughlin, president of the Office and Professional Employees International Union; John DeConcini, president of the Bakery, Confectionery, and Tobacco Workers International Union; William Winpisinger, president of the International Association of Machinists and Aerospace Workers; and Alexander Barkan, former national director of the AFL-CIO's Committee on Political Education (COPE). Barkan, a longtime close associate of AFL-CIO president George Meany, served as chairman of the advisory council for several years. After his retirement from COPE, he went to work for American Income as a labor consultant and as the full-time manager of the labor advisory board. Al was one of the most politically influential labor leaders in the country. He was a fierce political operative who played a key role in national Democratic Party affairs for many years.

> **Al Barkan was a great labor leader. Barkan was a tremendous force in convincing many, many people to become associated with American Income Life. After Al died, Jules Pagano was the next person that they hired. Jules came out of the CWA. He's the full-time executive director for this AIL labor board in Washington. He is Rapoport's right arm in Washington, which is what we wanted.** *— Hank Brown*

We had no official connections with any union, and I never talked to any labor leader about his union doing insurance business with American Income. I talked to the union leaders about how I could help with their particular programs, in those areas where it was perfectly legal for us to be helpful. I was the catalytic agent for the company, because the union leadership trusted me.

> **I was an official with the Communication Workers of America when I first met B. Whenever B came to Washington, he would ask me and several other labor leaders to come to the hotel and have a drink. We had great discussions. B always wanted to know if there was anything that he should be doing to help**

labor or if we had any advice for him. Sometimes he would
have advice for us. He always kept the discussion at an intellectual level that was exciting. —*Jules Pagano*

We didn't just talk, we also acted. For example, we waived payment of
premiums by union members during an authorized strike. That provision
was unique in the insurance business. American Income was the first company in the United States to allow employees to deduct automatically from
their paycheck a contribution to the AFL-CIO's Committee on Political
Education. We included COPE literature in our mailings to all of our policyholders, and we distributed other AFL-CIO material through our agents.
American Income developed a college scholarship program for the children
of union members. We provided mortgage grants that made it possible for
several unions to construct headquarters buildings, and we contributed to
the strike funds of unions engaged in lawful strikes.

I attended and made a point of being visible at all of the state AFL-CIO
conventions, where we hosted a hospitality room. We knew all of the top
people in the international. The local union presidents saw me in the company of the top national union leaders and with prolabor politicians. When
our salespeople went out to see the local union presidents in their respective
areas, whether California or Pennsylvania or wherever, and identified themselves as representing American Income, the presidents remembered, "Oh,
yeah, that's Barney Rapoport's company. I saw him at our convention. Our
national president is on his labor advisory board." That broke the barrier
down and allowed the salesperson to get in the front door to talk business.

We asked the business agent for the union local if he would put out a
mailing because we were a Union Label company. We asked, "Since your
members are going to buy additional insurance, wouldn't you rather they
bought it from a union company than a nonunion company?" Only we put
it a little more bluntly; we would say, "rather than a scab company." We appealed to their sense of worker solidarity, and that was critical. We learned
always to market through a third-party endorsement. We operated best when
there was a social reason for the existence of the institution we were marketing through. When we strayed from that approach and tried to sell insurance
to members of rural electrical cooperatives, the effort flopped. Our agents
couldn't find a strong common bond among members that could be used
as a selling tool. There was no group consciousness.

Impressed that American Income was a union company, the local union
leader mailed our literature with a cover letter on union letterhead introducing American Income to his members. The unions did not recommend
American Income policies, they simply introduced the company to their

members. Enclosed in that mailing was a response card addressed to American Income. Six to 8 percent of those cards were returned. Company sales representatives called on the people who returned the response card. They sold policies to about half of those people.

We estimated that 80 percent of our prospects already had some type of supplemental policy, so the "be union, buy union" approach often persuaded them to switch. We dealt with 40,000 locals, so it added up to a lot of money in the end.

> When I think of American Income and the union movement, I think of Samuel Gompers's philosophy. He said we should reward our friends and punish our enemies. We talk about this, but too many of us deal with nonunion banks, nonunion insurance companies, nonunion brokerage houses, and nonunion business in general. It is incumbent upon the union movement to reward employers who believe in and accept their employees' right to organize and bargain collectively.
> —*John Kelly, labor leader*

In addition to people like Hank Brown and Al Barkan at the national level, we recruited former labor leaders in every state to work for American Income. As one of them once told me, American Income was the repository for retired labor leaders. We had so many retired labor leaders working with us that it was difficult to distinguish between our company and the labor movement. Nearly all of them made wonderful contributions to the growth of the company. One in particular who stands out in my mind is the late Oscar Jager.

I met Oscar through Chuck Caldwell, a COPE staff member who had once been on Senator Yarborough's staff. A former assistant to the legendary United Auto Workers president Walter Reuther, Oscar was a talented writer who used his self-taught skills to further the interests of the labor movement. Oscar had been a speechwriter for Reuther as well as for a number of other labor leaders, and he edited several union publications. He did a lot of work for the United Mine Workers. Oscar had little formal education; he just had natural talent. He could sit down at a typewriter (he was a two-finger typist) and whip out terrific commentary in a matter of minutes. His ideas just flowed to the page.

When we met, Oscar was doing press work for a congressional committee, and he had a private consultant firm editing newsletters. I liked him immediately. We had a long talk that night. At one point, Oscar said, "Why don't you let me do a labor letter for you?" He talked about what he thought it could do for American Income's expanding labor union market. The idea was to print and circulate a newsletter with brief capsule stories of interest to labor leaders. For example, the newsletter would have summary reports about AFL-CIO executive committee meetings, the status of federal and state legislation that might affect labor, and news about the activities of prolabor members of Congress. Oscar recommended that since American Income would print and distribute the newsletter as a service to union leadership, subscriptions should be free. I liked the idea and told Oscar we would do it.

We called the newsletter the *AI Labor Letter*. The company and its state general agents underwrote it. The newsletter attracted an amazing amount of attention as soon as the first issues appeared. Labor leaders from all over the world requested permission to reprint items from that newsletter. The *AI Labor Letter* turned out to be the most effective public-relations piece ever done with the labor movement outside the movement's own efforts.

Obviously, we wanted to help our business, but it helped our business a lot more than we ever anticipated. There was no advertising of any kind. We just made clear that it was sent to union members "with the compliments of American Income Life Insurance Company, a Union Label company." The newsletter gave us access to anybody in labor we wanted to see. The company's representatives could call a labor leader and honestly say, "I'm representing American Income, the company that publishes the *AI Labor Letter*. I'd like to come by and see if you'd like to be on our mailing list." When our representative was in the labor leader's office, he or she talked about insurance. The newsletter was all about access.

We sent out approximately 40,000 copies of the newsletter every month. We did not do business with a fourth of the people who received it, but that was beside the point. The fact is that American Income was better known by labor leaders than Prudential or Equitable as a result of that newsletter.

I was delighted by the success of the *AI Labor Letter* in generating new business, but the real objective when we started was to use it as a vehicle to advance my political objectives. When a prolabor senator such as George McGovern, Birch Bayh, or Alan Cranston had four or five years before they were up for reelection, we wanted to keep their names in front of the labor leadership with stories about how supportive they were of labor's legislative goals. The *AI Labor Letter* publicized their activities to the labor movement during a period when they weren't campaigning. We did that for a number of senators.

Of course, it was in the political arena that my interests had long been the same as labor's. I have worked closely with COPE and other labor political organizations in support of more candidates for public office than I can remember. My political contact with labor leadership across the country has cost me millions of dollars in personal money for political contributions. That doesn't include what my general agents and my state general agents contributed. We made available a sizable amount of money every election year in political contributions for labor-endorsed candidates. I am sure that some people think that I gave money to elect or reelect prolabor candidates to Congress because I believed it would help my business with labor. In truth, I contributed money to prolabor politicians because those are the candidates I would have supported anyway. I was helping those same candidates before I ever thought of having an insurance company that caters to labor unions. The labor leadership knows my political history, and that is another reason I have earned their trust.

I can say honestly that I have never used my political connections with labor or with anyone else for any personal gain or profit. It is true, however, that my political connections and my close ties with labor sometimes made it possible for me to get things accomplished for the company in a faster way than otherwise. My friendship with Senator Edward Kennedy, for example, certainly made it possible for me to get access to the state officials in Massachusetts to make a case for American Income when we were trying to get into that state.

When American Income wanted a charter to operate in Massachusetts, I met with the president of the state AFL-CIO and asked for his advice. He said to me, "We don't need any more insurance companies here. I think we would have to protest your application."

We kept talking, and Senator Edward Kennedy's name came up. So, I said, "Well, Teddy Kennedy's a good friend of mine."

The man looked skeptical and replied, "Well, of course, everybody says that. I don't believe you know him. I'll tell you what. Why don't you get the senator on the telephone and show me? If you reach him, and he says you're okay, we will help you get that state charter."

I said, "Now, I didn't tell you that Ted Kennedy would endorse my company. He probably doesn't even know the name of my company, but I can assure you that he knows me, and that's all I was telling you."

I accepted the challenge and made the telephone call to Kennedy's office. Luckily, he was in and able to take my call. When Teddy came on the line, I asked him to talk to the labor official. Teddy told him that I was an honorable person and that we were good friends. When he hung up the telephone, the fellow laughed and said, "Okay, you've got our support." We did $1 million the first year we were in Massachusetts. That's the way it sometimes works out. My social and political contact with top labor leadership and with the political friends of labor gave the company easier access to the labor market. Let me emphasize that Senator Kennedy did nothing himself to get us our approval, nor did any other politician. The state made its decision on the merit of our application, but we had avoided a potentially powerful source of public opposition to that application.

Our business with labor unions eventually spread throughout the whole country. That was when we started really doing business in states like Ohio, which had nearly 3 million union members at the time. We went into the state of California at the beginning of the 1970s. California has the most union members of any state in which we operate, which means that we did more business there than we did in any other state. By the time we entered California, our reputation with the labor movement was so well established that we had no difficulty breaking in there.

In 1963 we were taking in about $6 million or $7 million. Ten years later we were bringing in $31.5 million. Nearly all of that growth was the result of our success with labor. At first we were ignored by the industry. We were so small that my fellow insurance executives here in the Southwest didn't pay any attention to our new labor orientation. The truth is I have never had much of a relationship with other insurance company executives. That is not intentional; I have been a working president, and I just didn't have the time to go to association meetings and do all the things that make executives think they're busy, when they ought to be running their companies and trying to get more business.

When we began to attract substantial business from union members, however, some of our competitors tried to jump in. These companies portrayed themselves as serving union members, but the companies weren't unionized; their agents weren't unionized. It was just a merchandising gimmick, and it didn't succeed. Our competitors soon discovered that they can't wake up one morning and say, "I'm a union company; I'm going to be in the union business." There has to be a history behind a company to enable it to do that. The average executive in the insurance business, of course, is sort of scared of unions; he just doesn't understand them. That's why no company, to my knowledge, was as successful in the supplemental union field as our company. By the time it got around that American Income was a Union Label company serving the union members in that state, our competition got nothing but the crumbs.

Obviously, my decision back in the early 1960s to enter the labor market reaped profits for me and for my company. I can say sincerely that my relationship with labor has also given me a deep sense of personal satisfaction. It provided me with an unusual opportunity through my business to contribute to causes that promote and benefit the labor movement. Despite all of the ups and downs of the movement's history, I remain convinced that the American free enterprise system needs the labor movement to guarantee democracy on the job and fairness to workers. I am proud of the labor movement, and I am proud of my relationship with it.

It's great to do well by doing good.

7 ▶ *Vietnam and the Politics of Tumult*

I have long had a reputation in Texas as a "radical business-man," a term many people think is an oxymoron. I plead guilty to being a businessman, but I don't think I'm especially radical. I will admit to being something of an anomaly, however. To my fellow business executives, I was never more of an aberration than in those politically turbulent years of the 1960s and early 1970s. I was an anti–Vietnam War millionaire in Texas, a state where the vast majority of businessmen strongly supported the war in Southeast Asia. I was a businessman in an open-shop state who actively promoted a labor union for his own employees. And I served as the financial angel for an antiestablishment and, in some respects, antibusiness newspaper, *The Texas Observer.*

The reality is that I'm not radical in any way. I used to describe myself as a moral puritan and a social radical, but that really isn't true. I tend to agree with Thomas Jefferson that a revolution is good for society every so often, but I wish that revolutions weren't necessary. Actually, I don't think they have to be. Revolution and violent protest often are the direct result of elite intransigence and greed and the refusal by the members of the power structure to understand and accept the need for constructive and tangible change. Few times in our history has the power structure in this country been more intransigent than it was during the second half of the 1960s and the first half of the 1970s. That intransigence was embodied in those years by our unwise military action in Indochina.

The War in Vietnam

Our military intervention in the civil war in Vietnam during the decade beginning in 1965 and ending with the fall of Saigon in April 1975 was a national disaster that damaged this country more extensively than any other event in American history, with the exception of our own Civil War. I believe that the Vietnam War was a worse disaster than the American Civil War for the reason that absolutely nothing good resulted from it. The American Civil War ended slavery in this country. I have yet to hear a credible argument on behalf of some good outcome of the Vietnam War. I recently heard one of the architects of our policy in Vietnam, when asked to identify a positive result of that war, claim that our intervention made it possible for Hong Kong, Singapore, Taiwan, and the other so-called Asian Tigers to remain free and to develop into the economic and industrial successes they are today. That answer stunned me. It was the first time I had ever heard that particular reasoning. Certainly, no one said it quite that way during the war. I wonder how many parents and spouses and children who lost loved ones in Vietnam appreciate that their sons, husbands, and fathers died so that Singapore could have a healthy economy?

I truly hated that awful war. I have not changed my mind about it to this day. The United States simply had no national interests at stake there. I acknowledge that at the beginning of the war most Americans (and I include myself) were caught up in the so-called Munich syndrome, believing that an aggressor nation had to be stopped as early as possible or we would all pay the consequences of a much larger war. But we didn't stop to evaluate whether the Munich model was relevant to every case of military conflict in the world. It isn't, and it wasn't in Vietnam. The vast majority of Americans knew nothing about Vietnamese history and culture, which meant we did not understand the real nature of the conflict. We didn't even understand that the Vietnamese and the Chinese are ancient rivals with fundamental nationalistic differences that even communism could not resolve. That reality, along with our military stalemate, was readily apparent by the time the Vietnamese Communists caught us off guard with the Tet Offensive in February 1968. Yet the war continued for several more bloody years.

> **B was one of those who early on saw the folly of Vietnam as sharply as anyone that I can recall. He hated the war with a passion.** — *George McGovern, 1972 Democratic party nominee for president*

This isn't a book about the Vietnam War, nor am I an expert on Southeast Asian affairs, but I must dwell on the war here because that war dominated my political decisions and actions as a concerned American citizen during the late 1960s and early 1970s. I have to admit that my son being draft age had something to do with my feelings about that war. I'm not embarrassed to say it, nor do I believe that my fears about Ronnie's future mean that my opposition to the war was selfish. That my son was very much at risk forced me to examine our involvement in the Vietnam War to a degree I might not otherwise have done, and for that, I am grateful.

I was solid in my support of the antiwar movement, and I had a deep respect for the young activists from the so-called New Left who provided most of the energy for the movement. I helped them as much as I could. I provided financial support, for example, to Sam Brown's Vietnam Moratorium Committee, which organized a national mass demonstration for peace on October 15, 1969. I thought the Vietnam Moratorium Committee was one of the most enterprising of the student organizations.

I did have my problems with elements of the New Left, however. I was disturbed by the hostility that some of the New Left showed toward Israel. I also thought that many New Left activists were extremely naive about the real nature of the governments in the Soviet Union, the People's Republic of China, and Fidel Castro's Cuba. In addition, the rise of the New Left was in some ways a reaction against the political pragmatism of the Old Left, especially of the labor movement. Unfortunately, the resulting antagonism between the activists in the New Left and the older stalwarts of the labor unions hurt the progressive cause in general, and it was one of the reasons for the Democratic Party's overwhelming electoral defeat in 1972.

Labor shared responsibility with the New Left for the hostility that existed between them. Labor union support for the war in Vietnam was a bitter disappointment to me. It was one of the few times in my life that I felt alienated from the movement.

AFL-CIO president George Meany was a war hawk, and he thought Vietnam was wonderful. There was a real blind spot with Meany and the people around him about the incredible mistake we had made in Vietnam. B knew the war was a disaster from the beginning, so he worked hard with labor leadership to convince them that they were wrong on that issue. — *George McGovern*

My frustration with labor during this period was evident in a letter I wrote in May 1967 to *Texas Observer* publisher Ronnie Dugger. Referring to the rigid prowar stance taken by the labor leadership, I wrote that I was "tired of getting excited about the CIO of the 1930s and then having it become part of the Establishment in maintaining the kind of anachronistic hierarchy that makes it as obnoxious as any other narrow, vested-interest groups."

Although I gave money to several antiwar groups, the organization in which I was most active was the awkwardly named Businessmen Executives

Move for Peace in Vietnam (BEM), which was started in August 1967 by Henry Niles, an insurance company executive in Baltimore. Niles was a fascinating man. He was a Quaker and the father-in-law of Staughton Lynd, a Yale professor who caused a sensation when he openly violated a State Department travel ban by traveling to Hanoi during the war. Harold Willens, a Los Angeles businessman whose efforts on behalf of world peace were unending, recruited me to become one of the leaders of BEM. I had met Willens as a result of my association with the Center for the Study of Democratic Institutions. Like me, Harold was the son of Russian Jewish immigrants, and his family had little money when he was growing up. He meant well, but he was impulsive and excitable and he tended to jump from one project to another.

I joined BEM in September 1968. Other Texans who were deeply involved in BEM included Bob Childers, a businessman in Houston who died prematurely in a tragic accident in the early 1970s, and my friends J. R. Parten and Fagan Dickson. In all, BEM recruited about 2,500 businesspeople who considered Vietnam to be a terrible mistake. The national leadership included people like former Federal Reserve chairman Marriner Eccles, Gimbel Brothers executive Bernard Weiss, former SEC chairman J. Sinclair Armstrong, Xerox executive Chester Carlson, and Gordon Sherman, president of Midas Muffler. Our mission was in the title of the organization. We were businessmen who wanted to end U.S. involvement in the war in Vietnam.

Because of the title and because we were businesspeople who wore suits and didn't have long hair or beards and all of that, we were much more effective opponents of the war than the kids who confronted the police in the streets. Those of us who had been young radicals in the 1930s had been greatly influenced by Veblen's theory of the leisure class. We had wanted to call attention to our ideas, not to our style of clothing or to the length of our hair.

BEM was well organized. We got the attention of many businessmen who had never been involved in public issues. We weren't radical, in the sense that we didn't want to destroy the system; we wanted to preserve capitalism. We sponsored dinners with speakers and we had cocktail receptions. One of the events that we staged was BEM's third national conference, held in Washington in May 1969. It was memorable for me because I arranged for my close friends Senator Ralph Yarborough and John Henry Faulk to be speakers. Ralph treated the BEM membership to a good old-fashioned tub-thumping speech in his east Texas populist style. John Henry was also a sensation as he explained the views of his fictional Cousin Ed Snodgrass on the Vietnam War. I'll never forget the howls of laughter from the audience when Cousin Ed declared that "them Pentagon boys know that you can't depend on them people [the Vietnamese] to fight each other unless you stay right there and keep your eyes on 'em and keep their minds on their business."

Most of us in BEM supported and helped to finance Senator Eugene McCarthy's bid for the presidential nomination in 1968. He was the featured speaker at some of our dinners. Several military leaders were among our most active members, including General David Shoup (former commandant of the Marine Corps) and Rear Admiral Arnold True. Former diplomats Benjamin Cohen, Roger Hilsman, and Edwin Reischauer were members. I served on the BEM executive committee and worked as its finance chairman. I also represented BEM as a speaker against the war at several colleges around the country. I remember in particular my speech at Creighton University in Omaha, which attracted one of the largest and most enthusiastic crowds I have ever addressed.

My speeches emphasized three main points: that the war was unwinnable, that America's actions there were immoral, and that the war was an economic disaster for the country. With respect to the latter point, President Johnson lied to the American people when he asserted that we could have that war and still have prosperity and not have to pay for it with higher taxes. We cannot greatly increase our defense spending and cut taxes and have a healthy economy. We cannot do it. I thought we learned that then, but we did not. President Ronald Reagan did the same thing and ran up the biggest national debt in American history.

The war also caused me to become active in another antiwar organization, the Businessmen's Educational Fund, which was an outgrowth of BEM. Harold Willens formed the group in 1969 to lobby against the increasing power of the military-industrial complex. My main involvement in BEF was to sponsor John Henry Faulk's commentary on the BEF syndicated radio program "In the Public Interest" in 1972.

Eugene McCarthy (1968)

Because of my strong opposition to the Vietnam War, I was attracted to a number of antiwar or so-called dove political candidates in 1968. The best-known antiwar candidate that year was Senator Eugene McCarthy of Minnesota. I was among McCarthy's most enthusiastic supporters in his effort to win the Democratic nomination for president as an antiwar candidate. During the primary campaign, J. R. Parten and I hosted a luncheon for Gene in Houston. I had not met him prior to that visit. I was impressed with him immediately. He has a wonderful sense of humor, and he is a gifted storyteller. The thing that most people don't understand about McCarthy is that he's a poet, and he's one of the most charming people to be around. He is also an intellectual, which is a characteristic that I find enormously appealing in a politician. Unfortunately, it is also a rare characteristic in the political world. Gene and I have been good friends ever since that campaign.

> **B's position against the war could have hurt his insurance business, but he did not back off, and he was very visible. He really had to challenge the position of the labor movement on the Vietnam War, for example, and that could have proven very costly to him. He and I have been together over the years on what I consider to be all of the critical issues.**
> — *Eugene McCarthy*

As was so often the case in those years, J. R. Parten and Palmer Weber were my closest allies and advisors in the political battles of 1968. We were deeply involved in the reelection campaigns of Democratic senators George McGovern of South Dakota, Frank Church of Idaho, Birch Bayh of Indiana, and Joseph Clark of Pennsylvania. We made personal financial contributions to and raised money for several of these dove candidates in the hope that their reelection would hasten the end of the war. I don't know how many hundreds of thousands of dollars I raised that year, because I worked for every single dove senator running. I was ubiquitous; I was all over the political landscape.

In addition to McCarthy's campaign and the Senate reelection campaigns, I supported antiwar challengers to incumbent hawk senators. The one with whom I became most involved was Alan Cranston, who became one of the closest friends I ever had in the U.S. Senate. I first met Alan in Washington early in 1968. At that time American Income had a contract with a public-relations firm owned by Bob Maurer. Bob invited me to a small dinner party for Cranston, who was the Democratic candidate in California for the U.S. Senate. Alan and I had a strong rapport almost immediately. I learned that his Republican opponent was Max Rafferty, a right-winger who was state superintendent of the public schools. The incumbent Republican senator, Thomas Kuchel, was supposed to have been unbeatable, but Rafferty upset him in the Republican primary. Cranston had won his primary easily because he had been the only Democratic leader with the guts to challenge the supposedly invincible Kuchel. Alan told me at the dinner that he needed to raise an additional $10,000 to continue his campaign. The next morning I called Palmer Weber, and he and I quickly raised the money Alan needed. He defeated Rafferty in the general election and soon became one of the most influential members of the Senate. He was always grateful for my help, and from that day forward we were close personal friends.

Those of us in the McCarthy campaign got a tremendous boost when Lyndon Johnson withdrew from the presidential race in March 1968. I was the master of ceremonies for an Israel bond dinner at Waco's Temple Rodef Sholom the night Johnson made his announcement. A few minutes after eight o'clock someone handed me a note with the news that President Johnson had just declared that he would not be a candidate for reelection. I announced this news to the audience. It was a total surprise to us all. Some in the audience gasped in astonishment. I had a personal feeling of exhilaration, not because I got any pleasure out of Johnson's downfall but because I believed that his withdrawal from the race meant that peace in Vietnam was just around the corner.

Historian Eric Goldman wrote a book titled *The Tragedy of Lyndon Johnson.* Goldman was right, Lyndon Johnson was a tragic figure. He did more in terms of good domestic policy than any president we've ever had, better even than Roosevelt. Nobody has ever accomplished more in the area of civil rights than he has. I certainly would have supported Johnson against any Republican, but in an election between Johnson and Gene McCarthy, my support was for McCarthy. Johnson's tragic downfall was Vietnam, of course. He misled the American people about the nature of that war, probably because he had been misled himself. In the meantime, young men were being brought home in rubber bags.

Chicago and the Humphrey-Muskie Campaign

In August 1968 I took Audre and our 21-year-old son, Ronnie, a student at Oberlin College, to the Democratic National Convention in Chicago to work for Gene McCarthy's nomination. Although Vice President Hubert Humphrey seemed to have enough delegates to win the nomination, his lead was thin and insecure. Humphrey had not been a candidate in any primary, so most of his delegates were officially unpledged or were pledged to favorite-son candidates supporting Humphrey. There were a large number of delegates loose in the convention who had been elected as representatives of the late Bobby Kennedy. Also, George McGovern declared his candidacy two weeks before the convention with the hope of being the compromise candidate if the need for one arose. Hovering over all of this was the specter of a major and potentially violent antiwar demonstration in the streets of Chicago.

It was an exciting, depressing, fascinating, and frustrating experience. It was like no other political convention I have ever attended before or since. I was emotionally invested in the McCarthy campaign; it seemed to me literally that thousands of Vietnamese and American lives were at stake. We worked at a feverish pace to turn the tide for McCarthy's candidacy. We had meetings around the clock trying to raise money and to persuade uncommitted delegates to vote for McCarthy. The lobby at the Drake Hotel, where we were staying, was at all times like the New York City subway at rush hour. The Drake was where most of the labor union leaders also were housed. They were all Humphrey supporters. The area around the convention site was a war zone, with large numbers of heavily armed police and security agents wherever we turned. Young antiwar protesters numbering in the thousands heeded the call of peace activists David Dellinger, Rennie Davis, Abbie Hoffman, and Tom Hayden and flocked to Chicago. The mood was incredibly tense. Those of us on the McCarthy side really thought the world was going to come to an end if Gene didn't win the Democratic nomination.

During the evening of August 28, Al Barkan, Ronnie, and I sat in our hotel room and watched on television as Humphrey won the nomination. I remember that Ronnie, who was deeply upset by the outcome, denounced Humphrey and declared that he would not support him in the coming campaign. Al Barkan scolded Ronnie and asked him how he could not support a decent man like Humphrey, who had done so much in his career to help working people and the underclasses. I watched in sorrow as my son and my best friend in the labor movement argued heatedly. Their disagreement symbolized for me the deep division in the Democratic Party in 1968.

Meanwhile, there was chaos and violence on the streets. We could not see it from our room in the Drake Hotel, but the police and the antiwar demonstrators were rioting in front of the Conrad Hilton Hotel on Michigan Avenue. As the videotape of the riot flashed on the television screen, the sight of the Chicago police beating and kicking those kids horrified me. It was an outrage. Later, I saw some of the bruised and battered young people sitting on the floor of the hotel lobby. Several of us who had raised money for McCarthy put together a fund to pay their medical bills. That was as bad a night as I have ever experienced in public life.

A few days after the convention in Chicago, I attended a meeting in Austin of about 400 liberal Democratic leaders and antiwar activists who wanted to create an organization to take control of the Texas Democratic Party by 1970 or 1972. We decided to call ourselves the New Democratic Coalition of Texas, but that was about the only meaningful subject on which we could agree. We passed a number of resolutions, most of which were irrelevant to our primary purpose. One resolution called for the abolition of the Texas

Rangers, another urged the governor of Texas not to reappoint controversial attorney Frank Erwin to the University of Texas Board of Regents, and another demanded that the police be prohibited from carrying automatic weapons. We could not agree, however, on the most important issue: whether we should support Hubert Humphrey in his campaign against Richard Nixon.

Those of us from the old guard, including Maury Maverick, Jr., and Ralph Yarborough, who had fought for years to be recognized as the true and loyal Democrats in Texas, argued that the New Democratic Coalition had to endorse the national party's presidential ticket. The loyalty issue had been our main weapon against the conservative Democratic Party establishment, which had refused in 1952 and 1956 to support the national party's presidential candidate. A younger group of participants, most of them white, middle-class college students, who knew nothing about those earlier struggles, were adamantly opposed to Humphrey because of his support of LBJ's Vietnam policy. After much debate and pleading, we succeeded in striking a sentence from a resolution stating that we did not "seek to bind our members' consciences in the pending national election by any declaration of endorsement or preference." We finally agreed to issue a statement that some of us would support Humphrey, while others had not made up their minds. Even that wishy-washy resolution raised a hue and cry of protest from those participants who were there only because of their antiwar stance.

The meeting was depressing to me because of the tunnel vision of the moral absolutist antiwar group. I wrote Ronnie Dugger, who had joined the anti-Humphrey faction: "I feel like chucking it all, Ronnie, and going out to the Center [for the Study of Democratic Institutions] and just read and write the rest of my life, and, really, not caring very much if one appreciates what I write. Guess I'm getting old, tired, and frustrated."

The hard-core antiwar people really gave us hell about our support of Humphrey. They insisted that there was no difference between him and Nixon. To most of them, social, economic, and racial justice issues were unimportant or nonexistent. The only issue was the war and Humphrey's support of it.

Anybody who knew about Nixon's demagoguery during his 1946 congressional campaign against Jerry Voorhis and his 1948 Senate campaign against Helen Gahagan Douglas, and his record as a member of the House Un-American Activities Committee, also knew how stupid it was to see no difference between him and Humphrey. I got mad at Gene McCarthy for leaving the mainstream of the Democratic Party after he lost the nomination to Humphrey, a man who had been responsible for some of the most important social legislation ever enacted. Gene refused to endorse Humphrey until it was too late, and even then his endorsement was weak. There was a world of difference between Nixon and Humphrey, and we almost lost our world because of what Eugene McCarthy and his followers did. Gene is not very pragmatic, and I have to admit that he probably wouldn't have made a good president. I really believe that if Gene had come out full force for Humphrey and urged his followers to vote for him, Humphrey would have beaten Nixon.

I was not among those McCarthy supporters who refused to back Humphrey. I joined with a number of Democratic Party activists to put together an organization to manage the Humphrey-Muskie campaign in Texas. Ralph Yarborough agreed to head up the campaign, and I agreed to be the finance chairman. Fred Hofheinz, the son of Houston's flamboyant judge Roy Hofheinz, served as the state chairman. Working closely with the labor movement around the country, I raised funds for Humphrey. Audre and I gave him a lot of our money. I was proud of Ralph Yarborough during that campaign. He traveled across the state giving speeches on Humphrey's behalf. To everyone's surprise, we carried Texas for Humphrey, and Yarborough deserved much of the credit.

After Nixon's narrow victory, I wrote Hubert Humphrey a confessional letter of sorts: "I would be less than honest with you if I didn't say that at the outset I was not a Humphrey supporter until the conclusion of the Convention: my concern with the war and the subjective considerations involved when one has a 21-year-old-son were the reasons. Reflectively, I was wrong. My sins of nonsupport for you in the pre-Convention days I hope were expiated by my total commitment in being your State Finance Chairman. Sophocles surely had someone like yourself in mind, Mr. Vice President, when he said: 'I was born not to share in hate but to share in love.'"

I believe Hubert Humphrey would have made an outstanding president. He was a pragmatist who could bring people together. He was a real leader. During the 1972 presidential campaign, someone said that the problem was that when George McGovern entered a room, nobody noticed. I can assure you that when Hubert Humphrey was in a room, it lit up. As an old Spanish philosopher said, "In order to give light to others, one must first set fire to himself." Well, Hubert Humphrey was always on fire. I loved his enthusiasm. I think that enthusiasm is an indication of energy and desire. I think that many people who have a reputation for being deep and introverted really just lack energy. They just don't care enough about people. I like people who are demonstrative. When I see you I'm going to put my arm around you. I may even hug you. When I meet somebody that I care for, I want to demonstrate, both physically and emotionally, what my feeling is for that person. Hubert Humphrey was that kind of person. He would give you a bear hug every time he saw you.

The Yarborough Defeat (1970)

After we carried Texas in the 1968 presidential election, I felt optimistic about Ralph Yarborough's chances for reelection in 1970, especially given the widespread attention that he had received as leader of the Humphrey campaign in Texas. I had hopes that Ralph's loyal service in support of the Democratic ticket in 1968 might dissuade serious challengers from entering the Democratic primary, but that was not to be. John Connally (who had retired as Democratic governor and then became a Nixon crony) and his allies had no intention of giving Ralph a free ride. They knew that as a prolabor liberal in a conservative state, Ralph was vulnerable. They also understood that Ralph's courageous stand against the Vietnam War gave them an issue that would be easy to demagogue.

During the early years of the escalation of U.S. military involvement in Vietnam, Ralph Yarborough took a hawkish position and vocally supported LBJ's actions. His position on the war was not much different from most of his colleagues in the Senate, especially those from the South. I made several trips to Washington to urge Ralph to look more closely at that insane war and the real nature of our role in it, but my pleadings had little effect on his thinking. At least that's what I thought until August 1967, when Ralph gave his first speech on the floor of the Senate about Vietnam. Reacting to a widespread rumor that the U.S. military was planning an invasion of North Vietnam to cut off Viet Cong supply lines, Ralph gave notice to the Johnson administration that he would oppose expansion of the war. "Any land invasion of North Vietnam," Ralph declared, "would be . . . an utterly indefensible step. It would be escalation gone mad. . . . This . . . is a course of near madness, one that I must speak out against." It wasn't a condemnation of U.S. policy in South Vietnam, but it signified a profound change in his thinking. I was elated by this development. I immediately sent him the following message: "It is always difficult for me to write you, Senator, on the Vietnam situation. You already know how I feel and think. I commend you for . . . expressing the horrendous consequences that would befall America and the world were we to attempt an invasion of North Vietnam. There are thousands of Texans who look to you for leadership. They have wanted you to say these things for so long. In the midst of the Great Debate . . . we have a tendency to overlook the fact that people are getting killed. I hope and pray that this is only the beginning of a series of statements from you relating to the Viet Nam situation."

Ralph had turned the corner, no matter how slowly, and he gradually moved closer to the dove side of the debate over the war. It was exceedingly difficult for a senator from Texas, which has a passionately promilitary tradition, to oppose the war. I understood that. It was for that reason especially that my respect for Ralph grew and deepened as he moved decisively toward the antiwar side. He would pay an electoral price for his stance, however.

As the time approached for Ralph to return to Texas in 1970 to stand for reelection to his third full term in the Senate, I slowly realized that he was facing a difficult campaign. Nixon was in the White House, and he had anointed Houston congressman George Bush, Ralph's unsuccessful 1964 opponent, as the Republican Party's brightest hope. We also heard substantive rumors that Ralph would attract a primary election challenge from the conservative faction of the Texas Democratic Party. From 1964 until 1968, it had been taken for granted that John Connally would run against Ralph, but by 1970 Connally was a partner in the Houston law firm of Vinson, Elkins, and he apparently was not interested in a Senate seat. We didn't know who Ralph's primary challenger would be, but we knew Connally would find someone to make the race.

On January 6, 1970, Houston businessman Lloyd Bentsen, Jr., announced his candidacy. A former congressman from the Rio Grande Valley of Texas, Bentsen was forty-eight years old, tall, handsome, and wealthy. He made it clear that he would hang the antiwar movement around Ralph's neck. In his announcement speech, Bentsen accused Ralph of "partisan sniping" that had undermined President Nixon's efforts to end the Vietnam War. Bentsen charged that Ralph would "never be satisfied until we have run out or been driven out of Vietnam." Now we knew what we were up against, and it wasn't encouraging. Armed with the full and active support of John Connally's political organization, Bentsen was a formidable candidate.

If we beat Bentsen, we still faced another young, handsome, and rich candidate in George Bush, who would be a stronger foe in 1970 than he had been in 1964, when Ralph had benefited from LBJ's landslide victory over Barry Goldwater. Elected to Congress in 1966 and reelected in 1968, Bush was a more seasoned and mature candidate, and this time he—not Ralph— had the power of the White House behind him.

Those of us in the Yarborough camp tried to organize early for the coming battle, but we couldn't get Ralph's attention. My letters to him in the summer and fall of 1969 asking for guidance about campaign plans usually ended with the following plea: "I would appreciate an immediate answer . . . time is growing short. I want to go to work, but we do need a plan." After several letters went unanswered, I finally sent one outlining a campaign fund-raising plan and ended it thusly: "Is there any objection? I really want to go at my job of being chairman full blast; consequently, since we all sometimes overlook answering mail, may I proceed on the basis that if I do not hear within ten days from this date, I can assume no response is an indication that I should go ahead with this project?" Or I would call him in Washington and beg, "Ralph, you've got to get back home and campaign."

He would reply, "Well, I'm busy up here. Look what I'm doing for the people. Look at my voting record. It's a one-hundred-percent voting record for the people."

I would respond that it made little difference how he voted if the people never saw him or got an opportunity to know him on a personal basis, but he never understood that. He didn't know how to backslap, and he did not know how to do the things that people want a politician to do. So we were late getting started, and it cost us dearly.

In addition, the big urban newspapers in Texas that pictured him as an antibusiness labor candidate were killing Ralph. I was especially incensed by that charge. Ralph had the enthusiastic support of such highly successful and wealthy businessmen as J. R. Parten, John de Menil, Arthur Temple, and Walter Hall, men who had made a fortune in the free enterprise system. Parten strongly opposed federal interference in his business operations, yet he was Ralph's most important and loyal supporter. In fact, Yarborough was a great admirer of the entrepreneurial spirit, and he wanted a healthy business climate because it provides jobs. Nevertheless, too frequently during that campaign I received letters from business executives who had supported Ralph in the past but who were now convinced that he was somehow antibusiness.

When the president of an insurance company in Dallas resigned from Yarborough's reelection committee with the complaint that the senator was trying to destroy the insurance industry by favoring a moderate national health insurance plan, I had to respond in writing, "I am so bored with people in our industry, and people in the business community generally, expostulating that Senator Yarborough is 'anti-business.' He is the most pro-business senator I know of, BUT he is even more PRO-people. His great intelligence enables him to be . . . perceptive in understanding that, if we don't make the system work, it can't endure. It is my sincere belief that . . . any legislation that he initiates is with the thought of extending the most benefits to the most citizens of this country. With that kind of attitude, our system cannot do otherwise than survive and prosper."

That was a mean and dirty campaign. Bentsen's campaign ads showed a film of student protesters confronting the police outside the National Democratic Convention at Chicago in 1968, with the narrator stating, "Ralph Yarborough is against the war in Vietnam." Of course, there was no relationship between the riots and Yarborough's position on Vietnam, but the ads implied that Ralph had endorsed the Students for a Democratic Society (SDS) and their cohorts in the radical left who had confronted the Chicago police. Other ads falsely claimed that Ralph was an ultraliberal who opposed school prayer and supported compulsory school busing to advance racial integration. That was the kind of campaign they ran against Ralph.

I'll never forget election night in 1970; we somehow thought we just might be able to scratch out a victory. Ralph and I were sitting alone in his library at his house in Austin listening to the election returns. We wrote the vote totals down as they came in from each county. The first return came in from some east Texas county, the name of which I don't remember now. Frowning, Ralph looked at the figures and said, "Barney, we have lost the campaign."

I said, "Ralph, what are you talking about?" His head drooped down. I could not believe it. It was a county where he had always been strong, and he could see immediately that he was not getting the votes. More returns came in, and he was right. It was a sad and depressing night.

We raised plenty of money in that campaign. As Yarborough's finance chairman, I don't make that claim to avoid my share of the blame for the defeat. Truly, a lack of money isn't what beat us in 1970. Bentsen's demagoguery about Ralph's stance on the Vietnam War cost us a lot of votes, especially in east Texas. I also believe that Yarborough beat himself. He refused to pay attention to the campaign until it was too late. When he finally went to work, he insisted on controlling every little detail of the campaign. Ralph was what we now call a micromanager. He not only wrote his own speeches, but he even wrote his own press releases.

The truth is that Ralph was not a politic man; he neglected his constituent services, and he didn't know how to be nice to people on a personal level. During his last term as a senator I don't know how many times I received complaints from financial contributors he had managed to offend or alienate because he didn't answer his mail. That was not the fault of his staff; he had good people who did their best for him. Ralph insisted on handling most of his own mail, and he just couldn't keep up. When Ralph did allow the staff to draft documents, the drafts were frequently lost in the piles of disorganized paper that he kept scattered across his desk and on tables in his office. The few times that I dared to speak to him about this problem, Ralph responded with lengthy speeches about how he didn't have time to keep his desk organized. He was fighting the people's fight (which was true), and he was working twenty-four hours a day to get essential legislation passed.

The point is, I could never really have a dialectical conversation with

Ralph Yarborough. He was as stubborn a man as I have ever met. I could never change his point of view. If I started a conversation with him, he would have a preamble that lasted about forty-five minutes, and then I had about thirty-five seconds left to say something. Then he would respond for another forty-five minutes.

Ralph was in his late sixties when he left the Senate in January 1971, but he kept burning with a desire to return to public office in 1972, either as a U.S. senator or as governor of Texas. The problem with the governor's race that year was that Lieutenant Governor Ben Barnes, the popular red-headed boy wonder of Texas politics, appeared to have a lock on that job. The Sharpstown Bank scandals had not yet brought Ben down. I urged Ralph to go after John Tower's seat in the Senate. Tower's election to his first term in the Senate in 1961 had appeared to be a fluke because of the circumstances of a winner-take-all special election. He had drawn a weak opponent for his re-election bid in 1966. I believed that as a Republican Tower could be beaten, and that Ralph's strong name recognition combined with a unified wing of progressive Texas Democrats behind him would carry the day. It never occurred to me, however, that Ralph would lose the Democratic primary.

I agreed to serve once again as Ralph's finance chairman, but it became clear to me early on that Ralph's bad habits had only gotten worse since his defeat in 1970. He assembled a group of dedicated and enthusiastic workers in Austin to run his campaign, but they were mostly young and inexperienced and badly in need of a full-time campaign manager. Unfortunately, Ralph insisted on managing his own campaign, which meant that there was no campaign manager because a candidate has too many other duties to carry out.

In addition, Ralph's campaign speeches, which he insisted on writing himself, were rambling, off-center, and hard to follow. The speeches also were full of irrelevant personal attacks against Lyndon Johnson, John Connally, and Lloyd Bentsen. LBJ, of course, was in retirement back on his ranch and completely out of the picture. As Nixon's secretary of the treasury, Connally had little influence in a Democratic primary. Bentsen was fully engaged in making his way in the Senate. None of those political giants had any desire to protect John Tower, and none was close to Ralph's primary opponent, Dallas attorney Barefoot Sanders. Ralph's fixation on old enemies was so disturbing that I reluctantly sent him this message on January 20, 1972: "This is a difficult letter for me to write, Ralph. I know full well about Bentsen and LBJ and Connally. I think we should never forget, on the other hand we have a specific objective and that is, to win a Senate seat for the people. At this point we have one opponent and that is Barefoot Sanders. I think we ought to run against him. Later, our opponent will be Tower and we ought to run against him. It seems to me that every time we mention the name of an individual other than the opponent that it might cost us some votes." Like so many other letters I wrote Ralph, that went unanswered as well as unheeded. Ralph continued to rail against his old enemies, and I am convinced that it cost him dearly.

Ralph not only tried to manage his own campaign, but he also served as his own fund-raiser and treasurer. He insisted on keeping the donor list himself. I couldn't even get copies. He insisted on running our fund-raising meetings, which always resulted in much wasted time because of Ralph's need to give unnecessary speeches. He served as his own exclusive liaison with labor, despite my deep and extensive connections with the unions in Texas. I finally had enough. Ralph's mismanagement and paranoia got so bad that I decided to relinquish my position as his finance director. I wrote him on March 6, 1972, "I don't know why, Ralph, that you are more difficult to work with this year than you ever have been before. It doesn't look to me like you want a state finance chairman. That's fine with me, just don't hold me accountable for the results. You have taken all my enthusiasm, and I don't operate well on a perfunctory basis. I would not do anything to embarrass you, and will keep the title for as long as you want me to, as long as we both understand the truth; which is, that you have constrained me to a situation that does not lend itself to success." I received no reply to that letter either.

I was not surprised when Barefoot Sanders pulled off a major upset by beating Ralph in the primary. Sanders went to defeat in the Nixon landslide in November. John Tower had lucked out a third time, and Ralph had beaten himself once again. It was his last campaign.

The charge that Ralph Yarborough actually had a negative effect on the healthy development of the liberal wing of the Texas Democratic Party is absolutely true. Yarborough's commitment to his own campaigns and his commitment to his own career was so intense that it prevented him from doing the work that was necessary to help us build the liberal wing of the Texas Democratic Party. He negated anything that was not directly supportive of his reelection. He was wrong to do that. The reason was that he did not trust anyone. I know that he trusted his beloved wife, Opal, but I doubt that he trusted anyone else. His paranoia was sad and disturbing to us all, and it did more to defeat him than anything his opponents ever did.

I tried to talk to him about it once, just before the 1970 campaign. A friend of mine wanted to be appointed U.S. attorney in Dallas. He had headed the Veteran's Administration in Waco. He was a wonderful and competent man, a real liberal and a Yarborough supporter. When I visited with Ralph in his Senate office in Washington to discuss his support for this man's appointment, he jumped up out of his chair and said, "You are in cahoots with Lyndon against me." I didn't know what the hell he was talking about. I was stunned. Apparently, this man was identified with Johnson somehow in Ralph's mind, and he accused me of pushing him on behalf of Johnson, who was by then retired to his ranch in Texas and very much out of politics. I did not even know Lyndon Johnson. I was a Yarborough man, and Yarborough men did not have a relationship with LBJ. Besides that, I had worked hard and visibly against the Vietnam War, so I was obviously not one of the LBJ crowd. But Ralph saw Johnson conspiracies all around him. It was a sad thing to witness. When Ralph made that accusation, I just stood up and walked out of his office. There was no point in arguing with him. Once he had his mind made up, that was it; there was no way to convince him otherwise.

Despite those all-too-human frailties, all Texans can take pride in Ralph Yarborough's record as a progressive member of the Senate. Yarborough was the sponsor or cosponsor of every major piece of educational legislation passed into law during the 1960s. They included landmark bills such as the Elementary and Secondary Education Act of 1965, the Higher Education Act of 1965, the National Defense Education Act of 1959, and the Vocational Education acts of 1963 and 1968. Ralph played key roles in the passage of the Cold War GI bill and the Bilingual Education Act. He was a tireless advocate for the conservation of our natural resources. Neither the Padre Island National Seashore nor the Guadalupe Mountain National Park would exist if Ralph had not been in the U.S. Senate.

In the early 1980s Audre and I decided that it was important that the students who go to the University of Texas at Austin are forever aware of Yarborough's contributions to Texas and the nation. To help insure that his achievements continue to be recognized, we endowed the Ralph W. Yarborough Professorship in Economics. In addition, shortly before his death in January 1996, we helped raise the funds necessary to acquire the core of his rare Texana library for preservation in the University of Texas Center for American History, where it can be used and enjoyed by students and the general public.

Lloyd Bentsen

I was bitter when Yarborough lost his Senate seat in the 1970 primary. The campaign against Ralph had been especially mean, even by Texas standards, and I held Lloyd Bentsen, Jr., personally responsible. After Ralph's defeat, I toyed with the idea of funding a Democratic Party re-

Senator Lloyd Bentsen, Jr., with B and Audre. CN 10484, Rapoport (Bernard) Photograph Collection, Center for American History, The University of Texas at Austin.

building committee to help elect the Republican candidate George Bush in the general election in November, not because I favored Bush but because I wanted to cast a protest vote against Bentsen and the John Connally Democrats.

A surprising thing happened, however. About nine-thirty one night, not long after the primary election, we received a telephone call from Marge Lacy, one of our neighbors. Marge had gone to school with Lloyd Bentsen's wife, B.A. She said that the Bentsens were visiting and that Lloyd was wondering if he could come over to talk. We were getting ready for bed, but Audre and I were intrigued, so we said okay.

> **We didn't like Lloyd Bentsen. He ran a very dirty campaign against Ralph. We were quite upset about it. Bernard and I were shocked that he wanted to come to our house at that time of the night to meet us.** —*Audre Rapoport*

When I opened the door, he stuck out his hand and announced, "I'm Lloyd Bentsen. Can I come in and visit with you?" We shook hands, and I invited him in. As soon as he sat on the couch, he went straight to the point.

With a solemn expression on his face, he said, "Mr. Rapoport, I want your support against George Bush."

"Well, you know I'm very mad about what you did to Ralph," I replied. "I know that," he responded, "and I fully understand why."

We talked for at least an hour, maybe more. Bentsen said that he regretted some of the tactics he had used against Ralph. He explained, however, that early in the campaign Ralph had publicly accused his father, Lloyd Bentsen, Sr., of being a crook and swindler. Bentsen's father had made a fortune as a land developer in south Texas. In the late 1940s Bentsen Senior had been embroiled in lawsuits stemming from his development activities. He also had been involved in a controversial land deal with Allan Shivers, who at that time was lieutenant governor of Texas. Arguing that his father had never been convicted of a crime, Bentsen looked me straight in the eye and said his father was a decent and honorable man. Ralph's accusations had so enraged Bentsen that he had decided to take the gloves off and go after him. "That's only an explanation for the mudslinging," Bentsen said. "I realize it's still not an excuse."

Bentsen then argued that Ralph's time had passed, that Texas and the nation were becoming more conservative politically, and that Texans wanted a moderate voice in Washington. "Ralph Yarborough could not beat George Bush this November," Bentsen asserted. "Moderate and conservative Democrats will not vote for him. I can beat Bush, but only if leaders such as yourself, J. R. Parten, and others on the liberal side help me. I know you don't really want Texas to have two Republican senators."

Admitting that he was a conservative, Bentsen claimed that his conservatism was not the closed-minded version. As a businessman who had made his own way in the insurance industry, he suspected that his economic views were similar to mine. He was not an ideologue, he said, but a pragmatist in the tradition of Sam Rayburn, who had been his mentor during his years as a congressman. He wanted to get things done for Texas, and with the Democrats solidly in control of the Senate, he would be an effective representative in Washington for the state. As a Republican in the Senate minority, George Bush could not be effective. Texas would lose influence. Bentsen admitted that he and John Connally were friends and that the former governor was helping his campaign, but he was not John Connally's puppet.

"I can assure you, Bernard, that I will be my own man. Anyone who knows me, knows that I will set my own course. I am also a loyal Democrat who will work effectively with the party's leaders in the Senate, some of whom I have known well for many years."

I found his arguments to be persuasive. I was enormously impressed that he would journey to the home of one of Ralph Yarborough's closest longtime supporters to make his case in a respectful manner yet with honesty about his own views. It was a gutsy thing for him to do. I could sense that he was an honest person. His integrity was quite apparent. I liked him, but I wasn't happy about it. I wanted to dislike him at that particular point. Nevertheless, he persuaded me to support him.

A few days later, I learned that Bentsen paid a similar visit to J. R. Parten at his house in Madisonville and that he had also won J.R.'s support. If he had not made those personal visits to our homes, J.R. and I probably would have financed a rebuilding committee effort and it might have been a different election. Bush was a formidable candidate who had President Nixon's full support. The Republican Party leadership wanted that Senate seat badly, but Bentsen outsmarted them and beat them. Much to my delight, he became an outstanding senator.

Sissy Farenthold

Ralph Yarborough's ill-starred bid for the Senate was not the only campaign in which I was active that spring of 1972. As my influence and interest in the Yarborough campaign waned, I turned most of my attention to the gubernatorial contest in the Democratic primary, where progressives were rallying in support of state representative Frances "Sissy" Farenthold's crusade against the state's conservative political establishment. A women's rights advocate, peace activist, and civil libertarian from Corpus Christi, Sissy had attracted popular attention as a reformer in the Texas Legislature during the Sharpstown banking scandal. Her gubernatorial campaign was an open challenge to the conservative good-old-boy state political establishment and its candidate, Lieutenant Governor Ben Barnes.

Sissy's campaign was another in which J. R. Parten and I played an active and significant role as a team. We were both early and enthusiastic supporters. John Henry Faulk initially got J.R. and me interested in Sissy while she was in the Texas Legislature. It was well known at that point that Sissy, who had earned a law degree from the University of Texas law school, was thinking about running for a statewide position, attorney general being the most likely. Although neither of us had ever met Sissy, she had some ties with J.R. She was the granddaughter of Judge B. D. Tarlton, J.R.'s real-property professor when he attended the University of Texas law school, and the daughter of Dudley Tarlton, a lawyer in Corpus Christi whom J.R. had known well for many years. Parten was won over to Sissy during his first meeting with her, when they had an opportunity to discuss her political views. "I am convinced that Sissy Farenthold is a real Democrat," Parten told me on the

Frances "Sissy" Farenthold, during the 1972 campaign
for governor of Texas. CN 10752, Farenthold (Frances)
Photograph Collection, Center for American History,
The University of Texas at Austin.

telephone. One of J.R.'s primary concerns was civil liberties, and he worried that the Nixon administration and its allies at the state level posed a serious threat to our basic freedoms. "Sissy understands the need to defend and protect our constitutional liberties," J.R. said. "I believe she deserves our support if she runs for a statewide office."

After I had an opportunity to visit with her, I too became a fan. She is an intelligent woman and a quality person. A few weeks after my first visit with Sissy, I drove to Austin to attend a state labor union meeting. On the way, I decided to have breakfast with J.R. at his weekend home in Madisonville. He was complaining that Houston attorney John Hill, whom he wanted to run for attorney general in 1972, wouldn't run "if Sissy Farenthold is in the race. You've got to talk to Sissy about running for governor instead of attorney general."

By this time, Ralph Yarborough had decided to run for the Senate rather than for governor, which left that race open for a liberal candidate. After I got to Austin, I called Sissy and told her what J.R. had said. She asked me what I thought.

"Well, I really don't think you ought to run for attorney general," I replied, "because we've got John Hill and he has an excellent chance of winning. We really need a good candidate for governor. J.R. and I think you should take on Preston Smith and Ben Barnes. You can count on our help if you do."

Sissy replied that she had wanted to run for governor, but when it looked like Yarborough would run, she had backed off. Now that he was running for the Senate, she would reconsider the governor's race. Of course, that's the office she went after. It's interesting to wonder what might have happened if I hadn't stopped for breakfast with J.R. that morning.

I agreed to serve as Sissy's finance chairman. It was a labor of love because she is such a fantastic person. My former UT classmate and political comrade Creekmore Fath managed the state campaign. The joint financial support that J.R. and I provided helped make Sissy's race possible. At the beginning of the campaign, I joined with J.R., Houston art patron John de Menil, and Houston banker Robert Lanier to loan $60,000 to the Farenthold campaign. At a particularly critical juncture a few weeks before the election, J.R. and I contributed the funds needed to keep her state office open.

Sissy ran her campaign without a professional public relations person, without billboards (she opposed them), and with only a little radio and television time. In addition to her opposition to the Vietnam War and her support of George McGovern's presidential candidacy, Farenthold demanded that the Texas Rangers be disarmed because of their record of suppressing Mexican-American and labor union protest, called for strict gun control legislation, and argued for the enactment of a corporate profits tax. She ran a populist campaign that struck a chord with a lot of voters who were thoroughly disenchanted with the corruption in Austin. So many college students volunteered to work for Sissy that her campaign resembled Gene McCarthy's 1968 children's crusade. One reporter described her staff as a "zealous, if disorganized, band of newly enfranchised students and old Yarborough hands."

The last week of the campaign, Creekmore Fath called me and said that he was certain that if I could only raise another $25,000, Sissy would make the runoff. So I went to Bob Lanier's Main Bank in Houston and talked them into giving us the money. A couple of days before the election, some newspapers reported polls indicating that Ben Barnes and rancher and former legislator Dolph Briscoe, Jr., of Uvalde each had about 31 percent of the vote and that they would be the runoff candidates. We believed Sissy was doing better than that, but you never know until the votes come in.

On May 7 Sissy surprised nearly everyone by receiving 28 percent of the vote and leaping ahead of Ben Barnes to wind up in a runoff with Briscoe. It was a stunning defeat for Barnes, who had been heavily favored. Briscoe, whose campaign spent more than $900,000 to Sissy's $212,000, finished well ahead of Sissy but failed to get enough votes to avoid a runoff.

J.R. and I helped to finance Farenthold's runoff campaign, but we could see the writing on the wall. We knew that the Texas political establishment, with which J.R. and I had battled for so many years, was scared to death by Sissy and that they would do everything possible to defeat her. She had sneaked up on them during the primary, and that wouldn't happen again. We also knew that it would be almost impossible for Sissy to attract enough votes from Barnes and Smith to overtake Briscoe. With the incumbents defeated, many people felt that the main goal had been achieved. Another factor that hurt us was the scheduling of the runoff on Saturday, June 3. Our college activists, who were scattered for summer vacation, had generated much of our energy. We were bound to lose votes simply because those students were away from the college towns where they had registered to vote. For those and other reasons, Dolph Briscoe beat Sissy soundly in the runoff.

McGovern Campaign

My active support for Senator George McGovern was a natural thing for me. I knew George personally. He was among the peace candidates I had helped in the 1968 election. In addition, the antiwar organization in which I was most active, Businessmen Executives Move for Peace in Vietnam, had transformed itself into a McGovern campaign support group.

> I got to know B when I was a brand-new senator in 1963. I had known about him before that when I was in the House of Representatives, but he and I really became friends early on in my Senate career. — *George McGovern*

Although I endorsed McGovern's candidacy in April 1972, my formal entry into the McGovern camp occurred on May 1, when I attended a campaign fund-raising party in New York City. J. R. Parten and I were among a group of forty prominent people, including entertainers Shirley McLaine, Warren Beatty, and Barbra Streisand, and General Motors heir Stewart Mott, who attended the party to demonstrate their support for McGovern and to raise $1 million for his campaign. J.R. and I agreed to work as a team to raise money for McGovern's Texas campaign.

> B was one of my key contributors in 1972, but beyond that he raised a lot of money, not only in Texas but elsewhere. He talked to people in the labor movement. Nineteen seventy-two was the only presidential campaign in which the AFL-CIO refused to endorse the Democratic presidential nominee. That centered almost entirely on the Vietnam War. B worked hard with the labor leadership to convince them that they were wrong about me. I had a strong record of support of workers in this country. I think the AFL-CIO's own records indicated that I voted with labor about ninety percent of the time. B knew that I had written a doctoral dissertation on the Ludlow Massacre during the Colorado coal strike of 1913-1914. He saw that I was the natural candidate for people who made their living working with their hands. — *George McGovern*

I attended the 1972 convention in Miami. That was a wonderful event, especially compared to our experience in Chicago four years earlier. After McGovern was nominated, I attended a meeting with several people to talk about the selection of a vice presidential nominee. Someone said that it would be great if we had a woman on the ticket. When I said, "What about Sissy Farenthold?" everyone thought that was an interesting idea. Sissy was eager to do it, so I gave a party for her, and we generated some excitement. I went to McGovern and asked him if it was okay if we promoted Sissy for the ticket. McGovern said, "Go ahead and do whatever you want to do." I believed that he wanted her nominated because it would produce a lot of fun and excitement in the convention. The nominee can always stop anything like that if he really wants to. I didn't know it, but the people around McGovern had already chosen Senator Thomas Eagleton of Missouri, and the unions were really pushing Eagleton.

Sissy might have won the nomination if we had taken it seriously in the beginning. I was taken by surprise when McGovern did not object to her candidacy. If I had known that he would not oppose her, I would have gone to work a couple of weeks before the convention, and we might have had Sissy on the ticket. I went down to the California delegation, where Alan

Cranston introduced me to Willie Brown, who was then Speaker of the California House. Brown asked, "How many votes do you want for Farenthold?" I replied, "I'll take forty from California." Just like that he gave us forty votes for Sissy. I don't know what would have happened if she really had had the votes. I don't know what McGovern would have done. But it made us feel good that Sissy did so well at the convention.

I spent some time at the convention in Miami with Rennie Davis. An SDS leader, he was one of the eight antiwar leaders who had been tried in 1969 on the charge of conspiring to cause a riot at the Democratic Convention in Chicago. In Miami, Davis asked me for financial help to support his work on behalf of the rights of elderly people. I gave him some money for that. Davis's father was an economist who had served on the Council of Economic Advisors under President Truman. Rennie and I had an interesting argument about the pros and cons of free enterprise. I don't know whether I did the right thing or not, but I noticed a few years later that he was selling insurance for some company in Denver, Colorado. Most of the Chicago Eight eventually settled down. Jerry Rubin, who was the obnoxious loudmouth of the bunch, became a stockbroker. Radical today, conformist tomorrow: the system is always going to get you.

I was delighted by McGovern's successful bid for the nomination, and I approved of his selection of Eagleton as his running mate. Eagleton was a promising young Democrat who could contribute much to the party. I was outraged, however, when a controversy arose soon after the convention about Eagleton's medical history. As a result, pressure built on McGovern to dump him from the ticket. Only a few days after pledging his complete support for Eagleton, McGovern removed him from the ticket and replaced him with former Peace Corps director Sargent Shriver.

What they did to Tom Eagleton was terrible. I thought McGovern should have kept him on the ticket. It was a year when McGovern could not win anyway, and he might as well have stood on principle. I would have advised him to keep Eagleton, but I did not have the opportunity. McGovern was no different from most politicians. Once they get the nomination or win the office, they draw much closer to the people in their innermost circle, the people who are the professional political operatives, and they tend to ignore their other old friends. I think that is a mistake, but I understand it. Those are the people who have the experience and practical knowledge. They are the experts, or at least they are supposed to be experts.

I don't know how much money J. R. Parten and I raised together for McGovern. I must have given McGovern $50,000 and raised hundreds of thousands of additional dollars. I really went all out for that campaign. J.R.

and I had luncheons and gatherings for him in Houston, where we had thirty or forty people we could depend on for large contributions. John de Menil was probably the most important member of that group.

The most successful fund-raising event J.R. and I hosted in Houston was a luncheon for Sarge Shriver at the Sheraton-Lincoln Hotel on September 13, 1972. Though only twenty-five people attended, it was a successful event. Bob Lanier, a future mayor of Houston who had gone to law school with Sissy Farenthold, asked during the dinner if J.R. and I thought we could raise $15,000. All of a sudden Parten slapped the table and declared that he would donate $25,000. John de Menil and I matched J.R.'s pledge, and suddenly we had raised $75,000 with three people. When that kind of tempo is set, then everybody else ups theirs. We eventually raised about $250,000. That was a lot of money in 1972, and it was desperately needed by the campaign. At that time it was the most successful luncheon ever held in Texas for fund-raising, especially in terms of dollars raised per person.

We still needed more money than that to run the Texas campaign, so Parten, Menil, Lanier, and I went over to Lanier's Main Bank and signed a note for $100,000. We used that money to start the Texas campaign. After the luncheon, Shriver and his wife, Eunice, and I went into a small private room with their press spokesman. He asked me, "Mr. Shriver is going to be interviewed. What do you think he ought to talk about?" Before I can open my mouth, Eunice is telling him what he ought to talk about. And here I live in Texas. So I said, "Well, now, Eunice, I think he's got to talk about oil." I tried to give Shriver that advice, and he took some of it. But, boy! Eunice Shriver is one dominating person, I'm telling you. She wanted to run the show; there's no question about that. Anyway, Shriver told reporters that he had just come from "a very enthusiastic luncheon of men of means."

The McGovern campaign's codirectors for Texas were Taylor Branch, a young man from Atlanta, Georgia, who had been a protégé of Congressman Allard Lowenstein, and a Yale law student named Bill Clinton. Branch, who later wrote two outstanding books on the civil rights movement, made the financial decisions for the Texas campaign, while Clinton ran political strategy. Clinton's future wife, Hillary Rodham, was also working in Texas for McGovern, but I did not get to know her until after she and Clinton were married in 1975. I saw much more of Branch during that disastrous campaign because of my role as a fund-raiser, but I also met with Clinton from time to time. He struck me then as one hell of a bright kid, a really intelligent person with an attractive personality. Tall with a really bushy head of hair, Clinton was memorable in his physical appearance. He was impressive and seemed to me to have a promising political future, although I can't say honestly that I was among those who saw a future president of the United States whenever he came into view. We all worked hard in that campaign, but we knew it was a lost cause.

> **B recruited John Henry Faulk to travel with my daughter, Carrie, on the so-called *Grasshopper Special* in 1972. They went into the toughest states in the country for me.**
> — *George McGovern*

George McGovern has been my close friend ever since that campaign. I helped him in his 1974 Senate reelection campaign, and I helped him in 1980 when he was defeated in the Reagan landslide. He is a decent, compassionate, and intelligent man.

> **The thing I remember most about B in those early days was that he was not only a genuine liberal but also a genuine humorist. Hubert Humphrey used to be described as the happy warrior, which phrase also fits B Rapoport one hundred percent. He never let politics interfere with laughter. When I think of him, I think of him throwing his head back and laughing.** — *George McGovern*

During the Watergate hearings it was revealed that President Nixon's domestic policy chief John Ehrlichman had compiled a list of 490 individuals considered to be enemies of Nixon. Ehrlichman had given the list to White House special legal counsel John Dean, who was told to submit it to the IRS commissioner with instructions to conduct special tax audits of those listed. When that Nixon enemies list appeared in the newspapers, I was not surprised to discover my name on it, along with J. R. Parten and Frances Farenthold, as well as such nationally prominent McGovern supporters as Shirley McLaine, Gary Hart, and Pierre Salinger. The use of the IRS to harass and embarrass Nixon's political opponents constituted one of the articles of impeachment drawn up by the House Judiciary Committee. When a reporter asked for my reaction to being on the list, I told him that it was a real honor.

8 ▶ *The Texas Observer*

The Texas Observer, published fortnightly in Austin, Texas, has been a journal of free voices in my home state ever since its founding in 1954. My close association with the *Observer* has always mystified some of my business associates because its writers have not been shy about attacking people and positions that I support. Indeed, it is often labeled "muckraking." I have to admit that the *Observer* has angered me more times than I can remember, but I always get over it. That's because I agree with the *Observer*'s position on issues far more often than I disagree. I also understand, despite temporary irritations, that the *Observer* plays a fundamentally healthy role in the civic life of Texas. It has long been the state's leading journalistic advocate for social, economic, and racial justice.

The *Observer* was founded by activists from the liberal wing of the state's Democratic Party who had worked hard but unsuccessfully to elect Ralph Yarborough governor of Texas in 1952 and 1954. That group of activists included J. R. Parten; Houston attorneys Jesse Andrews, Bob Eckhardt, and Chris Dixie; Austin attorney Creekmore Fath; Dallas attorney Otto Mullinax; and a cadre of politically progressive women led by Minnie Fisher Cunningham and Frankie Carter Randolph. A few of those activists, especially Parten and Cunningham, had suffered a long string of disappointing defeats dating back to W. Lee O'Daniel's election as governor in 1938. Eckhardt, Dixie, Fath, and Mullinax had been former colleagues of mine in the Progressive Democrats of Texas at the University of Texas.

Yarborough's defeat in 1954 marked an emotional transformation in Texas politics. Many of his supporters felt that his campaign had been treated unfairly by the state's newspapers. Parten in particular believed that the state's major news media were engaged in a conspiracy to impose a blackout on liberal candidates. Parten's view was shaped by his experience in 1946. The largest state radio network refused to sell air time to Homer Rainey's campaign, and most of the state's largest circulation newspapers actively opposed Rainey's election. After that experience, Parten hoped that a loyal Democrat would either purchase one of the urban newspapers or create a new one. Most of the Texas liberals shared Parten's view. The 1954 campaign experience convinced these activists that Texas needed a major news journal to disseminate political and public policy information that the state's conservative newspapers either refused to print or distorted for partisan purposes.

Led by Parten and Frankie Randolph, an heir to a lumber and banking fortune, several of the more affluent and prominent leaders among the liberals decided in September 1954 to underwrite a news journal. Frankie Randolph had played a major role as an organizer and worker for Yarborough in Houston. She and Parten and their associates agreed to buy the old *State Observer* from liberal publisher Paul Holcomb to create a new weekly journal to be called *The Texas Observer.*

The Texas Observer group knew nothing about running a newspaper, so their first task was to recruit an editor. Someone suggested that they interview Ronnie Dugger, the former editor of the University of Texas newspaper, the *Daily Texan.* Only twenty-four years old, Dugger had written a progressive political column for the *San Antonio Express* while attending graduate school at Oxford University. Dugger met with Randolph, Parten, and other members of the group in October 1954. He was on his way to Mexico to work on a fishing boat in Tampico and to write a novel, so he was not keen about taking the job. When he was offered the position of editor, Dugger accepted, but only after it was agreed that he would have exclusive control of the contents of the journal. Dugger published the first issue of the *Observer* on December 13, 1954.

The Texas Observer soon became the iconoclastic voice of liberal politics in Texas, featuring Dugger's passionate and incisive editorials and investigative reports on important topics that establishment newspapers preferred to ignore. In time, the *Observer*'s influence extended far beyond the borders of Texas, especially with the ascent of Lyndon Johnson to national power. It was the only journal that was doing hard-nosed investigative reporting, especially on the Texas Legislature, which badly needed exposure.

Dugger eventually recruited to the *Observer* talented writers such as Willie Morris, Larry Goodwyn, Billy Brammer, Molly Ivins, Kaye Northcott, and Jim Hightower, among many others. The paper soon became required reading for Texas politicians from every point on the political spectrum. Never a profit maker, the *Observer*'s financial losses during the first few years were largely subsidized by donations from Randolph, Parten, Jesse Andrews, and Houston philanthropist Nina Cullinan.

My connection with the *Observer* goes back to the late 1940s, when it was still the *State Observer*. That's when I met two of the truly great women in Texas liberal politics, Minnie Fisher Cunningham and Lillian Collier. Unfortunately, many Texans have forgotten who they were. They were dedicated liberals and strong supporters of the *State Observer*, although not financially, because they didn't have any real money. I never knew Frankie Randolph (she was prominent during the 1950s, when I was living in Indiana), but I do know that without Mrs. Randolph there is no question the *Observer* would not have survived its first year. Ronnie Dugger once told me that she personally covered the *Observer*'s annual deficits for several years. I think her contributions totaled about $250,000. It is to her credit that the journal survived.

Because of illness, Frankie Randolph was no longer active by the time my close relationship with the *Observer* began. Ronnie Dugger has often said that I took up the slack when she had to withdraw. I first met Dugger in 1962. Fred Schmidt urged him to come to me for financial help. As usual, the paper was in dire financial trouble.

> Fred Schmidt told me there was this insurance company executive in Waco named Bernard Rapoport who might help support the *Observer* if I would ask him. I drove to Waco, and we met. We went to a cafeteria that was down in the basement of the building across from American Income's offices. We went through the food serving line and got a table. Barney asked me if I wanted to buy any insurance. I answered no. He laughed and said, "Okay, now we have discussed business, so you're my lunch guest. Now let's talk about what you want."
> — *Ronnie Dugger*

I knew Ronnie was there to solicit financial support. He was even more intense and candid then than he is now. When I asked him what he wanted, he said that he was there to seek my help for the *Observer*. "But I think I should tell you something," he warned. "I've thought a lot about life insurance, and I've concluded that it's essentially a social service," Ronnie argued. "It depends entirely on actuarial tables, and there is no competitive function that's valid. Everyone should have life insurance, and the cost of it should be the same in the same circumstances."

I told him that he had an interesting idea. He wasn't finished, however.

"After much thought," Ronnie continued, "I've concluded that the whole process of insuring people's lives should be socialized. There's no reason why it shouldn't be a part of Social Security."

After telling me my business should be nationalized, he stopped talking

Ronnie Dugger and B at a Texas Observer *fund-raiser in the late
1970s. CN 10486, Rapoport (Bernard) Photograph Collection, Center
for American History, The University of Texas at Austin.*

and just looked at me, probably wondering if I was going to throw him out
of the cafeteria. Of course, I agreed with him completely and told him that.

I wanted a way to give the *Observer* some money, but I was not able personally to help the paper at that time. I noted that a lot of companies were
running public service ads in other magazines, so I decided that if they could
do it, so could American Income. I told Ronnie that we would buy ads in
the *Observer*. As I recall, our first ad, which appeared in the December 13,
1962, issue, cost $100 a month. That seems now like a tiny amount of money,
but it was a major windfall for the *Observer*. Through the rest of the century,
the company continued to buy advertising in the *Observer*.

There were a couple of times during that period, however, when I failed
to renew the ad contract. The *Observer*'s business manager from the early
days (until he died a few years ago) was Cliff Olofson, a wonderful soft-
spoken man who was devoted to the *Observer*. Whenever our advertising
dropped off, Cliff would call me. "Barney," Cliff would say, "can you do it
again?" I would always reply, "Not if you don't come have lunch with me."
So he would drive up to Waco, and half the time he was late because his beat-

up old car would break down on the way. That was Cliff Olofson. He was never deterred when it came to fulfilling his mission of keeping the *Observer* alive. Cliff would sit in front of my desk and say, "You know, Barney, I don't know whether the *Observer* is going to make it or not, but if we can count on your ads, I think we can do it." That kind of pleading had no relationship to begging. Rather it made me understand that in his view, this little paper committed to truth would determine whether our society would continue. That was the way he believed; he was concomitantly simple and so very complex. I don't think Cliff ever spent one second of his life thinking about himself. When he died, the *Observer* lost a part of its soul.

In 1968 I increased the size of our ad, which provided additional revenue. The following year, when Ronnie Dugger asked me for more help, I expanded our advertising to a full page. After I bought my first full page, Ronnie wrote me a typical Dugger letter: "Whammo! We may make it into the black and the sacred terrain of the non-money-losing self sustaining free-enterprise socialistic idealists by the middle of next year!"

I was criticized severely by other business executives for advertising in the *Observer*. I still get a lot of criticism for supporting the journal. That does not bother me. I have always been criticized for supporting liberal candidates and liberal causes. On the other hand, many times readers of the *Observer* will write letters to the editor attacking me for things I say in my public service messages in the journal and criticizing Dugger for publishing it. I have always believed that it is essential to the preservation of our society that we maintain a conservative voice, a liberal voice, and a middle ground. I decided that our company could serve the people of this state by being the primary financial support of this paper.

There never was a period when the *Observer* was not on hard times. It faces a crisis every week. That makes life exciting, and it provides the motivation to produce the best kind of journalism. From the time I got involved in the early 1960s until the mid-1980s, J. R. Parten and Walter Hall were the two people with whom I worked to keep the *Observer* afloat financially through its periodic crises. Whenever the *Observer* was in trouble, Dugger would talk to J.R., and he would talk to Hall. I was always the last one he would talk to; whatever he didn't get from them, I always made up the difference. At one point in the 1970s, the three of us made a loan to the *Observer* that rescued it from certain bankruptcy.

The three of us made up our minds that the *Observer* was not going to go under, and that's what kept it going. For example, when the fundamentalist evangelical minister Lester Roloff of Corpus Christi filed a libel suit against the *Observer* in 1974 because of an exposé it had printed about his activities, Parten and I raised the money to pay the *Observer*'s legal fees. The Roloff suit was a serious threat to the *Observer*'s continued existence, because the newspaper had no funds to pay for its own defense. I circulated a letter warning that the *Observer* would not survive without immediate outside financial support. The response was wonderful. We received a large number of $5 and $10 donations from college professors and students, newspaper reporters, writers, public schoolteachers, librarians, and labor union members. The Oil, Chemical, and Atomic Workers Union was especially supportive.

The thing I really love about the *Observer* and the reason it has my continuing support is that I can't tell the staff what to do even though I'm their primary financial support. I know that if I can't tell them what to do, nobody else can. I like that.

> **Barney has been with us through all our ups and downs. He has never once asked that the *Observer* do anything or not do something editorially; he has never sought to affect our endorsements or our crusades.** —*Ronnie Dugger*

Ronnie Dugger and I are close friends, and we share intimacies. Dugger knew that my support would never make me think that I could tell him what to do. Shortly after I ran my first full-page ad in the *Observer,* he ran an article attacking the insurance industry! I have to admit that the industry had some bad practices that needed exposing. I thought that was okay, and I applauded the *Observer* for it.

> **You are always a great one for not asking me any favors—you know how much I appreciate that, Barney . . . but by damn it, I am going to make you one promise anyway. When . . . I get my study done . . . for socializing the life insurance business . . . in the U.S., I am going to tell about the only life insurance company president in U.S. history, surely, who took a newspaper ad with the same newspaperman in the same conversation during which they were agreeing the insurance business should be socialized!** —*Ronnie Dugger, letter to Bernard Rapoport, October 31, 1969*

Dugger never asked me to approve any editorial policy, but we frequently discussed what I thought the *Observer* should not be doing. At one point I thought the *Observer* was becoming too literary and too focused on places like Central America. If I want to be literary, I can read *The New Yorker*. If I want to know about Central America, I can read *The Nation*. When I read the *Observer,* I want to know where the dirt and corruption are in Texas.

The *Observer* is best when it focuses on state issues. Its indigenous Texas quality is what makes the *Observer* unique and special. It needs to stick to Texas stories. I told that to Ronnie, and he listened to me, but he and his successors have continued to give too much space in the *Observer* to literary criticism and international issues.

Over the years I have also suggested to Dugger that certain topics deserved some investigative attention. One time I urged the *Observer* to do an essay about the dangers of allowing bank holding companies to operate in Texas. I think bank holding companies are a bad idea. Ronnie agreed, so he asked me to write it. Shortly after I wrote the article, my lawyer, Pat Beard, went to the First National Bank in Dallas, which was the largest bank holding company in Texas at that time, to borrow a couple of million dollars for the company. One of the vice presidents of the bank pulled that issue of the *Observer* out of his desk drawer, pointed to my essay, and asked, "Is this the guy you want me to loan money to?" Incidentally, he didn't give us the loan, but I got it somewhere else. I should also add that his bank was among those that collapsed in the 1980s, although I certainly don't take credit for that.

What has remained constant throughout the *Observer*'s history is the fear of the accumulation of power in too few hands. From my point of view, that more than anything else makes the *Observer* deserving of support. The *Observer* also has always had a sharp eye out for corruption. It has probably exposed more graft, more ill doings of politicians in Texas, than all the state's daily newspapers combined.

Dugger's strength is in his total commitment. A sense of outrage at injustice flows from his pen right onto a piece of paper. That is his outstanding characteristic to me. He's an excellent writer, although not a great writer, but when it comes to an instinctive feeling for people, he doesn't have to take a second place to anybody I have ever known. We have the same general objectives, but often we take different routes to get to those objectives. Ronnie is more of a purist, and I am more of a pragmatist. Unfortunately, I think he is committed to being too pure, and that does seem to make him appear to be a little bit phony. He really isn't phony personally, and I don't believe he is aware that his behavior might seem phony. But he desperately wants to be pure, and he wants to set the standards for that purity. That gets him into trouble once in a while. He and I fight about that, because I know I'm not pure and I know he's not pure; the difference is, I don't want to act like I am.

I feel about Ronnie Dugger the way I feel about consumer advocate Ralph Nader. God help the world if we don't have them, but God help the world if they are ever in a position of power. Ronnie has made a career out of baiting university regents, LBJ, and Lloyd Bentsen; he's made a career out of being critical of just about anybody who has any power.

Dugger was critical of everything Lloyd Bentsen, Jr., did. Bentsen's unforgivable sin to Ronnie, of course, is that he beat Ralph Yarborough. Even if Bentsen was for some policy Ronnie supported, Ronnie always assumed Bentsen was taking that position only for selfish or self-serving reasons.

I'll share a personal example of just how uncompromising Ronnie can be when it comes to Lloyd Bentsen. When I was raising money to pay the *Observer*'s legal expenses in the Roloff suit, I asked for a contribution from Senator Bentsen. Despite the unrelenting misery that the *Observer* had dealt him in print, Lloyd graciously sent a check for $100 to Ronnie. Without my knowledge, Ronnie sent the check back to Lloyd, telling him that his contribution (which had no conditions attached to it) didn't "feel quite right." He refused the donation. Ronnie's action embarrassed and angered me, and I told him so. I wrote him a letter to complain that he and I might not agree with some of Bentsen's political views, "but, doggone it, if . . . you and I aren't for trying to recruit more people to what we are about, then I missed the point." I also noted that Bentsen was not so naive as to think that a $100 contribution was going to change the editorial direction of *The Texas Observer*. I went so far as to charge that Ronnie's action had been the "starkest kind of insolence."

Dugger sincerely apologized for not consulting with me before returning Bentsen's contribution. He explained that his letter returning the check had been written in a respectful and nonconfrontational tone, but Ronnie also let me know that I had gone too far. He pointed out that he did not "regard level relationships among equal citizens in a democracy as susceptible to the characterization, insolent." That is pure Ronnie Dugger. It is one of the reasons I love and respect the man, despite his being so hardheaded. Lloyd Bentsen, by the way, sent the check back to Dugger with the explanation that he could just count it as a paid subscription. At the 1975 subscription rates, Lloyd's $100 bought him eleven years of the *Observer*.

As I have explained in the previous chapter, I was bitterly anti-Bentsen when he defeated Yarborough in 1970, but I have come to know Lloyd Bentsen, and I think he is a fine man. He has never been anything but honest with me. He is more conservative than I am on a few issues, but he has respect for my opinions and I have respect for his. I think he probably knew more about economics than anybody in the U.S. Senate when he served there. He ran his committee skillfully and was terribly effective. I also think he was an excellent secretary of the treasury for Bill Clinton. I'm an admirer of his now. Although Dugger and the *Observer* constantly jumped on Bentsen and I did not approve of it, that never made me think about withdrawing my support.

The *Observer* has had some poor editors, it has had some good ones, and it has had some great ones. One of the great editors was Ronnie Dugger himself. Obviously, Ronnie supplied the spirit and the intellectual thought that made it the tremendous paper that it is. He determined the editorial policy; there's no question about that. Anyone who knows Ronnie knows that is just the way it has to be. I wasn't in Texas when Willie Morris was the *Observer* editor, but I've known all of the others. Jim Hightower, who later served as Texas agriculture commissioner, was a tremendous editor of the *Observer.*

My favorite editor other than Ronnie Dugger was the unsinkable Molly Ivins. Molly is one of the great ladies of the world, and she is a gifted writer. She is not someone you would want to invite to a Baptist church picnic (her vocabulary includes more four-letter words than I ever knew existed, and she's not shy about using them), but that's one of the reasons I love her. I thought the *Observer* was the best reading in Texas when she and Kaye Northcott were its coeditors.

For those unfamiliar with her style and her capacity for friendship, I'll quote something of Molly's that warmed my heart when I read it. For some reason, when I gave a speech at a political meeting a few years back, my expansive personal style made an extremely poor impression on the famed British journalist Christopher Hitchens, who described me in his column in *The Nation* as an "old poseur." Molly's response was published in the *Observer:* "The 'old poseur' as Christopher Hitchens so gratuitously called him, has not only been an invaluable public citizen, but has performed innumerable acts of private charity, sometimes going to extraordinary lengths so that the recipient does not even know he has a benefactor. I doubt Hitchens would understand the delicacy of feeling that motivates such shifts. I am sorry Hitchens did not care for Rapoport's expansive style: myself, I never cared much for snotty Brits. Tell Hitchens to keep his ass out of Texas because they're a bunch of us down here who'd like to kick it from Waco to Luzbuddy."

Anyone who thinks that giving the *Observer* a large amount of money over the years has bought me influence over editorial policies has not been paying attention. I supported Bentsen; the *Observer* attacked everything he ever did. Likewise, the *Observer* printed articles that I thought were irresponsibly critical of Israel, which upset me deeply.

The *Observer* also was fiercely critical of one of my closest friends, Jim Wright, when he was Speaker of the U.S. House of Representatives. I thought Jim Wright was one of the best people in Congress. He was one of my heroes. When a group of Republicans, led by Representative Newt Gingrich of Georgia, launched a vicious smear campaign in 1988 to discredit Jim and to force him from the Speakership, the *Observer* printed a series of articles repeating many of Gingrich's false allegations. The *Observer* was

*Molly Ivins. CN 10499, Ivins (Molly) Photograph
Collection, Center for American History, The University
of Texas at Austin.*

wrong about Jim Wright. In my opinion, the *Observer*'s attacks on Wright played a major role in forcing him to resign from Congress in May 1989. It was a tragedy for Texas and the nation when he quit.

One of the allegations against Jim was that he had encouraged me and other financial backers to purchase multiple copies of his book *Reflections of a Public Man,* published in 1984, as a scam to get around House ethics rules that limited outside earnings. House rules exempted book royalties from those limits. It was true that I purchased several hundred copies of Jim's book, as did J. R. Parten, Boston University president John Silber, Southwest Texas State University president Robert Hardesty, and Democratic National chairman John White. There was nothing sinister about those purchases. Every year, for many years, J.R. purchased hundreds of copies of books and sent them to his friends. They were books on some public policy

Jim Wright with B and Audre in the late 1970s. CN 10499, Rapoport (Bernard) Photograph Collection, Center for American History, The University of Texas at Austin.

issue or historical topic. It is a practice that I have emulated and continued. I purchased 250 copies of *Citizen Power* by Alaska senator Mike Gravel in 1972, for example, and distributed them to my friends and associates. It is my understanding that Hardesty and Silber had Wright's book distributed to students at their respective universities. To imply that anything unethical was involved in their purchases was simply ludicrous.

> When *The Texas Observer* went after Jim Wright when he was Speaker of the House, I guarantee you that B just about came unglued. That incident really pushed B to the limits of his support for the *Observer*. —*Ben Barnes*

It should have been clear, especially to the *Observer,* that Gingrich's attacks were in retaliation for Wright's efforts to end the civil wars in El Salvador and in Nicaragua. They also had the purpose of destroying the most effective Speaker of the House since Sam Rayburn. Wright had been responsible for turning back some of the Republicans' pet initiatives, and the

Republicans were desperate to remove him. Gingrich's success in forcing Wright to resign ultimately led to Gingrich's elevation to Speaker of the House in 1994, where he soon engaged openly in the same activities he had accused Wright of doing. Thankfully, he too was forced out of the office. The Wright affair was not the *Observer*'s best moment.

Despite the ups and downs, I remain a firm supporter of the *Observer*. Texas needs it. That is why when Ronnie Dugger decided in 1994 to relinquish his control of the *Observer*, Audre and I gave $100,000 to the foundation that was created to own and manage it.

In the spring of 1997 I told a writer for *Texas Monthly* magazine that I had terminated my financial support of the *Observer*. The quotation in the resulting article attracted much attention. I really said it, and I meant it when the writer interviewed me. I was unhappy with the *Observer* at that moment because I felt that it had lost its direction entirely. It seemed to me that more and more of its space was filled with literary and art criticism and international news. As I have already said, I think that is a mistake. What I want from the *Observer* is hard-hitting investigative political reporting with a focus especially on the Texas Legislature and the other branches of state government. I thought it had drifted away from that. The quality of the journal had also suffered from the loss of Cliff Olofson.

In the blink of an eye, my careless remark to *Texas Monthly* brought the formidable Ms. Molly Ivins to my office in Waco. Molly really did a number on me. Talk about being made to feel guilty over forsaking a cause! She showed me no mercy. I changed my stance pretty fast. Molly walked out of my office with my pledge of a $20,000 matching gift.

> **B Rapoport is a force of nature—loud, blunt, profane, bull-headed. He talks a mile a minute, he's twice as smart as the average bear, and, I confess, he's a man I love dearly.**
> —*Molly Ivins,* Texas Observer

The Texas Observer has played a significant role in the public affairs of Texas. Although its circulation is small, I will bet you it has been quoted as often throughout the country as the *Dallas Morning News,* the *Houston Chronicle,* or *Texas Monthly.* The *Observer* has a well-deserved reputation for integrity in reporting. It has a prejudiced point of view on the side of a liberal political ideology, but I have never seen it purposely distort the facts to promote that ideology. I think it is a substantial credit to Texas. May it exist for many decades to come.

9 ▸ From Entrepreneur to CEO: AILICO in the 1970s and 1980s

By the early 1970s American Income's labor union business was growing rapidly. I certainly felt confident as we entered our third decade of existence. Nevertheless, the early 1970s weren't problem free. In fact, the company suffered a major crisis that forced me to make a dramatic change in the type of product we marketed and, soon after, to make a radical change in our management structure.

Sam Klein and the Bank of Louisville

My first crisis of the 1970s occurred at the beginning of the decade. For several years a bank in Waco had held a $3 million note of mine. Although I never missed an interest payment, I never made a payment on the principal. When the time came to renew the note, the bank management decided to charge a high renewal fee because they had grown tired of my not ever reducing the principal. They called my loan when I refused to pay the higher fee. Needing $3 million to pay my debt, I turned to some old friends who had a bank in Temple, Texas. It was too large an amount for their bank, so they went to one of the big Dallas banks to secure the loan for me. The Dallas bank initially responded positively. The next morning, however, the *Dallas Morning News* ran a story about my agreeing to serve as Ralph Yarborough's finance chairman for his 1970 Senate reelection campaign. After the story appeared, the Dallas bank suddenly changed its mind and refused to make the loan. The bank never said that my work for Yarborough was the cause, obviously, but I have no doubt that was the reason. Some of Yarborough's financial backers had experienced similar problems with Texas banks in the past.

That was bad news for American Income. Despite my good earnings from the company, I did not have $3 million in available cash to take care of the loan. I was beside myself with worry. I didn't know where to go or to whom to turn. Among the people I called for advice was Stanley Yarmuth, a friend of mine in Louisville, Kentucky, who owned a company called National Industries. Stanley urged me to call his father-in-law, Sam Klein, who was the majority stockholder at the Bank of Louisville. I rushed to Louisville, and Klein agreed to make the loan. If it had not been for Sam Klein and the Bank of Louisville, I would have been in deep trouble. Sam saved my company, and he continued to be my banker for many years.

There were times over the years when Sam could have closed me out on a moment's notice. Thank goodness his bank was not owned by a holding company. It was not a gigantic bank that treated its customers coldly. Sam just had a lot of faith in me, and he never bothered me. If he had not been the kind of person he was, there would not be an American Income today.

The Stock Crash Crisis

My second major financial crisis of the 1970s occurred in the summer of 1972. Because of a change in the formula that we used in reporting our financial status, our operating statement for the first half of the year seemed to indicate that we had lost a huge amount of money when we had not. Problems with our disability insurance policies necessitated the formula change.

Disability insurance policies are fraught with claim-related problems. A disability policy, for example, will not cover preexisting conditions. Nevertheless, the insured wants his money if he is disabled, no matter what the original agreement says. That often leads to a hotly contested disagreement, and it leaves a bad taste in everybody's mouth. The American public has developed an attitude that it's okay to beat the insurance companies. In addition, the state legislatures started enacting disability insurance for all of their citizens. People would buy accident and health policies from us, and they would have the state benefits, and they would have all of these ancillary benefits payable to them—they could make more money on disability than they could by working. They didn't have to pay tax on a lot of the disability money either. So the number of claims shot up and almost put us out of business.

Hank Brown, who was monitoring the labor market closely, advised us when union members needed new types of insurance policies or when certain types of old policies needed to be terminated. Hank had urged me to stop selling disability insurance and to focus more on a life insurance plan for union members.

We had some hellacious fights about getting rid of the disability policy, because the general agents made money selling
that policy and they didn't want to stop it. I wanted it stopped.
When Rapoport and I argued about the policy, I asked him
what he thought would happen when the average local union
official in Texas got fifty calls complaining about American
Income's disability policy. He'll put American Income on
the you-know-what list, and you don't sell no more policies.
I wanted American Income to sell what's called virgin pure
insurance. They're either alive or they're dead. They either
have cancer or they don't. They either had an accident or they
didn't. There's not much debate about that. If they're alive,
we don't pay on a death claim. If they're dead, we pay. That
way you don't get into disputes. —*Hank Brown*

When you are as intimate with a market as we were with the labor movement, you have to stay with clearly defined products with low potential for
disputes. Hank was especially sensitive to that because he spent so much
time out in the field and was forced to deal with some unhappy local union
officials face to face.

I walked into a boilermaker's office in Mississippi and handed
him my American Income Life card, and I got hit in the side
of the mouth. I had come out of a tough local and I wasn't
exactly a pansy myself, so we had a little lively brotherly conflict right there on his floor. We rolled around a bit and neither
one of us had really taken advantage of one another too bad,
because I didn't want to kill him. You know, after all, he was
my brother, and I was trying to do business with him. After
we got up, he told me why he had punched me. He had five or
six bad disability claims. I got on the phone with Rapoport,
and in about forty-five minutes we settled those claims. Rapoport paid through the nose. It was either that or lose the entire
state of Mississippi because this old boy was going to go to the
convention and tear up our como-se-llama. —*Hank Brown*

So, the problem with our disability business had resulted in this misleading financial report. I made a mistake by not announcing publicly the reason
for the change in our statement and not explaining how it gave a misleading
picture of our financial health. That was a costly mistake.

We issued the statement in July 1972, a day before the annual convention for our 300 general agents at Lake of the Ozarks in Missouri. When I got on a plane in Waco to fly to Missouri, American Income stock was about $30. While we were still in the air, I received a message reporting that our stock had plunged to $12. For someone who owns some 400,000 shares of stock, like I did, that is a considerable loss. I lost a little more than $7 million (in 1972 dollars) in one day. It gets your attention, I promise you.

I realized I might be in deep trouble, but I can honestly say that I didn't panic. I knew we had a great company, and I was certain we could turn the situation around. I knew what the company was really worth and that the financial statement was misleading. I also understood that we had to make a drastic change in our business product if we had any hope of surviving. That meant getting out of the disability insurance business.

Because of Hank Brown's concerns and warnings from others, I had thought about making the change for some time. I didn't know much about life insurance, but I knew that American Income would be better off as a life company. Unfortunately, as far as we could tell, no accident and health company (which we were primarily) had ever converted successfully to life insurance. Confronted with this catastrophic loss in stock price, however, I made the decision, on the flight to Missouri, that we had to make the change. What's the saying: necessity is the mother of invention?

> **You have to understand that Bernard does not know what reality is. What is reality to him is whatever it is that he wants. Here's a smart man who is very much driven to action, who can read people instinctively very well, who has a very powerful personality, and whose view of reality is whatever he wants it to be. Now that can be very, very powerful in the building of a company.** — *Charles Cooper, former president, AILICO*

When I arrived at the convention our agents were in an uproar. They knew what had happened, because the price fall was on the stock ticker. Here I've got 300 agents that I'm supposed to enthuse and make happy, and our stock price has just fallen by more than half. I'll never forget that meeting. I had to rewrite the agenda and redirect the whole meeting. Despite the bad news, I was the most enthusiastic person there.

One of the agents complained that he owned 100 shares of stock. I said, "Let's see now, you've lost $1,800, and I know you don't like that. Now, I've got 400,000 shares, and I've lost $7.2 million and I'm not exactly happy either."

He replied, "I really don't have a problem, do I?" When it came out that I had lost all that and still had the enthusiasm, the drive, and the will to continue, it infected everybody else.

> Bernard is the best I've ever seen in terms of hitting your buttons. During troubled times, when it comes to controlling people with force of personality, he is the best. When I first came on and we were cutting out the waste, a lot of the guys in the field talked revolution and opposition, and they started building a war chest to sue the company and that kind of thing. We were going to a meeting with a bunch of these guys, and I warned Bernard to be careful. He shook me off and said, "Aw, those guys are just talking. You just watch them when I get in there and see who stands up." Nobody did, of course. He had them cowed. It was just sheer force of personality.
> — Charles Cooper

I turned that meeting around and convinced people who were depressed about the company that we would survive by becoming a different kind of enterprise. It turned out to be one of the best conventions we ever had. I told them that I had made the decision that we were going to become a life company and that the subject was not even up for discussion. I explained that the disability insurance business provided no future for them or for the company. We had made a lot of foolish mistakes at American Income and we had done a lot of silly things, but we had vision. I must admit that the agents were skeptical, but most of them had been with me a long time. I've always been level with these people. I told them it could be done, and they believed me.

At the meeting in Missouri one of our state general agents, Ray Griffin, told me that if we could write a life policy that would pay the same commissions as our disability insurance, the agents could make it work. I agreed to do that. The advantage of having a small company and also of being the largest stockholder was that I could make a decision and implement it without going through committees and boards of directors and various bureaucracies. Within two weeks, we had that policy on the market. In twenty-four hours we did something that had never been done before or since in the insurance business, to the best of my knowledge. We converted an accident and health sales force to a life insurance sales force. It was tough, but we did it. We became a real life insurance company.

We developed a package that fit the needs of 90 percent of the union members. We brought out what we call a supplemental insurance plan, and we devised a supplemental cancer policy to go with it. American Income had sold a small number of life insurance policies from the start, so we already had the model for the policy that we now needed for our union market. The raw materials were there; all we had to do was make a finished product. That is where our merchandising know-how and technique came into play. The one thing I know how to do is merchandising, and that includes motivating our people. We revised the policy to pay a level of commission that would maintain enthusiasm in the sales force. Our sales agents just started selling the heck out of it.

We also had to retrain our public relations people to present this new package to the unions. That wasn't nearly as tough as we thought it would be, because the union leaders realized that in so many instances, when somebody died in the family, the member was left in bad shape not only emotionally but also financially. After all, the only way that the average American can protect his or her family is through life insurance.

The union leaders accepted the new policy with relief rather than with skepticism. They knew their people needed life insurance a lot more than they needed disability coverage, because the states provided disability insurance. They accepted it as a more sincere commitment on our part to serve the needs of their members. Over the years, that product has served the union membership better, and it certainly served us a lot better, because it's a trouble-free policy.

Despite our success in transforming American Income into a life insurance company, it took us until the latter part of 1977 to turn our stock-market situation around. In those days, the stock market forgave a company slowly. We simply were not accepted by the investment banking houses, even though we had good years in 1973, 1974, and 1975. Nobody in New York wanted to talk to me. Businesses have to go to New York to talk to investment bankers, and I could tell they were listening with one ear but they were not absorbing. They always said, "Well, let's wait another year," and another year, and another year.

After spectacular years in 1976 and 1977, we finally regained our credibility. We increased our new life premiums from $7.6 million in 1973 to $22 million in 1977. That inspired Eppler Guerin to circulate a good report on American Income. Then Rotan Mosle and, finally, John Muir and Company put out outstanding reports. That put the zing back into our stock. The major investment firms like Drexel Burnham and E. F. Hutton began recommending our stock for purchase to their customers. The investment banks and brokerage houses were incredulous. They just didn't believe we could turn it around.

After we were restored to the recommended lists, we took in more than

$33 million in new life premiums in 1978. It was highly unusual for a company of our size to achieve that kind of growth. By then, we were known as the fastest-growing life insurance company in the United States. We enjoyed spectacular growth from that point on.

New Management

By the mid-1970s we had developed into a company with an impressive degree of flexibility. An old-time baseball player named Wee Willie Keeler said, "Hit it where they ain't," and that's what we did. We went after those markets that the major companies ignored. In terms of the insurance industry, we were a peanut compared to companies like Metropolitan Life and Prudential, but by 1975 we had become a substantial company with $4 million in investment income. The company had reached the stage where it could survive even if it didn't do any new business.

Although survival was no longer a concern, it was clear that our profits should have been larger. We were doing well, but I felt that we could do better. I finally decided that I might be part of the problem. I realized something that most founders of a company never understand: it takes entrepreneurs like me to build companies, but it usually takes the MBA types to run them. I know I'm not a manager. I'm a builder. There's a big difference between a management type and an entrepreneur. Individuals like me really cannot run big companies. I don't like to have staff meetings, and I'm not the best delegator in the world. The truth is, when I was trying to run the company day to day, we had a surprise every fifteen minutes. American Income had been too much of a one-man show. I had been the working president ever since 1951, but I had not built the executive staff that a company of our size should have had; I was really tardy about that. Plus, I just wasn't paying close enough attention to day-to-day management. The result was that we were not doing our business as efficiently as possible, and our operational costs were way out of line. We had grown to become a large national company, but I was running it like a mom-and-pop grocery store.

In addition, I was making decisions that should have been made in consultation with a professional management team consisting of individuals who could look at things with a bit more detachment than I could. As the largest stockholder in the company, with 25 percent of the stock, I had a different perspective from a president who doesn't own much of the stock. In the latter case, when the president spends the company's money, none of it is out of his pocket. Every time I spent a dollar for American Income, 25 cents of it was my personal money. That colored things quite a bit.

When I can't do something myself, I hire the best person I know to do it for me. So in 1975 I began the search for a professional accountant to oversee our financial side and a professional insurance manager to run the operational part of the company. I went to a head-hunting company in Dallas, one of those places where you pay a fee, give them the characteristics you want in an executive, and they search out people for you. I chose that route because I'm an emotional guy and I tend to fly by the seat of my pants, so I thought it would be good to have professionals screen the candidates. They gathered a large pool of attractive candidates, and we interviewed a lot of people.

I found our financial person first. I brought in Ken Phillips as vice president and as our first professional comptroller. I hired Ken from Peat, Marwick and Mitchell, one of the big accounting firms. He was a certified public accountant who also had insurance experience. I was probably a few years too late in hiring a comptroller. The first thing Phillips said to me after he got the job was, "I know your type. You are used to running everything. You have to understand, I will run the accounting department." I said, "Yes, I know. That's the first area I'm letting go. Just run it the way you want to." That was the first time I had ever let go of a major component of our operation.

A couple of months after Phillips joined the company, I hired Charles Cooper as our senior vice president. Cooper has a bachelor's degree in economics and a law degree from the University of Washington. He learned the insurance business at the Capitol Holding Insurance Group, for whom he had handled the acquisition of five life insurance companies. Cooper served for a couple of years as chief operating officer of Georgia International Life Insurance Company, one of the companies he had helped acquire for Capitol. One thing that attracted us to Cooper was his role in resolving the postacquisition problems of Capitol's new subsidiaries, which meant that he initiated and supervised significant changes in the structure and management of those companies. He was highly recommended as someone who knew how to improve workflow systems and reduce operating costs.

> I came down and interviewed with Bernard. There were signs right off that the company had some problems. He took me around and introduced me to everyone. As we walked around, I saw that there must have been ten thousand applications sitting in stacks all over the department. There was a formidable logjam. It was easy to see just what a shambles the place was. But what was really exciting to me was the volume of paper that was coming in. You can easily clear a logjam, but you can't just go out and generate that kind of business easily.
> — *Charles Cooper*

I appointed Cooper senior vice president, and I told him that if he did a good job I was going to make him the president and I'd take the chairmanship of the board. Titles are not important to me in the sense that I'm the major stockholder. My concern is with the results. Charles did an excellent job, so in December 1976 he became president of the company.

My larger role really didn't change that much when Cooper and Phillips came in. It's funny, but after they joined us, I became busier than I had ever been. With the change in administrative structure, I had more time to work with the sales force and to maintain personal contact with union leadership. I was able to pay more attention to the state agencies. That's why we began to generate significantly more business than we had before the change. Because I learned so much from Cooper about the technical side of the insurance business, I was better prepared from an informational standpoint when working with the agency sales force.

Cooper and Phillips also brought American Income into the automation age. When they started, there were only two computer terminals in the entire company. We had purchased expensive new software that we used for a pilot operation. It had the capacity we needed, but with only the two terminals, we were fumbling around with it. Cooper and Phillips brought in a bunch of computer terminals and put the software to work in a way that allowed us to streamline a significant portion of our operation. Cooper also stopped several activities that were irrelevant or useless. In every company there's a ton of wasted effort. Quite often, a large company can make more money simply by stopping some of its daily procedures. Cooper was a master at that. He could find waste and cut out inefficiencies that I never saw. For example, we had a serious problem in our application processing department. Applications were stacking up, and the policies weren't being issued in a timely manner. It was costing us an enormous amount of money. Cooper solved that problem and several others, and he had to remove some deadwood to do it.

> It took me a couple of years before I could even get around to the claims operation. That was awful. I also had to fire a lot of people. The company was top-heavy with management. Everyone I terminated was an officer of the company. It was very awkward. Most really weren't competent, and a few just weren't honest. —*Charles Cooper*

Most people were skeptical that I would really delegate authority, but I did it. I understood that they knew more about running a home office in a minute than I would know the rest of my life. I had total confidence in them. I just told them to get the job done, and they did it on their own. They assumed authority and divided between the two of them the executive responsibilities necessary to manage the home office.

Because of Cooper and Phillips, American Income became a brand-new company in 1975. There was good news all around. In the first four years after they arrived, American Income's profits rose from $1.8 million (55 cents per share) to $11.3 million ($3.30 per share). The efficiencies they instituted and the changeover we made from disability to life insurance accounted for nearly the entire jump in profits. Individual life insurance premiums provided a much higher profit margin over other insurance products.

Kenneth Phillips left the company in the early 1980s to become CEO of a small insurance company in Dallas, but he left behind a much-improved accounting division.

Cooper stayed with us until 1999. He continued to do an excellent job of devising new insurance packages for our sales force. We seemed always to have the best product at the right time. In 1977 he led us into the credit union market, where we could use some of the same strategies we had perfected in our labor union business. We gained the confidence and endorsement of credit union leaders, and then we solicited their membership on an individual basis. Our entrance into the credit union market helped boost our premium income from $39 million to $58 million within two years.

> Bernard and I drove each other nuts, but we always operated in such a ying and yang way that it always worked. He doesn't like the blunt truth much, and I don't like bullshit much, but one of his favorite expressions is that bullshit makes the world go around, and he's right. So he supplied the bullshit and the idealism, and I supplied the blunt facts and reality. It worked well. — *Charles Cooper*

In 1979 *Texas Business* magazine declared that American Income was the fastest-growing insurance company in the United States. By then, we had more than $1 billion of insurance in force, assets exceeding $100 million, and nearly 1,100 sales agents. Bringing professional management to American Income was among the wisest business decisions I ever made.

10 ▶ *Politics, 1976–1984*

I didn't have any real money until the late 1970s. As the value of American Income increased, there was a corresponding increase in my personal wealth, but that was on paper only because my wealth was tied up in nondividend stock. The point is, I was cash short. I would borrow money every year, not only to live on but also to make contributions to the political and charitable causes in which I believed. Until the mid-1970s, my interest payments on those loans exceeded my income. After American Income's stock plunged in 1972, I was forced to reduce the size of my political donations. It was especially painful to suspend my donations to Jewish charities those four years.

The growing profitability of American Income after 1975 gave me the means to help more candidates financially than ever before. Before 1968, if I gave a candidate $100, I thought that was a tremendous contribution. By 1980 I was giving tens of thousands of dollars personally to state and federal political candidates. My donations went to candidates at all levels of government, but most went to Democratic candidates for the U.S. Senate. Despite my significantly enhanced financial situation, I continued to give more money than I actually had. If I liked a candidate, I would just write out a check for him. I never really looked at my checkbook balance. Being overdrawn at the bank was a badge of honor to me in those days, you see.

> **If you are a Democrat, you have to make a pilgrimage to Waco when it's time to run a statewide race. It's that not having him on your team knocks you out, but having him makes you a player in any game.** — *Greg Hartman, Democratic Party campaign operative*

Whenever a politician comes to me and says, "I want your advice, B. Should I run or not?" I always ask, "Did you file yesterday or the day before?" No politician ever comes to a contributor for advice; they come for affirmation and money. Most politicians are absolutely sure that he or she is the knight on the white horse and that the fate of humanity rests on their election. I've never known a politician who didn't feel that way to some degree.

Of course, I raised more money for candidates than I gave personally. How do I raise money? First, I have earned a reputation that gives me access to people who can afford to make donations. I have a long list. Those people get books from me each year, and they know I'm remembering them all the time. They know I respect them. I share my newspaper columns with them. I keep in contact with them. When I call them, they return the call. Access is important. In addition, I have to be a giver myself. Let's say I'm raising funds for something, so I donate $100,000 to the cause and that gets known. When I call people up, they know I am committed because I have already given my money. A lot of people give money when I call them, even though they may not be that happy about my cause, because they know I will give to their causes when they call. The quid pro quo is a factor in all fund-raising.

I also believe that the people I go to for donations know that I will not profit personally in any way from my political fund-raising efforts. They understand that I am involved in a cause because I believe in it for the common good, not because I am pushing a personal agenda.

There is one source I never went to for political contributions, and that is my office employees. I never tried to stir up the interest of my staff in political elections. I just don't think that is right. I don't ever want anybody who works for me to feel threatened. Obviously, I get a lot of publicity, so my employees know what I am doing, but I did not solicit political contributions from them.

I'm an expert on the subject of politicians. I have known hundreds of politicians in my lifetime. I have had the privilege of giving money to them, raising money for them, and working with them. In all my dealings with politicians, none has ever asked me to do anything that was illegal or unethical. My only complaint about many of our elected officials today has nothing to do with legality or ethics. Frequently I have had an elected official say to me, "I had to cast that vote even though I didn't want to cast it. My constituency demanded it." In that situation, it seems to me that the individual forgot that he or she must be the leader, not the follower. People want to be led, sometimes more than leaders want to lead. If our politicians would recognize that, we would have much better government today.

The thing the American public does not understand is that businessmen do not buy members of a state legislature or the Congress when they contribute to campaigns. What happens is this. If the politicians are aware of a businessman's integrity and know that he simply wants a better society, then his contribution gives him the opportunity to present his views to them. He influences them in the sense that when he talks with them their mind is open and he can reach them. What so many people never understand is that with all the money I've given to politicians, with all the supposed influence I have, all that really means is that I can get done today what someone else can get done tomorrow. I just get it done faster because they already know me. They don't have to check me out. I am talking about access, that's all. But if I wanted to get something done that was the slightest bit improper, forget it. That would get me nowhere with the kind of people I support.

> **The extent of Bernie's influence is just amazing. I doubt that there's any private citizen in the United States who's never been in government and who isn't a Washington lobbyist who can walk in unannounced in as many offices in Washington as Bernie.** — *Charles Terrell, insurance executive*

Influence is really about access and the ability to get information to these people in a timely and visible way. Let me give you an example of how this works. The Veterans Hospital in Waco was without air conditioning until 1974. Anyone who has been to Texas during the summer knows how hot it is. Imagine being ill enough to be hospitalized and having to stay in a room or ward without air conditioning in Texas in August. By the 1970s most of the people in the hottest parts of the country were used to having some type of air conditioning at work and at home, which made it seem even hotter when they were someplace that didn't have it. Various groups in Waco tried without success to get the Nixon administration to support the air conditioning of the Veterans Hospital. I finally went to Washington and gave the information to California senator Alan Cranston. One of the problems had been that money had been allocated for this purpose by Congress in previous sessions but Nixon's Office of Management and Budget (OMB) had impounded the money before it could be spent. Several weeks later, I received this note from Senator Cranston: "I struck a blow for Waco today! The VA hospital there will at long last get air conditioning. My amendment further provides that if OMB impounds the money, then no money can be spent to run the air conditioning apparatus in OMB headquarters in Washington. That will make those bureaucrats think twice about letting the veterans swelter in the hospital!"

I had raised money for Cranston's election campaigns, and that gave me influence in the sense that when I talked to him his mind was open and I could reach him. That's exactly the point. I'm certain the hospital would have been air-conditioned eventually, but access made it happen sooner rather than later.

I'll give you another example. In 1977 President Jimmy Carter nominated a friend of mine named H. K. Allen to be the vice chairman of the Export-Import Bank. A personable man and competent banker, Allen was chairman of the board of the Temple National Bank. During the hearings on his appointment, Senator William Proxmire, chairman of the appointments committee, and Senator Adlai Stevenson III, vice chairman, announced their opposition to Allen's nomination. Allen knew that I had access to some of the key Democratic senators, so he asked for my help.

I went to Washington and met with Alan Cranston, who agreed to support Allen's nomination. Then I met with Michigan senator Don Riegle, who was also on that committee. Riegle agreed to support him. Then I went to see a few other senators. About two days later, Riegle called me and said that his staff had checked on Allen's background and had determined that he was not qualified for the job. I told Riegle, "Now look, Don, that staff report is wrong, but let's assume that Allen's not a genius. I'm going to tell you something about Jimmy Carter. All of the people that he has appointed have not been particularly competent, and they haven't even been nice. At least this guy's very nice. That makes him at least fifty-percent better than any of the other appointments." Riegle laughed and said, "Okay, I'll go with him." The real votes were six against Allen, two for Allen, and six for Rapoport, which I gave Allen. I unlocked that nomination for Allen, and it was because I had respect and access. Allen, by the way, did a very good job.

Texas Business magazine ran an article in 1980 that included me among the twenty most powerful people in Texas. I brought the article home to show my wife. When Audre finished reading it, she said, "Honey, would you take out the trash?" I was indignant: "Audre, here I am one of the twenty most powerful men in Texas, and you want me to take out the trash?" She smiled and replied, "Honey, I want you to take out the trash, and I want you to put that article in with it."

I am politically active in nearly every state because I care about the entire country. The senators from California or Indiana or Maine can have as much or more effect on my life and business as the senators from Texas. The same is true for House committee chairs and the House leadership. Texans or not, what they do or don't do can make a difference to all of us, no matter what congressional district we live in. I am more actively involved with candidates for the U.S. Senate than with House members because there are only 100 senators. It is easier to know them personally, and I like that. Generally, I give my money to and support Democratic candidates for the Senate and the House who have a deep concern for social programs and education, are prolabor, and are friendly to Israel. I do not support any candidates, even if they are pro-Israel, who have the right-wing fundamentalist attitude that there is only one way to God.

A list of all or even most of the candidates who received my support during the 1970s and 1980s would make this book much longer than it needs to be, and it would make for boring reading. I will mention a few of my favorites, however, to indicate the type of political leaders I support. Most are no longer in office.

Although I am most involved with the U.S. Senate, I have always had a number of good friends in the House as well. As I have already said, Jim Wright is one of the best friends I have ever had. I always supported former Texas congressmen Jack Brooks, Charlie Wilson, and Bob Eckhardt in their campaigns. Former congressman Jake Pickle and I went through the University of Texas together. Jake is a fine person, and he was a top-notch congressman. Martin Frost of Dallas continues to be an outstanding member of Congress who is strong on all issues of deep concern to me, especially Israel. I have been delighted by his ascendancy to a spot in the House minority leadership. I knew and supported Henry Gonzalez from San Antonio for many years. I hated to see him retire in 1997, and I was saddened by his death in 2000.

Marvin Leath was the congressman from Waco for several years. I didn't like the way he voted, but I like him personally. Leath's predecessor, Bob Poage, wasn't as personable to me as Marvin Leath is. From my perspective, Poage voted badly on nearly every issue, and he was not even good on Israel. I couldn't abide the way he voted. After Leath retired, Chet Edwards took his place. Chet's votes are much more to my liking than those of his two most recent predecessors.

In the Senate, Henry "Scoop" Jackson of Washington was a good friend of mine. Although he was a hawk on defense issues, he and I were close because of his support of Israel. I have always been close to George McGovern. I helped James Abrouzek of South Dakota get a seat on the Judiciary Committee in 1975. In New Mexico, Joseph Montoya and I worked closely together. Birch Bayh of Indiana is a good friend. His son is now in the Senate, and I am a big supporter of his. In Arkansas, David Pryor and Dale Bumpers attracted my active support, and I developed excellent relations with both. In Tennessee, I was extremely helpful to Senator Jim Sasser when he beat Bill Brock, and he and I are good friends. I was upset when he was defeated for reelection.

I was probably one of Don Riegle's most important contributors in Michigan. Alaska's Mike Gravel and Oklahoma's Fred Harris were two of my favorites. In Vermont, Pat Leahy and I continue to be close. I helped John Glenn in every one of his campaigns in Ohio. I also supported Ohio's Howard Metzenbaum, even though he was the most antibusiness senator of all. Howard was almost the captive of Ralph Nader, but he was so good on social issues that I just had to support him. In Louisiana, Russell Long was a good friend despite his conservatism.

Although I was associated with a number of senators during the 1970s and 1980s, I would say that in terms of interest, time, and money I was most involved with Edward Kennedy, Walter Mondale, Frank Church, and Alan Cranston.

Teddy Kennedy

I did not know Ted Kennedy personally until he called me in January 1969 to ask for my help in his bid to be the majority whip in the Senate. Kennedy served on the committee on labor and public welfare, so he and I had several mutual friends in the labor leadership. They had urged him to call me for help. Ted told me that he needed just one vote to become the majority whip, and he believed that I could play a key role in getting that vote for him.

"Senator, if you want my help," I said, "I'll be glad to give it to you, but you need to know my record. I've been involved in twelve gubernatorial races in Texas the last twenty-four years, and I've lost every one of them."

Ted laughed and said, "Well, Barney, I think you have a chance to win this campaign. The one vote I need is Ralph Yarborough's."

Ralph was still in the Senate, and he was chairman of the Labor and Public Welfare Committee.

"If you know anyone who claims that they talked Senator Yarborough into doing anything," I said to Ted, "then you can be darn sure they are not very truthful." But I promised I would give it a try.

When I called Yarborough, he told me that he had already pledged his vote to Russell Long. Ralph Yarborough was as ethical and as moral a man as I have ever known, and his word was his bond. Still, I believe Ralph respected me, and when someone gives you his respect, then you usually have influence with that person, so I made my pitch. "Ralph, I just want to ask you one question. When you gave Long your word, did you know that Kennedy was going to be in the race?"

Ralph said, "No."

I said, "Well, don't you think that the conditions have now changed? Senator, you have every moral and ethical reason to change. Every one of your colleagues knows that you were always strongly supportive of John Kennedy and that Ted is one of your most dependable allies on the labor committee. Between Long and Kennedy, who do you think will work the hardest to further the social welfare and labor agenda that we support?"

I must have talked to him for more than an hour. "Look," Ralph finally said, "I know you're making some sense. I promise I'll give it serious thought."

Ralph didn't tell me what he would do, but the next day Kennedy was elected the majority whip in the Senate. The vote was secret, so I never asked Ralph how he voted. Kennedy won by one or two votes, so I've always believed that Ralph's was the deciding vote. Kennedy thought that too. When I saw Kennedy a few days later—he had asked me to come up to Washington for lunch—it was the first time we had ever met. Ted gave me a firm hug and said, "Barney, you finally found a winner." From that point on, I became a member of Ted's circle of outside advisors and fund-raisers.

After Ted Kennedy became the Senate's majority whip, I was among those who wanted him to be a candidate for the Democratic presidential nomination in 1972. After he decided against challenging Nixon, I hoped that he would run in 1976. With the Republicans in disarray as a result of Watergate, it was clear that the Democrats had an excellent chance to recapture the White House. As the 1976 campaign drew nearer, I changed my mind. Although the Watergate scandal presented the Democrats with a golden opportunity, the political environment that resulted did not favor a Kennedy candidacy. Ted's involvement in the tragic Chappaquiddick affair was a significant problem.

The Democrats needed a squeaky clean candidate with no hint of scandal in his background. In my view, Minnesota senator Walter "Fritz" Mondale was the most suitable alternative to Kennedy. I had worked with Mondale often as a result of his being on Yarborough's labor committee. He had a solid voting record in support of education and social welfare and issues important to labor. I was among those who pushed hard on Mondale early in 1974 to enter the presidential race. I raised a bunch of money for him to carry out the necessary preliminary activities, which included a heavy travel schedule to speak at meetings across the country. I arranged for Fritz to go to Mississippi to speak at a function hosted by my good friend Claude Ramsey, president of the Mississippi AFL-CIO. Fritz was one of the most liberal senators at that time, so he thought he was going to get lynched if he went to the Deep South, but he was well accepted and got national coverage during the trip. It was a huge success, and it looked like we were rolling.

After Ted Kennedy announced in September 1974 that he would not be a candidate for president in 1976, it seemed that Mondale had the nomination in the bag. That's why I was shocked when Fritz called me on the phone two weeks after the congressional elections in November and said, "You know, B, I really don't have it in me to do the things that have to be done to run for the presidency. I just don't have that burning desire." I was caught completely off guard. I admired Fritz Mondale a great deal, but his decision caused me a lot of consternation. It also left me without a presidential candidate.

Frank Church

With Kennedy and Mondale out of the race, I felt that Senator Frank Church of Idaho was the next best choice. Frank Church had long been on my list of favorite senators. He was a deeply intelligent, honest, moral, handsome, and personable man with an outstanding record in the Senate. He was surprisingly liberal for someone representing such a conservative constituency as Idaho. He had been an early critic of the Vietnam War, and he had a strong civil rights record. Frank had been elected to his first term in the Senate in 1956 at the age of thirty-two. He had recently won election to his fourth term, which meant that his high rank in seniority gave him prestige and power in the Senate. Frank was a dedicated family man. His wife, Bethine, was one of his most valuable assets as a politician. The daughter of a former governor of Idaho, Bethine was politically knowledgeable, outgoing, and dedicated to furthering Frank's career. She always called her husband Frostie. They made a terrific team.

I first met Frank in 1968 when I contributed to his reelection campaign. I helped him raise money for Cecil Andrus's Idaho gubernatorial campaign in 1970. Andrus later served as Carter's secretary of the interior. Working on other projects of mutual interest in the early 1970s, we became good friends. By 1973 I was looking closely at Frank as a possible presidential candidate for 1976. In March 1973 I arranged for Church to come to Houston and meet the small group of political campaign donors with whom I had worked during the 1972 presidential race, including Bob Lanier and J. R. Parten. Texas attorney general John Hill, Texas land commissioner Robert Armstrong, and oilman George Mitchell also attended the meeting. The senator was tremendous; a gifted speaker, he impressed everyone, especially J.R., who became a real enthusiast for Church.

Despite my high regard for Frank Church, I finally decided to support Mondale for the nomination. It was a tough call, but it seemed to me at the time that Fritz Mondale really wanted the nomination, while Church was undecided. That is why I was so dumbfounded when Fritz suddenly announced that he would not run.

The same day that Mondale told me he was out, I called Frank and gave him the news. I urged him to take Mondale's place. Frank asked if we could get the money. I told him that we could raise it. He promised me that he would give serious thought to the idea, but he had just won a tough reelection campaign back in Idaho and didn't have his feet back on the ground yet. Two months later, he became chairman of the Senate's select committee on intelligence, a job he had lobbied hard to get. Frank called me and said that he would have to put off any decision about the 1976 presidential campaign until the committee completed its work.

That news was disheartening; it was obvious that the Church Committee would be entangled for many months in a highly controversial investigation of the FBI and CIA. I knew Frank wanted to enter the presidential race, but his investigation of the illegal covert activities of our intelligence community was something that he believed took precedence over his personal political ambitions. As someone who had long urged just such a congressional investigation, it was hard for me to argue against that view. I admired Frank even more for taking that position. For most of 1975, I sat back and waited and watched helplessly as several of Frank's competitors, including Scoop Jackson, Arizona congressman Morris Udall, and Georgia governor Jimmy Carter, launched their campaigns.

In September 1975, when it looked like the Church Committee was nearing the end of its work, Frank finally agreed to let me host a dinner in Washington to bring together some of his probable financial supporters to evaluate the potential for mounting a credible campaign. At that dinner, Frank stated that he was almost certain that he would enter the race, but he would not permit the creation of a formal campaign organization until the committee hearings were completed. He did not want anyone to think that his highly publicized investigation of the CIA and FBI had been conducted as a ploy to enhance his presidential aspirations. Two more months passed while we waited for Frank to make his move.

On November 11 and 12 I attended a series of meetings in Washington with Frank and Bethine and several of his closest advisors and financial backers to determine how much money he would need for a presidential campaign and how we would raise it. Several of us at the meeting agreed to work together as an informal campaign organization. Henry Kimelman, a wealthy businessman residing in the U.S. Virgin Islands who had helped Frank raise money for his Senate campaigns, accepted the unofficial post of national finance chairman. I had worked with Henry during the McGovern campaign in 1972.

On December 11 we officially registered as the Church for President Committee. As it would turn out, however, because of delays in completing the intelligence committee's work, Frank did not announce his candidacy formally until March 18, 1976. By then, Jimmy Carter's campaign was on a roll. Nevertheless, we still believed that if Frank could pull off victories in the May and June primaries in Nebraska, Oregon, Ohio, Rhode Island, and especially California, and if the convention opened with no candidate having enough votes for the nomination — two big ifs — Frank might sweep into the convention with just enough momentum to get the prize.

That strategy failed to take into account two developments. The first was Governor Jerry Brown's surprise entrance into the race, killing our chances in California. The second was our lack of success at raising money. Frank's eleventh-hour entrance into the primary battles caused us severe problems on the fund-raising front. Most of the big contributors had made their pledges to other candidates. It was obvious from the beginning that raising money was going to be extremely difficult. We wanted to launch a direct-mail campaign to solicit contributions, but we didn't have the money to pay for it. It takes money to get money. I traveled all over the country to raise the money Frank needed to get the campaign off the ground. That took precious time that we really didn't have.

Despite his financial woes, Frank surprised the national media by winning Nebraska, the first primary he entered. Scoop Jackson had withdrawn from the presidential race shortly before the Nebraska primary, so we were able to grab some of his support within labor. Frank followed Nebraska with wins in Oregon, Idaho, and Montana. Suddenly it looked like we might be able to pull off a political miracle, or at least that is what we let ourselves think. Our hopes died quickly, however, when Frank lost to Jerry Brown in Rhode Island and California. The eccentric Brown quickly became a news media darling, while Frank could do nothing to attract media attention. One problem was Frank's personal style, which came across on television as a little uptight, stuffy, and self-righteous. Ronnie Dugger's characterization of Church in a letter to me in May 1976 highlighted our problem. "I'm sorry Church has come through so persistently prissy and churchy," Ronnie wrote. "If you could tell him for God's sakes stop praying and start rapping it might help him. He's so . . . sanctimonious."

Unable to raise the large sums of money needed for television advertising, ignored by the journalists covering the campaign, upstaged by the colorful Jerry Brown, and falling too far behind Carter in delegates, Frank finally had to throw in the towel.

Jimmy Carter

Looking back on the 1976 primary campaign, I still believe that if Frank had entered the race a year earlier, we could have raised enough money for him to give Carter a real fight. Frank Church would have made a great president. There is no doubt in my mind that he would have done a better job than Jimmy Carter. Despite my sharp disappointment that none of my preferred choices (Kennedy, Mondale, or Church) received the nomination, I attended the 1976 Democratic Convention in New York. I was delighted, of course, when Carter selected Mondale to be his vice presidential running mate. Mondale's presence on the ticket revived my flagging interest in the campaign, and I worked hard that fall for Carter's election.

After Carter won the presidential election and was inaugurated in January 1977, I had every reason to expect that during the next four years the country would benefit from having a Democratic president working closely with the Democratic majority in Congress. By the end of Carter's first year in office, however, I had some deep concerns about his leadership ability. I was pleased with Carter's support of human rights and his nonmilitaristic foreign policy, but his domestic program was a mess. He seemed unable to present his policies with the dynamic style that is required of a leader if he is to be effective. Carter was also inept in his relations with Congress. In my view, many of Carter's problems were the direct result of the mediocre quality of the people who filled his administration. Carter's top aide, Hamilton Jordan, with whom I met a couple of times to discuss the political situation, was at the top of the mediocre list.

Carter's relationship with organized labor was lukewarm at best. He had little interest in labor's issues and seemed to view organized labor with suspicion. The only thing that shielded Carter from labor's open hostility was his secretary of labor, Ray Marshall, who did an outstanding job despite the circumstances.

> I didn't meet Rapoport until I was secretary of labor. He made an appointment to talk with me in Washington. Although I had never met him, I knew who he was. During that first meeting, Rapoport said he just wanted to meet me and that he wanted me to know that he had a strong relationship with labor and unions. So we talked about labor law reform, which we were in the process of getting at that time, and about employment, unemployment, and economic policy—an area he has always had a great deal of interest in. I was the point person in our

administration for employment training, job creation programs, and the like. He liked the kind of employment training
things that we were doing. I saw him several times after that.
— *Ray Marshall*

Labor did everything it could to elect Carter president, but he never consulted labor when formulating his various domestic policies. Obviously, the
labor leadership wanted to feel like they were part of the decision-making
process. That would have been the smart thing for Carter to do. If the labor
leaders had felt like they were part of the policy deliberation, they would
have been more supportive even when the policies weren't the ones they
had advocated. Carter never understood that.

BRILAB

My opinion of the Carter administration plunged in 1978 as a
result of an unhappy personal experience I had with Carter's Justice Department and the Federal Bureau of Investigation when they entangled me
in their BRILAB program, an elaborate sting operation designed to uncover
allegedly corrupt practices in union insurance plans. "BRILAB" was the ab-
breviation for the code name of operation "Bribery-Labor," which was conducted across the country and resulted in the conviction of several people,
including New Orleans Mafia boss Carlos Marcello.

My association with BRILAB had its origins in a bad business deal I made
in California several years before. One night in 1969 or 1970, I was in Los
Angeles having dinner with Sigmund Arrowitz, president of the Los Angeles AFL-CIO. Sig mentioned that he wanted me to meet a close friend of
his, Joe Hauser, who was in the insurance business. Hauser was a Polish
Jew and Holocaust survivor. He had been in the Malthausen concentration
camp during the war. After immigrating to the United States and doing a
series of odd jobs, Hauser eventually opened an insurance brokerage in Los
Angeles.

Sig assured me that Hauser was an expert in pensions and in union contract health and welfare programs, areas in which American Income was
not involved. Hauser was eager to branch out into the supplemental insurance field, which was our main business. Sig suggested that I should enlist
Hauser's help because he was popular with all the labor people in California.
I respected Sig's judgment, so I called Hauser and worked out a business
arrangement. I paid him $25,000 to help us attract new business in Califor-

nia. I had no idea that Hauser was a con artist and swindler. My innocence cost me the $25,000 that I lost when Hauser was unable to deliver any new business to us. After a long period of nonperformance, I finally wrote him off.

> **The first time we met Joe Hauser I could tell he was as phony as a three-dollar bill. It was obvious to me, but Bernard thought he was great. Unfortunately, it turned out that I was right. He was a jerk. He wasn't anyone you would want to be around.** —*Audre Rapoport*

Eight or nine years passed without my having any contact with Hauser. During that time, I heard that he had been in jail for insurance-company fraud in California, but I didn't know any of the details. Then in 1979 I learned that Hauser and his partners had been convicted in Phoenix, Arizona, of looting millions of dollars from the insurance premiums of Teamsters union members. In June of that year I was surprised to get a phone call from him. He told me that he was out of jail and needed my help. He promised me that he had learned his lesson and was desperate to rebuild his life. I've helped a number of people who have been in jail because I think that is how the criminal justice system should work. The courts put people away to be rehabilitated. When they get out, these people should have an opportunity to reenter society and start over.

> **When I was at UCLA we had a big manpower training project jointly with the Teamsters. It was a very innovative program. But one of the guys got laid off when they restructured it. So I called Barney and told him that I had a good guy who was badly in need of a job. He said, "Okay. I'll fix it." And I said, "Oh, one other thing Barney. He's an ex-felon." He replied that it didn't matter, and then he gave me a sermon about how one can be resurrected and changed and you've got to believe in people. And he gave the guy a job, just over the phone like that, when he really needed it. He wants to help people, especially people who messed up and really need another chance.** —*Fred Schmidt*

Hauser also gave me an eloquent spiel about how he's a Polish-Jewish immigrant and a Holocaust survivor and that he had suffered the unimaginable. He knew my parents were Russian-Jewish immigrants, and he made an appeal to me on that basis. It was an Academy Award performance. Because of my background, I have acute empathy for immigrants. I don't care if they are Jewish, Chinese, Mexican, or what. I'm especially sympathetic if they're Russian Jewish. It is a particular soft spot for me because of Mama and Papa. I know the hardships that they went through.

Hauser said that he had a license with the California insurance department to do business. I was impressed with that, because it is extremely difficult to get a license from the California insurance authority. Hauser also said that he had a contract with Prudential. I told him that he had it made, because Prudential was the largest and finest insurance company in the country.

Hauser asked me if I would introduce him to some labor leaders in Texas. He had some pension plans from Prudential that he wanted to show. I told him that American Income was not involved in the type of pension plans he was selling; however, I thought that Harold Grubbs, who worked for American Income in Houston, might be able to recommend someone. Grubbs was a former official with the plumbers and pipefitters union. I told Hauser that I would call Grubbs to see if he had any interest. I suggested that he and Grubbs might be able to work together and that they could split commissions. Grubbs could be the contact man and Hauser could be the technical man. That type of arrangement is normal in our business.

I didn't know it, of course, but the FBI was taping my telephone conversation with Hauser. Also unknown to me, the FBI had recruited Hauser for the BRILAB operation. In return for an early release from prison and about $50,000 plus expenses, Hauser agreed to help the FBI trap elected officials and labor leaders accepting bribes.

I called Grubbs and explained to him that Hauser was a convicted felon and a Jewish immigrant and that I would really appreciate it if Grubbs could give him a chance. Grubbs said that he would be happy to do it. When Hauser called me back, I told him that Grubbs had agreed to work with him. Hauser later claimed that I put him in touch with Grubbs knowing that Hauser wanted to use bribes to get business. After that phone call, I never heard another thing from Joe Hauser. I never even knew that he came to Texas to meet with Grubbs. I never once discussed with Grubbs any details of anything he was doing with Hauser. As far as I was concerned, I had done something to help a man get another chance, and that was the end of it. I certainly had no plans to do business with him, but only because we didn't handle the type of policies he was selling, not because he was an ex-felon.

Grubbs subsequently introduced Hauser to L. G. Moore, a labor leader and former member of the Texas Amusement Machine Commission. In November 1979 Moore introduced Hauser to Billy Clayton, the powerful Speaker of the Texas House of Representatives. In that meeting, Hauser and Clayton discussed how Prudential could win a bid for the state employees' insurance contract, which was worth something like $90 million. At the end of the meeting, Moore gave $5,000 he had received from Hauser as a political contribution to Clayton. The FBI subsequently charged Clayton with accepting a bribe, but Clayton argued that he had intended to return the money to Moore. He said that he had temporarily taken the money only to avoid embarrassing Moore in front of Hauser. He denied that he had accepted a bribe.

When the news broke about Clayton and several other people who were indicted as a result of the FBI's sting operation, I was shocked to find my name mentioned in the stories. Some of the news stories repeated Hauser's false claim that I knew that he was looking for people to bribe. I was stunned and outraged, not only by Hauser's outrageous lie but also by the revelation that the FBI had tapped my telephone and used me for their entrapment purposes. I have never been charged with a crime, yet the FBI still tapped my telephone. The FBI never contacted me, before, during, or after the affair. I have never been contacted by any law enforcement agency about BRILAB, yet here was my name in the newspapers. Why did they have Hauser call me in the first place? I would have preferred that if they wanted to use me, they should come to me and ask my permission. But I can say this: I would not have permitted it. I am never going to be a party to an attempt to set somebody up in an entrapment scheme.

The FBI had nothing on Harold Grubbs. I've known Harold Grubbs for years; in all of our dealings he was always honorable and forthright about everything. Apparently, Hauser offered Grubbs $1,000, and he said no. Then Hauser raised the ante several thousand dollars. It is one thing for the government to target a person if it has evidence linking that person to some crime, but it is terrible to try to entice people into committing a crime without any prior suspicion or any evidence of any type about that person. The government has no right to prey on people's weaknesses with entrapment lures. Government is supposed to be supportive of those weaknesses that we as human beings have. That is necessary for a civilized society.

I resented deeply that my name was asssociated with the scheme. Hauser was such a liar. During the BRILAB trial of Carlos Marcello in New Orleans a couple of years later, it was proven in court that Hauser fabricated key portions of his tape recordings when he was working in Louisiana. He had no credibility. The affair was a farce. If I introduce you to John Doe and tell you that John Doe is a good friend of mine and then John Doe later asks you to go hold up a bank, I don't want you coming back to me and saying that you held up a bank with this guy because I told you he's a friend of mine. That is how ludicrous this thing became. I was indignant, and I felt badly for Billy Clayton and the other Texans who were entrapped.

Billy Clayton and I had been on different sides of the political road, but he had my sincere sympathy and my help. The average American has no understanding of what goes on in a politician's office. It would be embarrassing to have a tape recording of all the conversations I've had with politicians, although there has never been anything that they or I should have to be ashamed of. For one thing, we all have a tendency to brag. We tend to talk like we are a little more powerful than we really are; we like to exaggerate. That's part of life. Clayton said that he took the money to keep from embarrassing Moore, and I believe him. A jury believed him as well. Clayton and several other people who were indicted in this affair later won acquittals in court.

One of the things that gave me encouragement during that affair was the indignation shown by the judge in the Clayton trial when the tactics the FBI used were revealed in court. All Americans should be shivering in their boots to know that our government would countenance such action on the part of federal employees. We know now that if the FBI wants to contrive evidence against us, they just go ahead and do it.

What I learned in the 1970s about the illegal and immoral activities of the FBI and the CIA was profoundly disillusioning. I think a lot of Americans felt the same way. Frank Church's investigation did an outstanding job of uncovering many of those outrageous activities. I admired and appreciated his work in that area. It was one of the reasons I hoped he would be president. But as I watched Frank's hearings just two years earlier, I didn't realize how evil the FBI could be. I assumed that because I was innocent and had never been involved in anything of a malevolent nature, that was sufficient protection. Two years later I learned how wrong I was. It would not be my last bad experience with a federal investigation, but more about that later.

Kennedy's Challenge

My dissatisfaction with the Carter administration reached its peak in 1979. His domestic policies were not working, and he refused to take decisive action to control the runaway inflation and the extremely high interest rates that hit the country in late 1979. I told my friends that I would love to be for Carter in 1980, but if he did not take action in the economic sphere, I hoped another Democrat would challenge him in the primaries. I had friends on the verge of bankruptcy as a result of the administration's stupid policy of letting interest rates run amok. I realized besides causing harm to the country's economy, Carter's policies were making it unlikely that the Democratic Party could retain the presidency or even the Congress. That is why I was delighted when Ted Kennedy announced that he would challenge Carter for the 1980 Democratic presidential nomination. I quickly made up my mind to support Kennedy.

My decision to back Kennedy displeased many of my friends in the Democratic Party, but most of them understood and accepted my position. Among those I was most concerned about was the secretary of labor, Ray Marshall, because I thought he was doing an excellent job. In December 1979, when Ray heard about my support for Kennedy, he wrote me a letter expressing his disappointment, but he added, "I understand the pressures you are under. I also consider Ted Kennedy to be a friend, but do not think he would be as good a President as Jimmy Carter has been or will be during the next five years. Of course, this doesn't change anything between us. I fully understand your position."

I was Ted Kennedy's finance chairman in Texas for his 1980 campaign against Carter. It was a poorly organized campaign; neither Ted nor his campaign managers took Texas seriously. From the beginning, Kennedy's people were convinced that Texas was too conservative and that Kennedy could never win here. I think that was a mistake. By the time we got Kennedy's campaign started in Texas, he was already behind in the polls and had lost several primaries. We could have raised a lot more money than we did; we had an important function in Houston sometime in the middle of April. I asked Ted to come down. It was a salute to Billy Goldberg, the state Democratic chairman, and we had all the Democratic leaders there. Vice President Mondale and Governor Jerry Brown came down, but Kennedy didn't. That was a serious mistake. To raise money for someone like Kennedy, who was not particularly popular in Texas with the people who have money, we had to have the candidate in person. When people get with the candidate, somehow their pocketbooks loosen up. Many Texans think Ted Kennedy is some wild-eyed radical, and he really is not. He has a multimillion-dollar trust fund, so he's certainly interested in preserving that. He is as committed to this economic system as anyone else.

Compared with our other campaigns, I would say Kennedy's fund-raising was a complete flop. One of my best friends in the labor movement, the late William Winpisinger, was president of the International Association of Machinists and Aerospace Workers at the time and one of Kennedy's strongest supporters, but we received little help from the unions. Despite labor's problems with Carter, they didn't give Kennedy any money. But then they didn't give money to anybody in the primaries.

How does anybody ever get elected in this country! Campaigns are so poorly run that candidates get elected in spite of themselves and in spite of their staffs. When the Kennedys run, a certain imperiousness permeates their staff; they make it seem like they are bestowing an honor by accepting

Senator Edward M. Kennedy with Audre and B. CN 10490, Rapoport (Bernard) Photograph Collection, Center for American History, The University of Texas at Austin.

your support. I like Ted personally, but I don't like to work with him as a candidate, because there is so little cooperation. All the people in my situation have felt the same way. Fred Hofheinz, the former mayor of Houston, wanted to be Kennedy's state campaign manager. The campaign wanted someone other than Hofheinz, because he had been a little controversial as Houston's mayor. I told Kennedy I didn't want the job, because I didn't think a Jewish person should head his campaign in Texas. We had enough problems as it was, and I didn't want to create any more. I'm pragmatic; I wanted him to win. I urged Kennedy's staff to bring Hofheinz onboard. It took them maybe an extra month to decide to make him the state manager, and during all that time nothing was happening in the campaign.

By the middle of June 1980 I was telling some of Kennedy's campaign leaders that it was time to give up and concentrate on the platform at the convention. I also realized that with Kennedy's chances so slim, we now had no choice but to rally behind Carter. "Otherwise," I warned, "I think we are going to come out of this so divided that we are going to end up with Ronald Reagan." During Kennedy's challenge to Carter, I made a deal with my friend Jim Calloway, an independent oilman in Houston who raised money for Carter, that if Kennedy won, Calloway would help me raise funds for him. If Carter won, I would help him raise money for Carter. Despite my unhappiness with Carter, I never considered abandoning the Democratic Party or being neutral in the election, especially when it became clear that Ronald Reagan would be the Republican nominee. I simply could not stand the thought of a Reagan presidency. As I told Calloway and others during the primary campaign, if Carter won the nomination again, I would be his most ardent supporter against Reagan, and I was.

The Election of 1980

As I had promised, after Kennedy lost I threw my support to Carter's reelection effort. I helped Jess Hay arrange a major fund-raising dinner in Dallas that attracted a large number of donations. The problem was that there was no spirit in Carter's campaign. There was drive, but no spirit. I sensed it in New York during the convention. Any objective observer had to have sensed that Carter could not be reelected. I didn't come away from the convention feeling that we were going to lose, but in retrospect, I can see that we had no chance. Jimmy Carter is a man of substance, but he had no style; he could not evoke an emotional response from the people. The campaign also had to contend with the issue of those impossibly high interest rates, which broke a lot of small businessmen and small farmers, and the heated emotions generated by the Iranian hostage crisis. I also underestimated Ronald Reagan's ability as a campaigner and the degree to which his personality would appeal to the American people.

Shortly before the election, *Time* and *Newsweek* were predicting a close vote, but I knew by the first week in October that we were going to lose the presidency. I knew that we couldn't carry Texas, and without Texas, there was no chance for Carter to win. When I talked to the labor leaders here in Texas, I could see their lack of enthusiasm. The rank and file didn't want to go all out, and when they don't want to go all out, they are not going to respond to their leadership. I knew that Carter was beaten, but I thought we could keep control of the Senate. I turned away from the Carter campaign effort and concentrated instead on the reelection campaigns of Cranston, Church, McGovern, Bayh, and the other Democratic senators who were under siege.

Many think of B primarily as a fund-raiser, but I think of him as a brilliant political strategist. I don't know how many know how busy he was during 1980 or how much ground he

covered. If he wasn't in South Dakota mapping the McGovern campaign, he was in Idaho helping Senator Church. From there it was Indiana for Senator Bayh, and then he stopped in Iowa for Senator Culver, and finally the campaign ended with B in New Hampshire with Senator Durkin. — *Charles Wilson, former Texas congressman*

Those reelection campaigns were extremely nasty. The Republicans, mainly working through a right-wing political action committee called the National Conservative Political Caucus (NCPC), dumped enough dirt on Democrats in 1980 to fill the Grand Canyon. The NCPC invaded Idaho at least two years before the election. They spent an enormous amount of time and money calling Church a radical proabortionist whose vote in support of the Panama Canal Treaty had been part of a vast Communist conspiracy. They were masters at manipulating the silly emotional issues that devious leaders use against decent, good people. They divert the voters' minds from the substantive issues that really affect them, such as the growing economic disparity between rich and poor, the decline in the quality of public education, and the escalating cost of health care. Instead, the Republicans and their NCPC puppets distracted the voters with all their abortion and Moral Majority junk, issues that aren't the business of government in the first place. If a woman wants an abortion, it is none of my business and none of your business, and it's none of the government's business; that's her personal business. I'm not happy when any woman gets an abortion, but I'm not going to sit judgment on her either.

Despite the demagoguery, I remained cautiously optimistic about the Senate races until election day. On the day before, I talked to Frank Church, and his polls indicated he was nine points ahead of his challenger, conservative Republican congressman Steve Symms. In Wisconsin, Gaylord Nelson told me that his lead was fourteen points. I didn't think that race was even close. In South Dakota, McGovern's polls indicated an extremely tight race, but he believed he would squeeze through with a victory. I really thought they would all win. What the polls failed to anticipate was the extremely low turnout of Democratic voters because of the lack of enthusiasm for Carter. The polls weren't wrong; if the same percentage of people had voted as had voted previously, Carter still would have lost but the Democrats would not have lost the Senate. As a candidate, Carter turned out to be too big of a burden for vulnerable Democratic senators. In Idaho, for example, Frank Church received 180,000 more votes than the president. He lost his Senate seat by a margin of a little more than 2,000 votes. Birch Bayh had a similar situation. No candidate can win when his party's presidential candidate is losing by millions of votes. Even worse, in Church's case, was Carter's decision to concede his defeat publicly several hours before the polls had closed in Idaho, which undoubtedly persuaded many Democrats who were still at work not to bother to vote.

On the night of November 4, when I realized that the Democratic Party was losing control of the U.S. Senate, I thought about the Senate being under the thumbs of men like Jesse Helms and Strom Thurmond. It depressed me, because some of the people who were defeated were among the best leaders we have ever had in the Senate. Church, McGovern, Bayh, and Nelson were giants brought down by right-wing pygmies, ideologues of mediocre ability and limited vision. I was remorseful about the way the elections turned out.

One of the few bright spots was in California, where Alan Cranston won an overwhelming victory. Fortunately for Cranston, California is a liberal state on social issues like abortion. Also, California is so large and diverse that it is difficult to win statewide elections based on issues with narrow appeal. In addition, Cranston was the best-organized politician I have ever known. He fully understood that $1 received a year before the campaign is worth $10 the last month of the campaign, because the last month of the campaign is when the money is wasted. Having plenty of early money allows a candidate to make more effective use of the money; Cranston had more than $1.5 million raised a year before he ran in 1980. Cranston was a natural-born leader. He became party whip during his second term in the Senate. I have known some really great senators, but you don't see greatness like that anymore. He actually won more votes in California in his Senate race than Reagan did for president in 1980. He attracted about 4.7 million votes, the largest vote total anyone had ever received in a U.S. Senate election.

Alan Cranston and the 1984 Presidential Campaign

It wasn't long after Reagan's election that the various leading Democratic senators who had survived the 1980 election, or at least had the good fortune not to have been up for reelection, positioned themselves to make a run at the party's presidential nomination in 1984. As a Democrat who had won an overwhelming victory in Ronald Reagan's home state, Alan Cranston soon had his eye on that nomination.

Alan Cranston had a fascinating background. Not many people know it, but he was a foreign correspondent in Europe during the late 1930s and was among the first Americans to recognize the danger that Adolf Hitler posed to world peace. He published an unexpurgated English translation of Hitler's *Mein Kampf* in an attempt to educate the American public about

B and Audre with Senator Alan Cranston, early 1980s. CN 10500, Rapoport (Bernard) Photograph Collection, Center for American History, The University of Texas at Austin.

Hitler's evil. During World War II, Alan worked to get Jewish refugees into the United States, and he was an early supporter of Israel. In the 1950s, while Alan was building a business, he became one of the most stalwart supporters of Cesar Chavez's effort to organize the farmworkers in California. He was also deeply involved in the civil rights movement and a supporter of Dr. Martin Luther King.

I helped Alan in his election campaign in 1968, and I served as national finance chairman for his reelection campaigns in 1974 and 1980. When Alan ran for majority whip of the Senate in January 1977, I made a number of calls on his behalf. He was deeply respected by his Democratic colleagues, who chose him as their whip four sessions in a row.

In 1982 Alan decided that he wanted to run for president. I honestly didn't think he had a chance, but he wanted to be president, and he was serious about the campaign. I pledged my support and agreed to serve on his national steering committee, which included Willie Brown, Speaker of the California House of Representatives, author Norman Cousins, *Rolling Stone* publisher Jann Wenner, and Cesar Chavez. Harris Wofford, who later served as senator from Pennsylvania, was cochair.

Alan's campaign counted heavily on his status as California's favorite son. California has the largest block of delegates at the Democratic National Convention. We also knew we could depend on his supporters in the entertainment industry in Los Angeles to provide a critical base of financial support to get his campaign up and running. In Texas, I had to get twenty people to donate $250 each to his campaign so that he could be eligible for federal funding. We were able to do that in a number of other states. As a strong supporter of the nuclear freeze movement and the strategic arms limitation (SALT) agreements, he believed that his work to stop the arms race would make him an attractive alternative to Mondale and John Glenn, both of whom had weak records on that issue. J. R. Parten, for example, threw his support behind Alan because of his opposition to the nuclear arms race.

We had fun in that campaign, but it did not last long. It soon became obvious that the campaign was going nowhere. Alan lacked the charisma that voters seem to want in presidential candidates. He did not come across well on television, and his speaking style was a little too professorial and dry. He was one of the most intelligent senators I have ever known, but he did not generate any excitement on the campaign trail. After he bowed out, I gave my support to the eventual nominee, Walter Mondale.

The problem with Mondale was that everything came too easy for him. He was appointed attorney general; he was appointed to the Senate, and once you're in, you're the incumbent. He is a marvelous person, but it's like life: I really had to grub for my success, and I think I appreciate it more than somebody who got there easily. Although I don't think Walter worked as hard as he should have against Reagan, it was a moot point, because Reagan was too popular to defeat in 1984.

It would be another eight years before my party would reclaim the White House. I had no inkling in 1984 that a good friend of mine would be the person who would achieve that long denied victory.

11 | ▶ *Israel*

I am a Zionist. My commitment to the idea of a Jewish home-
land is total, but to be honest, it was not until I was well into my thirties that
I was able to sort out my conflicted thoughts and feelings about the need
for a Jewish homeland. My ambivalence about Israel was to some extent the
result of the split between my mother and father over the issue of Zionism.

My mother and her mother, my grandmother Bobo, raised me to love all
things Jewish. Bobo was the devout member of the family, and she probably
had more influence on me than she did on any of her other grandchildren. It
was from her that I developed my feelings for the spiritual side of Judaism.
Every Saturday, Mama and Bobo took me to the Aggudeth Jacob synagogue,
about twenty-five blocks from our house in San Antonio. At the synagogue,
we prayed often for the establishment of a Jewish state in Palestine. At home,
Mama kept a little blue box in which we put our pennies. When the box
was full, Mama would send the pennies to the Jewish National Fund to help
purchase land in Palestine for Jews. To please Bobo, I always put some of
my pennies into that little blue box.

> Bernie's Jewish roots are very important to him. He speaks
> often of his mother and his grandparents, and it is obvious that
> he has deep feelings about them. He believes that his success
> is a tribute to them and that he is what they would want him to
> be. The legacy is very important to him. This is one of the keys
> to understanding Bernie. — *Ruth Cheshin, Jerusalem Foundation*

When I was six or seven, Mama invited a nice young Jewish lady from
Wisconsin by the name of Golda Myerson to stay at our house while she
raised money for the Jews in Palestine. This was in 1923 or 1924. I don't remember her visit that well, but I do recall that she and Mama collected old
clothes that they sold at a rummage sale to raise money. Many years later

B and Golda Meir in Israel in the early 1970s. CN 10488, Rapoport (Bernard) Photograph Collection, Center for American History, The University of Texas at Austin.

that nice Jewish woman became prime minister of Israel. By then, she had changed her name to Golda Meir.

Papa did not share Mama's and Bobo's enthusiasm for the Jewish religion, although he did have an appreciation for Jewish culture. The only time I can recall Papa ever going to the synagogue was for my bar mitzvah at age thirteen. As a Marxist, Papa scorned religion as the "opiate of the masses." When I was a kid, he and his little group of radicals spent many hours at our house, arguing about Zionism until late in the night. These old radical Marxist Jews were not interested in a homeland in Palestine. Their concern was for the plight of the world's workers.

Although Papa and I had a difficult relationship, he dominated the formation of my worldview, so as a youth I generally assumed his outlook on politics and religion. As it turned out, however, my mother's religious views were ingrained in my emotional makeup to a degree that I was unaware of at the time. I didn't understand it, but I felt it. A brief passage in my diary, written when I was nineteen, reveals the inner turmoil I was experiencing about my religious beliefs: "I guess I'm an atheist," I wrote. "How I despise it!"

When I was at the university, most of the students with whom I associated were internationalists and pacifists, which bolstered my anti-Zionism. This was my extreme do-gooder stage, when I did not take human nature into account. I did not understand the need and the yearning people have to live in their own little world.

World War II and the Holocaust changed everything. The unprecedented horrors of Hitler's final solution left no Jew untouched. Six million human beings were murdered simply because they were Jews. Although my closest relatives had immigrated to the safe haven of the United States, I lost many members of my extended family to the German death machine. My uncle Boris Rapoport remained in Latvia instead of emigrating like my father and Uncle Foley. In the 1930s his son, who had migrated to Palestine in the early 1920s, could see that Hitler and the Nazis were a real threat, and he urged his father to leave Latvia. Uncle Boris refused because he did not want to give up his substantial property holdings. "Better to lose your money than your life" was my cousin's reply to his father's explanation. Unfortunately, that warning turned out to be prophetic. Uncle Boris was among those millions of innocent people murdered in cold blood by the Germans. My mother's family suffered similar losses.

My family and I did not know the fate of Uncle Boris and other relatives until after the war. I had abandoned my pacifism long before then. I could not contribute to the war effort in a military sense because of my leg, but I closely followed the progress of the war. News about the systematic attacks on the Jewish population in Germany and in the occupied countries awakened my nascent Zionism. Later, when information about the extermination camps and the mass murders became public, my feelings of solidarity with my fellow Jews took over. The experience of the Holocaust, added to the legacy of 2,000 years of persecution, created a desperate yearning among the Jewish people for at least one place on this earth where Jews can exist in relative safety and control their own destiny. I was not immune to those yearnings.

A few years ago, while giving a speech to a rather conservative southern group, I mentioned that my mother and father were Russian Jewish immigrants. Afterward, someone in the audience asked me what made Jews so different. My reply was that I really didn't know, but I suspected it was 2,000 years of Christian love. I am now a full-fledged, unapologetic Zionist. The state of Israel is a necessity in the kind of world in which we live.

My Jewish awakening was encouraged and abetted by Edward Fred, an Orthodox Jew I met in Waco in the late 1940s. Ed was a magnificent young man. I was so secular and he was so religious, yet we had a close friendship. A serious student of Hebrew, Ed taught me a lot about the Talmud. I can't read Hebrew, so Ed would read the Talmud out loud to me. He tried to bring me to orthodoxy, arguing that to be Jewish one must be Orthodox. I found his arguments interesting and challenging, but I was never able to make that religious leap.

In 1948, during the Israeli war for independence, Ed and I went to the radio station to get the latest wire-service reports on the battles. Audre and I sent whatever money we could spare to the Israelis during the 1948 war. We had rummage sales, and we sent old clothes through the United Jewish Appeal.

> **My family and I always supported the creation of a Jewish national state. It is important that the Jewish people have a homeland.** —*Audre Rapoport*

Soon after the 1948 war, Ed Fred traveled to Israel, lived in a kibbutz for one year, and then returned to Texas. In the late 1950s he moved to Israel permanently. He settled at Kiryat Bialik, changed his first name to Eliahu, and deepened in his orthodoxy.

> **Edward Fred was in some respects a great deal like Bernard at the time. He was an intellectual who was sort of trapped in a family business. His father died, and he had to take over the business. His younger brother had a jewelry business in Waco. It was Morris Jewelers, but it was the Fred family. That threw Bernard and Ed Fred together, the common background and Judaism. He was also very committed to Israel, as is Bernard, but one of the differences is that Edward elected to go to Israel and stay.** —*Hiram Friedsam*

One of the reasons I love Judaism so much is its concern for group salvation rather than individual salvation. I am also deeply attracted to Judaism's emphasis on the world today, not some mystical hereafter. I care about the world today and the society in which we live. I can't accept a concept like predestination, for example, because as long as you have life, you have opportunity, and as long as you have opportunity, you can change things. My real religion is that I say there is something greater than I am, and I call that God. Everything flows from that. I do not believe in an anthropomorphic god, one literally in a heaven with a beard and flowing robe. I think of God as a spirit that is something greater than we are. That is my religion. The rest of it I just develop through my own independent thinking.

> You cannot overestimate the importance of Bernard's commitment to Judaism. It is in some respects, in my opinion, a much stronger emotional tie than his politics or his economics or anything of the sort. — *Hiram Friedsam*

Late in his life, Papa became interested in Israel, especially in 1948 after the state of Israel was proclaimed and war broke out. By then Papa had become more conservative politically; he had abandoned his Marxism and his anti-Zionist views. A trip that he and Mama made to Israel in the early 1950s deepened his interest. Papa's conversion to Zionism was complete by the time of his death in May 1966. After Papa died, I discovered that his estate totaled about $35,000, and the entire amount was in Israeli bonds.

Papa was eighty years old when he died. He had been sick for about one year, and Mama took care of him like he was a little baby. He and Mama never had a day when they did not have an argument, which was typical for an immigrant family. When people have to struggle hard for everything, it creates more hardships and tensions. The funny thing is that Mama died about two weeks before Papa. It was one of those relationships where they couldn't live with each other, and they couldn't live without each other.

> When Barney's father died, I was invited to be a pallbearer. After the coffin had been lowered and all the people, many of them Mexican Americans, had walked away, Barney asked me to go with him back to the grave. Standing there by ourselves, he looked down at his old dad's coffin and said, "Good-bye, Papa. Franklin Roosevelt messed up your revolution, didn't he?" — *Maury Maverick, Jr.*

My moral and intellectual support for the state of Israel became total after its creation in 1948, but my financial support was limited severely by my personal economic circumstances. In the late 1950s, as I accumulated a little money of my own, I raised funds for Israeli bonds. A person buys Israeli bonds just like U.S. bonds. When you buy a bond, you are helping Israel but you also get a financial return. You are making an investment. With the assistance of state senator Oscar Mauzy, I helped get a law passed in Texas to allow banks and insurance companies to buy Israeli bonds. The State

Riva and David Rapoport with their son, B, in the early 1960s. CN 10495, Rapoport (Bernard) Photograph Collection, Center for American History, The University of Texas at Austin.

of Texas now invests in Israeli bonds. In 1994 Israel awarded me the Israel Peace Medal in recognition of my work on behalf of Israeli bonds. I was deeply honored. It's true that I have been responsible for selling hundreds of millions of dollars' worth of bonds, but so have many other people.

Fulbright and Israel

I could never support a political candidate who was against Israel. I have not, however, expected those for whom I have campaigned to agree with every Israeli policy or action. A good example of my outlook in this regard was my relationship with Senator William Fulbright of Arkansas, the controversial chairman of the Senate Foreign Affairs Committee during the Vietnam War. Senator Fulbright was a vocal critic of our military involvement in Southeast Asia. I admired his courage in speaking out against that immoral war despite intense hostility from the Johnson administration and from some of his own colleagues. I contributed funds to his reelection campaign in 1968 because of his antiwar stance. Although we were never close friends, he and I had many personal conversations. I reprinted some of his Senate speeches on the American Income page in *The Texas Observer*.

In the spring of 1973, however, I was shocked and disappointed by Fulbright's public statements about Israel during a televised appearance on CBS's *Face the Nation*. Fulbright asserted that Israel controlled the Senate and that the Senate would give Israel whatever it wanted, no matter if it ran counter to legitimate U.S. interests. About that same time, Fulbright also opposed Senator Henry Jackson's attempt to prohibit the granting of trade concessions to the Soviet Union unless it lifted restrictions on the emigration

B and Audre at the head table of an Israel Bond dinner in Waco in the late 1950s. CN 10487, Rapoport (Bernard) Photograph Collection, Center for American History, The University of Texas at Austin.

of Jews. I expressed my serious concerns to Fulbright about his statements and actions, particularly the claim that the Senate was subservient to Israel, which was not true then and is not true now. It is correct that most of Fulbright's Senate colleagues were supportive of Israel, but that support was based on moral persuasion and the pragmatic realization that Israel is the best instrument for the spread of democracy throughout the Middle East. Fulbright and his chief of staff were quick to assure me that he was not anti-Israel and that he wasn't pro-Arab, that he was just concerned with peace in the world.

A year later, in the summer of 1974, Fulbright's bid for a sixth term in the Senate was opposed in the Democratic primary by Arkansas governor Dale Bumpers. Although I liked Bumpers and had contributed to his campaign for governor, I supported Fulbright and was very much involved in that campaign. My support attracted national attention because of my strong association with the Israeli cause. Many of my Jewish friends, however, castigated me rather severely for continuing to support him. I remained concerned about Fulbright's views on Israel, but I took the position that I was doing the right thing. Although Israel is one of my primary interests, to have a healthy Israel in a world that has disintegrated doesn't serve any good purpose. I believed that Fulbright's opposition to the Vietnam War made us all indebted to him. Besides, I knew Fulbright to be a civilized man, and I agreed with nearly every other position he had taken on a wide range of domestic and foreign policy issues. I did not expect him to share my views on everything. Several of my Jewish friends, however, gave money to Bumpers, who won the election. I was shocked when Fulbright took a job lobbying for the Arabs after he left the Senate. That was a tremendous disappointment to me, because I had faith in the man and I had stuck my neck out for him.

Nevertheless, I have to say that to know the late Bill Fulbright is to know that he never was a racist or an anti-Semite. His votes against civil rights legislation, for example, were political expediency on his part. It was just one of the things that Southern senators were doing in those days. Ralph Yarborough, for example, would not speak out against the war in Vietnam at the beginning. I know that Ralph regretted that later.

Fagan Dickson and Israel

My unwavering support for Israel has led to strong disagreements with some of my other political friends and allies. The two disputes that stand out in my mind were with an Austin attorney named Fagan Dickson and with my old friend Maury Maverick, Jr. Of the two, my dispute with Dickson was by far the most disturbing.

Fagan Dickson was a liberal Democrat and Ralph Yarborough activist whom I met through J. R. Parten. Fagan and I worked together in several political campaigns and against the Vietnam War. When the United States gave Israel $2.2 billion in December 1973 to help rebuild the Israeli Defense Forces after the Yom Kippur War of October 1973, Fagan argued that the grant was illegal because it was in support of "the religious wars of the Jews." Later, he filed a lawsuit in federal court claiming that all U.S. aid to Israel was unconstitutional because the Constitution prohibits Congress from making laws "respecting an establishment of religion." He argued that Israel is a Jewish theocracy no different from the Vatican of the Catholic Church. I thought Fagan was wrong, and I did not hesitate to tell him so. Comparing the Israeli government with the Vatican is ludicrous. The Pope and the College of Cardinals control the Vatican; it is not a democracy by any definition of the term. Israel, on the other hand, is a multiparty democracy governed by a prime minister, a cabinet, and a parliament (the Knesset) who are freely elected by the people of Israel. The federal court saw the situation the same way and threw his suit out.

Fagan had a right to his personal interpretation of the Constitution, but I did not respect or understand one particular action that he took prior to his legal fight against U.S. aid to Israel. On February 18, 1973, Fagan placed a large advertisement in the *Austin American-Statesman* charging that the U.S. Congress was dominated by the Jewish lobby, that the Arab oil boycott in 1973 was caused by Israel, and that the Israelis were leading us into another Vietnam. Fagan got this nonsense from an anti-Zionist organization called Middle East Perspective, Inc. As far as I was concerned, the advertisement was terribly misleading, and it was provocative in a manner that would produce nothing but hatred. It was an appeal to the basest instincts of those with the intention to do evil. Fagan knew very well that Israel had never asked for American military advisors or troops, and more than twenty-five years later it still has not. His statement about the Congress was an insult to a group of independent-minded political leaders, some of whom had made courageous stands against the Vietnam War. Blaming Israel for the oil boycott was blaming the victim for the crime. I made it clear to Fagan that his use of such an inflammatory message had taken him beyond the bounds of decency and civility. As a Jew, I resented the advertisement; as an American, it infuriated me. I made my feelings known publicly, and the Austin newspaper subsequently printed them. I began to see Fagan as an apologist for the Arabs against Israel, and our personal relationship was never the same after that.

My argument with Maury Maverick, Jr., about Israel was qualitatively different from my dispute with Fagan Dickson. Maury's weekly column for the Sunday edition of the *San Antonio Express-News* covers diverse subjects ranging from the ecological benefits of growing lantana plants to the foreign policy of the United States. Not long after the Likud Party and Menachem Begin gained power in Israel in the late 1970s, Maury became a fierce critic of Israeli policies toward the Palestinians and their Arab allies. He expressed those criticisms too harshly, I thought, in his newspaper columns. Not surprisingly, many members of the Jewish community in San Antonio and elsewhere were outraged by Maury's writings and expressed their anger on the "Letters to the Editor" page of the newspaper, in some cases rather irresponsibly. A lot of my Jewish friends don't understand that Maury Maverick, Jr., is not anti-Semitic in any way, shape, or form. He sympathizes with the Palestinians because they are poor, and he sympathizes with poor people everywhere.

Maury had an equally negative reaction to his attackers. He responded in his column by accusing Jews of using their victimization in the Holocaust as a license for Israel to oppress the Palestinian people. That just escalated the controversy to an even higher level of tension. Maury's remarks disturbed me, so I criticized him publicly. In a letter to me, Maury replied that "Jews have become almost as reactionary as my fellow Episcopalians. Your father's generation was the conscience of America, but not today. God knows we need the spirit of those old time Jews."

I replied that I "certainly understand your motivation, Maury. I'm tempted to say you shouldn't discuss politics and religion, but then there would be nothing else to talk about. Part of my dismay at your editorials vis-à-vis Israel is that you detract so much from this essential work that you are doing." Not surprisingly, my advice to Maury on the subject of Israel has had no effect. He continues today to be a vigorous critic of the Israeli government, which disheartens me. Nevertheless, as I told Maury, "The only thing that I can't countenance is that when people that are as close as you and myself have a disagreement, that we would question one another's motives. I certainly never question yours. I might disagree with your conclusions, but that is the full extent of it." I meant what I said. Maury and I disagree on Israel, but I understand his motives and we are friends still.

The Jerusalem Foundation

Audre and I made our first visit to Israel in 1966. It was also our first trip overseas. As is the case with most of the firsts in life, this initial foray into the Old World made a profound impression on both of us.

B with students at Tel Aviv University in the late 1980s. CN 10492, Rapoport (Bernard) Photograph Collection, Center for American History, The University of Texas at Austin.

We were overwhelmed by the experience. The Israelis are a cosmopolitan and sophisticated people, and that surprised us. Equally impressive was the sense we had immediately of their steadfast determination and courage. It was love at first sight for me, and that love has only grown stronger ever since.

After that first visit Audre and I decided to do whatever we could to help the Israeli people improve their quality of life. It wasn't until the late 1970s that I had the personal financial means to take an active role in helping Israel. Audre and I have been pleased to foster and support a wide variety of educational and human welfare projects in different sections of that small country. In the summer of 1987, for example, we established the Rapoport chair in the Arane Graduate School of History at Tel Aviv University, Israel's largest institution of higher education. A significant portion of the money came from my company's general sales agents, who made generous donations for the endowment. Our purpose was to develop a research capacity at Tel Aviv University to study the influence of the American labor movement on American society and in turn its effect and relationship to other industrialized Western nations and to Israel. Funds from the chair have been used to sponsor scholarly exchanges between scholars at the university and U.S. labor leaders. In November 1997 I was elected chairman of the board of the

American Friends of Tel Aviv University, and my work with the university continues.

Audre and I are interested in all of Israel, but we have an especially deep affection for Jerusalem. In 1978 we became involved in the Jerusalem Foundation, which was the brainchild of Teddy Kollek, a dear friend of mine who was mayor of Jerusalem for nearly thirty years. Teddy (everyone who has had the privilege of knowing him calls him Teddy) is one of the most brilliant men in the world. Every president has recognized him for his contributions to fostering peaceful relations in the Middle East. Teddy and a group of his friends in Israel and in the United States created the foundation in 1966 shortly after winning his first term as mayor. Since then, the foundation has made outstanding improvements to the quality of life for both Arabs and Jews in Jerusalem.

> We try to become friends with every donor, but I don't know of any donor who has become a closer friend to me than Bernard is. Bernard expresses himself strongly and with passion. I love the way he waves his arms and moves his hands when he speaks. He is not reserved in any way, and I enjoy that very much. — *Teddy Kollek*

You have to remember that when Teddy was first elected mayor, Jerusalem was an officially divided city, the western half under Israeli authority and the eastern half under Jordanian control. After the 1967 war, Teddy found himself mayor of the entire city of Jerusalem. East Jerusalem was an impoverished and decaying area desperately in need of help. Basic services such as waste and sewage disposal and clean drinking water were almost nonexistent.

Teddy's city government made plans for improvements, but Jerusalem's tax base is so weak that public money was unavailable for many of the desired projects. He quickly forged a close partnership between the municipality and the foundation to attract private investment and funding for projects to modernize the whole city and to improve the quality of life for every citizen without regard for religious affiliation or ethnicity. At the heart of Teddy's effort was his deeply held belief that Jerusalem must be an ecumenical center, open and hospitable to every one of its varied populations, whether Jewish or Arab, religious or secular. It is this ecumenical philosophy that Audre and I found so personally compelling.

> Audre and Bernard Rapoport have a deep affection for Jerusalem. Almost every year they come for a visit, and sometimes

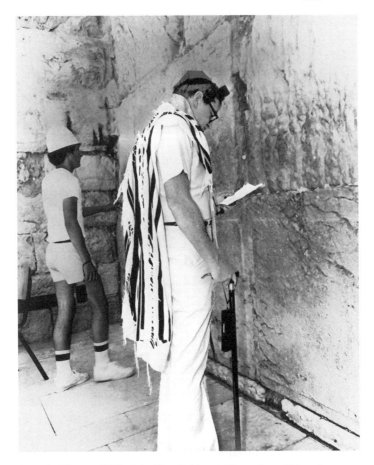

B at the Western Wall of the Temple Mount, Jerusalem. CN 10485, Rapoport (Bernard) Photograph Collection, Center for American History, The University of Texas at Austin.

they come twice a year. Their gifts reflect a constant theme of investing in the human infrastructure of Jerusalem. That indicates their interest in life: the Rapoports are interested in people, not things. They are most interested in projects that help both Jews and Arabs. —*Alan Freeman, Jerusalem Foundation*

By the year 2000, Kollek and the foundation had raised more than $360 million from donors in the United States, as well as many millions from donors in Australia, South America, and Europe. This money has been used to fund more than 1,400 projects, including community centers, parks, hospitals, libraries, and schools in every section of Jerusalem. The foundation has restored historic and religious sites, initiated social welfare programs, beautified neighborhoods, and spearheaded a cultural renaissance that has resulted in a multitude of new dramatic, musical, and fine arts programs and institutions. This good work has made a dramatic difference in the quality of life in Jerusalem. In Jerusalem, nearly everything one can see of a public nature has been built under the auspices of the Jerusalem Foundation. Teddy Kollek and his colleagues are committed to making Jerusalem beautiful and to educating the city's people, Arab and Jew alike.

Audre and I have had the honor of being a part of this effort. We have given several millions of dollars, and I serve as a director of the foundation's organization in the United States. My position as a director has been especially rewarding because it has allowed me to work closely with a group of wonderful people in this country, including former New York mayor Edward Koch, former ambassador Max Kampelman, Marty Peretz, and the late Annette Strauss, the former mayor of Dallas. The Rapoport Foundation does not give money to religious organizations, although Audre and I do, but it does give one-sixth of its annual donations to the Jerusalem Foundation and the United Jewish Appeal.

Givat Gonen High School

One of the most interesting Jerusalem Foundation projects in which Audre and I have been involved was the renovation and expansion of the Givat Gonen High School. We have given $1 million for its support. The school is in Jerusalem's Katamond section, the neighborhood served by bus route number 18, which was the target of two separate bombings by Arab terrorists in 1996. It is a poor area economically. Any child from the neighborhood can go to the school. Children from other areas of Jerusalem are also welcome, but they have to receive special permission from the municipality to attend. There is no public transportation to the school. Anyone wanting to come must get there on his or her own.

The purpose of the school is to have an educational institution for Israeli families who believe in the old Israeli style of socialism and who want peaceful coexistence with the Arabs. In addition, the school attracts children from all economic levels, thus providing a beneficial integration of social classes.

> **Bernard is now helping us build a major school in the city. It is a special school in a poor Jewish area that has social content in its curriculum. He has helped us equip the school with laboratories and computers.** — *Teddy Kollek*

Givat Gonen High School is the creation of a remarkable woman by the name of Yael Binyamina Levin, who also served as its first principal. Yael is now retired in an official sense, but she continues to work just as hard as ever for the school, including serving as the construction supervisor for the addition that Audre and I funded. Like most Israelis, Yael has strong political beliefs. It was politics that inspired her to found the school. After Menachem Begin's right-wing Likud Party came to power in 1977, Yael decided that Israel desperately needed an ideological high school with a curriculum and philosophy based on the tenets of the founders of modern Israel, the cooperative socialism of the kibbutzim and the Hisdarut. I have been active with Hisdarut, the Israeli labor organization, and many of its leaders have been close friends of mine.

Everybody told Yael that she was crazy, that the government would not help her, and that the Labor Party would not support Givat Gonen High School. Even Teddy Kollek, who is a good friend of Yael's, warned her that there was no money for the school because the municipality of Jerusalem had too many other pressing responsibilities. Yael's determination to put her educational project in one of the poorest areas in West Jerusalem, mainly populated with immigrants from North Africa who supported right-wing and religious political parties, made her problem even more difficult.

Yael refused to give up, despite having no money, no help, and no recognition and being surrounded by an unsympathetic and potentially hostile local community. After two or three years of dedicated effort, she finally attracted enough financial support from Hisdarut and a number of small donors to open the school. Yael named the new school after one of the socialist pioneers of Israel. It now has about 1,300 students.

I chose Givat Gonen school because we loved the teachers and the principal and the program they had. The Jerusalem Foundation gave us a list of projects, but Yael Levin was the one who sold us on it. The fact that it taught Israeli labor socialism especially appealed to me. Socialism in Israel is a combination of the best of socialism and the best of capitalism. I think that capitalism is the best economic system ever devised; socialism is the best social system. Capitalism acknowledges the greed instinct; socialism acknowledges the need for cooperation. It is when we integrate those two that we have a good system. That's what Israel really did.

In my opinion Givat Gonen is one of the most exciting educational projects in Israel. Yael had intended for Hisdarut to use it as a model for other schools in Israel, but that has not happened, largely because Hisdarut and the socialist movement have been seriously weakened in the last ten years.

The current principal of Givat Gonen School is Yehudit Shalvi, who served the school as a teacher for several years before assuming her current position upon Yael Levin's retirement. I am involved, as a donor and fund-raiser, in the rehabilitation and modernization of the existing structure and the addition of a large new wing. We also beautified the grounds and rede-signed the open space to make room for additional basketball courts and other recreational activities. All of the children in that community, not just the students at the school, are desperately short of playgrounds. The new open space at the school is available to everyone, whether or not they go to Givat Gonen.

Adjacent to the school is a small park that I funded and named in honor of my friend and colleague Al Barkan, the former chairman of American Income's labor advisory board who died in 1990.

> We were having breakfast with Teddy Kollek, and B told him that he wanted to honor Al Barkan with some project in Jeru-salem. Kollek told him that he should look at a particular area close to some schools that could be converted into a park that could be named for Barkan. B asked me to go look at the area. The neighborhood consisted of a group of rowhouses teeming with children with no place to play. We could visualize a park at this fairly large plot of ground that was overgrown and had garbage scattered about. The Jerusalem Foundation told us that it would cost about $250,000 to build the park. When I reported this to B, he pledged $100,000. The unions put up the remainder. Today it is a beautiful little area. When I was there recently it was full of students eating their lunches and playing. The flowers were blooming. It was nice. —*Morty Bahr*

Sheikh Jarrakh Medical Center Eye Clinic

Another Jerusalem Foundation project in which Audre and I are involved is a medical center in the Sheikh Jarrakh section of East Jeru-salem. The medical center, founded in 1982 to provide services directly to the Arab population in Jerusalem and the surrounding villages inside the old pre-1967 Green Line boundary, handles 2,000 to 3,000 patients at a main facility and ten branch clinics. It is a comprehensive medical center providing preventive as well as therapeutic care, with particular attention paid to women's special health needs. The center is not a hospital, and it does not treat medical emergencies. Only day surgery and outpatient ser-vices are provided. In addition, the center has a social service program for the homebound.

Audre and I first visited the clinic in 1984. I was interested in seeing the clinic because Arab physicians who treat primarily the Arab population of Jerusalem staff it, although it also has some Jewish patients. We met the medical director, Nafez Hamdi Nubani, a Palestinian who was trained in Egyptian medical schools. Dr. Nubani also has a master's degree in public administration from Harvard's John F. Kennedy School of Government. Audre and I were impressed with Dr. Nubani's efforts to establish a special medical program to help the people of East Jerusalem. Of particular interest to us was his discussion of the eye-care needs in the community. Based on his presentation, Audre and I decided to provide funds to equip a badly needed ophthalmology clinic for the medical center so that the Arabs of East Jerusalem can get good eye care. Instead of engaging in empty rhetoric about liking Arabs, we did something tangible. The Jerusalem Foundation has many similar projects in the Arab sectors. The foundation understands that Jew and Arab have to live together; there is no other way. We have made several visits to the clinic, and we keep in close touch with Dr. Nubani.

Day Care Center

We also provided the money for a child-care center in Jerusalem for Arab children as well as Jewish, many of whom are from Ethiopia. It is a wonderful facility. Named in memory of my mother, the Riva Rapoport Day Care Center is in the East Talpiot section of West Jerusalem. It mainly serves families in the immediate neighborhood, but it has built such a good reputation that some families come from more distant locations to place their children there. The fees are scaled according to the economic condition of the child's family.

> To see Bernard come and visit with the children in the day care center—and he does it on every occasion that he is in Israel—is to see a magical transformation in his personality. At one moment he is a big businessman, and the next he is relating to small children in the most warm and wondrous way. I can't relate to and play with children as warmly and with such expression as he does. It is quite outstanding. — *Teddy Kollek*

> Bernie has a wonderful time at the day care center. These children sit in his lap and he holds their hands and gives them hugs, and there is much laughter and singing. It is an emotionally rewarding thing to witness. — *Ruth Cheshin*

The Riva Rapoport Day Care Center, Jerusalem. CN 10482, Rapoport (Bernard) Photograph Collection, Center for American History, The University of Texas at Austin.

I was with him when he visited for the first time a day care center for infants that he was supporting financially. There were three rooms crammed with cribs of crying babies. If you know B Rapoport, you can picture the tears that were coming down his eyes when he saw how crowded the day care center was.

He immediately said, "Build another room, it's too crowded here. Send me the bill." —*Morty Bahr*

During our visit to Israel near the end of 1996, Teddy Kollek took Audre and me and our grandchildren on a tour of Jerusalem's new Biblical Zoo, which is on a beautifully landscaped site at the western edge of the city. This zoo features the animals that are discussed in the bible story about Noah's Ark and the Great Flood. I knew Teddy had hopes of persuading me to make a contribution to the zoo, but I did not find the idea appealing. I've never been interested in zoos. Our granddaughters wanted to go, however, so that was sufficient reason for me to go.

As Audre and I were walking around the grounds of the zoo, the first thing we noticed was that the place was full of Jewish and Arab children. There were hundreds of them. They weren't in separate groups; they were intermingling and putting their arms around each other and laughing and enjoying the animals. It made me once again realize that children every-where seem to want to love each other, while adults seem to want to hate each other. I could see that this zoo was an important place for these chil-dren to meet and to have fun together and to know each other. In addition, our grandchildren loved it. I suddenly became interested in zoos. As Teddy had calculated, Audre and I were hooked.

If Teddy really wants something and really pushes it, that usually is the decisive factor in our decision to give money. That's how much we respect him. —*Audre Rapoport*

Audre and I donated $1 million to support the building of an information center with a theater and a restaurant. I was so impressed by what I saw at the Jerusalem Zoo that when I returned home to Waco, I gave a major gift to our local zoo because I now understand that it can do the same thing the Jerusalem Zoo does. It can bring children from different races and ethnic groups together, and it can help unify our community.

Bernie Rapoport was troubled by the thought that the Arab community in Jerusalem was not being helped as much as the Jewish community. His was a strong voice in support of our projects in East Jerusalem. Bernie's first interest was in helping the children. He was very involved in our effort to establish day care centers and preschool programs, and he always made certain that these programs were for Arab as well as Jewish kids. Bernie always wants his money to go toward some tangible project or program that made a real difference in people's lives. He is not interested in symbolism or token actions, it is real results that he cares about. He chose the day care centers and the eye-care clinic because he realized that those were areas where help was really needed. —*Ruth Cheshin*

Awards and honors are nice to receive, but Audre and I have never sought that type of recognition. We get our satisfaction from seeing the results of our philanthropy. Nevertheless, both of us were deeply touched and honored in November 1994 when we were given one of the most wonderful awards we have ever received. The Jerusalem City Council bestowed its Ne'eman Yerushalyaim award on us, which made us honorary fellows of the city of Jerusalem, the highest honor Jerusalem can give to a nonresident of Israel. Ever since we first saw Jerusalem, Audre and I have felt a special bond with the city. As honorary fellows of the city, that bond is even more special.

Bernie is not a person who will write a check and disappear. He gets involved directly and maintains an interest, telephoning and writing letters and paying personal visits. I consider him to be a great personal friend, not just a donor to the foundation. He is one of us, no question about it. —*Ruth Cheshin*

I am in favor of a Palestinian authority, and I support Israel's relinquishing of the West Bank and the Gaza Strip to the Palestinians. I have a reflexive response whenever questions arise about Israeli policy. My initial feeling is that Israel is always right, but I have always been opposed to the building of Jewish settlements on the West Bank. Those settlements have a political rather than a social purpose, they are unnecessary, and they stir up resentment and hatred. They are rooted in the old Orthodox belief that God meant for the Jews to inhabit all of that land. God never shared that information with me, however. Although Israel is small, the Israelis do have enough land. They don't need to settle the West Bank. Israel has a lot of open land in the Negev that can be developed. The bottom line is that we have to have peace, and we all, Jews and Arabs, have to pay the price for it. If that means no settlements on the West Bank for Jews, then so be it. The problem with the Palestinians taking back the West Bank is that I don't know how they are going to finance it or how they are going to develop an economy.

I do have worries about returning the Golan Heights to Syria. The topographical aspects bother me, because it is extremely difficult to defend the Israeli land below the Golan if a hostile force attacks from there. The Syrian

B and the Israeli prime minister Yitzhak Rabin in Israel. CN 10757,
Rapoport (Bernard) Photograph Collection, Center for American
History, The University of Texas at Austin.

government is irresponsible, and I have grave fears about the threat it poses. I have been reassured somewhat by Teddy Kollek and many others in Israel that modern technology makes it simple for the Israeli army to monitor the Golan Heights. Modern weaponry also makes the Heights a much less formidable military post than it was thirty years ago.

I try to be neutral in the matter of Israeli politics. My strong sympathies have always been with the Labor Party, but I have been scrupulous about staying out of the politics of that country. We are all Jews, and I have a sense of solidarity with all Israelis no matter what their political affiliation. I have to admit, however, that former prime minister Benjamin Netanyahu severely tested my policy of strict neutrality. Netanyahu reminds me of an Israeli Jesse Helms. He did grave damage to the effort to get peace established between Jew and Muslim in the Middle East.

The election of Ehud Barak in May 1999 was an answered prayer. Netanyahu's strategy of building political support on a base of hatred for the Arabs and resentment of the old elite of Jews of European descent fell apart. I believed at the time that Barak's victory was a clear mandate for his government to continue the peace process initiated by the late Yitzhak Rabin. Barak is a tough former Israeli army general. I had confidence in his ability eventually to make a peace agreement that would not endanger Israel.

I was optimistic about the prospects for peace if the Barak government had been allowed to continue its efforts. It is difficult to maintain that optimism now that the religious hard-liners, led by Ariel Sharon, have come to power. As I write this, another infitada rages, and the peace process is in tatters. No one knows what the future will bring, but the peace process must be revived. There simply is no acceptable alternative to peaceful coexistence between Jew and Palestinian. I can only hope that peace returns as soon as possible.

All my life I have known that religious bigots to the left or to the right cause most of the real problems in this world. I have no empathy at all for fundamentalists, be they Jewish, Christian, or Islamic. When you become a fundamentalist, you stop thinking. I wish all religious leaders would tell their people, we believe what we believe but we are going to respect the right of others to believe what they want to believe. Why can't we do that? My beloved aunt Fania Kruger, the poet laureate of Texas, summed it all up for me when she wrote:

> If each of us be but a blade of grass,
> And touching one another, O comrade cherish
> Each neighboring blade, and let not hate enflame
> Life's field, or blade by blade, we perish.

Aunt Fania, as usual, you have said it best.

12 ▶ *A University Regent*

In November 1990 Ann Richards, one of the most dynamic human beings I have ever known, upset her heavily favored opponent, West Texas Republican businessman Clayton Williams, Jr., to become the second woman to be elected governor of Texas. Ann's exciting victory was a rare experience for me. Before her election, I had been active in twelve gubernatorial campaigns in Texas, beginning with Homer Rainey in 1946. With the exception of Mark White in 1982, the candidates I backed lost every election, sometimes by huge margins. It was disappointing and sometimes discouraging to be on the losing end of so many elections, but I was never tempted to take the politically expedient (and cynical) option of supporting only those candidates who were favored to win. The people I back for public office have to share my views on a majority of the issues of relevance to our society.

I had known Ann Richards for many years before her exhilarating victory in 1990. As a homemaker, first in Dallas and later in Austin, she had long been a grassroots activist and organizer for the liberal wing of the Democratic Party. In the late 1970s Ann was elected county commissioner in Travis County (Austin is the county seat), and she took a leadership role in the party, especially on behalf of women's rights. It was during that period that I got to know and like Ann. As was the case so many other times in my life, it was John Henry and Liz Faulk who made me realize that Ann was someone who deserved my encouragement and support in her political activities. I soon became one of Ann's most devoted fans.

In 1982 Ann was elected state treasurer of Texas, an office that she modernized and made more effective. It was as state treasurer that Ann first won national recognition as a rising political star. Her sensational keynote address at the 1988 Democratic National Convention made her a national celebrity and launched her on the road to higher public office. When she announced her candidacy for governor of Texas, I was among the first to pledge support.

Governor Ann Richards with B. CN 10491, Rapoport (Bernard) Photograph Collection, Center for American History, The University of Texas at Austin.

Ann's victory over Clayton Williams was an exciting event for me personally, because she was the first person to be elected governor of Texas with whom I had had a longtime friendship. Because I had been a key fundraiser for Ann, some of my friends asked me soon after the election if I had any interest in an appointment to one of the state commissions or boards. During the campaign, I had given no thought to any type of appointment. Some state commissions, such as the Parks and Wildlife Commission and the highway commission, have much prestige, and people lobby hard to get appointed to them. I have had a keen interest in seeing that good people are selected for service on state commissions and boards, but I have never had personal ambitions for any of those positions. The only board I had any interest in being appointed to was the University of Texas System Board of Regents. That stemmed from my desire to give something substantive and meaningful back to an institution that had done much for me and that is critical to the well-being of our state.

To be honest, until 1991 I saw the university as divided into two antithetical components, one that I loved and one that I disliked. The component I disliked was made up of the regents and the higher levels of the administration, which in my mind represented the conservative political establishment. The other component, the one I loved, consisted of the faculty and students.

I had a low opinion of most of the people who were on the board of regents from 1944 until 1991 because I thought most of them were reactionary old fogies who did not care about education. I felt that way because of what had happened to Homer Rainey. But when I became a regent and saw first-hand the complex and difficult problems that the regents have to confront, my thinking changed. That's not to say that I unfairly judged everyone who had served on the board since 1944. Let me be frank about this: the men who fired Homer Rainey were mean-spirited reactionaries, and some of their successors were almost as bad. I discovered, however, that some of the later regents were good people with the best of intentions who, in grappling with some complicated issues, tried to do what was right for the university.

The point is that I was so disgusted with what happened to Homer Rainey that I did not pay much attention to that bad component of the university for many years afterward. I even refused to join the Ex-Students Association, which I saw as an arm of the conservative political establishment. I had nothing to do with the university's executive administration until I joined the board. I never attended a commencement ceremony, and I didn't know the president or the chancellor.

I had radically different feelings, however, about the university's faculty. Without my education at the University of Texas, I probably would have spent my working life behind a jewelry counter. No one who succeeds in life is so good that he or she can do it alone. My teachers at the university made me dig deep down into myself to discover talent I didn't know I had. Ever since I left the university, I had hoped for an opportunity to help pay back my debt to the faculty.

I was fortunate enough in business to be in a position eventually to donate some money. My earliest financial contributions were two endowments in economics and three in liberal arts. One of the economics endowments is in honor of my mentor, Professor Edward Everett Hale, and one of the liberal arts endowments is named for Ralph Yarborough. The university honored Audre and me by naming one of the chairs in the economics department the Audre and Bernard Rapoport Centennial Chair in Economics and Public Affairs. That honor meant even more to us when the university appointed former secretary of labor Ray Marshall to the chair.

Appointment to the Board of Regents

Several days after Ann Richards's inauguration, Jane Hickie, who was helping Ann with gubernatorial appointments, called me and asked if I wanted to be appointed to any particular board or commission. I told her that the only job I wanted was to be a regent of the University of Texas

The University of Texas Board of Regents in 1991. Front row, left to right: Mario Ramirez, Louis Beecherl, Robert Cruikshank. Back row, left to right: Sam Barshop, Tex Moncrief, Ellen Temple, Bernard Rapoport, Tom Loeffler, Zan Holmes.

System. I knew that there were three vacancies on the board to be filled. I told her that if it wasn't possible to appoint me to the board of regents, I would understand, but I didn't want anything else. Jane asked if I would consider an appointment to the Coordinating Board for Higher Education. I told her that I wasn't interested in the Coordinating Board, so she said that she would call me back.

A few days later I learned that the governor had appointed Ellen Temple, a civic and cultural leader from east Texas, to the board of regents, so I assumed that the three new regents had already been selected. Jane called me again and started talking about some state commission or board. I interrupted her and said, "Jane, I'm not going to fall out with Ann if she doesn't do this, but it is the University of Texas Board of Regents or nothing at all. I don't need honorary or symbolic appointments. I already have had more accolades and honors bestowed on me than I deserve. What I want is a real job, something that will actually put me to work."

A few days after that, on February 1, 1991, Governor Richards appointed me to the university's board of regents, along with the Reverend Zan

Holmes of Dallas, who was the first African American ever appointed to the board.

Holmes, Temple, and I joined a board dominated by six appointees of former Republican governor William Clements: Louis Beecherl, Sam Barshop, Tex Moncrief, Tom Loeffler, Robert Cruikshank, and Mario Ramirez. Some of them are as active in the Republican Party as I am in the Democratic, so I feared that some partisan tensions might surface during our meetings. As we began that first meeting, I wondered how well we were going to work together. It took me about five minutes to learn that political partisanship had no place with these individuals in their work as regents. In fact, during my entire six-year tenure as a regent, no board member ever let personal political affiliation dictate decisions with respect to the university's affairs. That is the way that board must work. It is to the credit of all with whom I have served that no one ever wavered in recognizing that service came first. I don't think it is possible to get people who are more committed to the university than those who served on the board with me.

> B and I talked daily, and frequently twice a day, during his term as chairman. He examined all of my recommendations through only one screen: what was best for the University of Texas System and, particularly, what was best for our current and future students. Politics, politicians, and his own company were never given any consideration in the decisions that he made as chairman of the board of regents. — *William H. Cunningham, University of Texas chancellor*

Louis Beecherl, an independent oilman from Dallas, was the chairman the first two years I was on the board. He is one of the finest people I have ever known. Bob Cruikshank, an honorable man whose background is in finance, headed up the board's asset management committee. Tom Loeffler, who played football for the university during the Darrell Royal days, is a former Republican congressman. I jokingly tell Tom Loeffler that I didn't know there was such a thing as a nice Republican until I met him. Mario Ramirez, a physician from the Rio Grande Valley, is dedicated to improving the quality of life in his region. Tex Moncrief is an independent oilman from Fort Worth. Whatever is at the back of Tex's head comes out the front of his mouth, and I really like that. The sixth regent was Sam Barshop of San Antonio, the founder of the chain of La Quinta Motor Inns. Sam is an independent person who calls his own shots. Sam was a Clements appointee, but when Clements asked him to vote a certain way when a particular matter came before the board, Sam didn't feel that it was in the best interest of the university, so he did not do it. He is a dedicated and hardworking Republican, but he felt as I do, that the governor should not dictate university policy through the board of regents.

Shortly after I was appointed to the board, Governor Richards recommended that I vote for Bob Cruikshank to be chairman instead of Louis Beecherl, who is more conservative politically. She explained that Cruikshank might be a more moderate, open-minded chairman. I wasn't offended by her request, because the person who serves as chair of the board is a proper concern of the governor's. I joined with Temple and Holmes in support of Cruikshank, but Louis Beecherl won. I would have had a hard time opposing Louis after I got to know him.

With the exception of the vote on who should serve as board chairman, Governor Richards never tried to influence my decisions. In fact, I had very few conversations with her during the four years she was governor. On those rare occasions when we did speak, I sensed that Governor Richards was a little concerned that the UT System was spending too much money. I didn't agree with her. I don't believe she ever understood the economic realities of building a first-class university system of national rank.

When I came on the board, Hans Mark was chancellor. Mark did an outstanding job of upgrading the scientific and engineering programs of the university. About a year after I became a regent, Mark announced his retirement. He had an intuitive sense that it was time to turn the job over to someone else. His decision came as a shock to the other regents and me. There was no pressure from anyone on the board for him to retire. One of the things that impressed me about Mark was that even though he remained a presence on the Austin campus as a faculty member, after he retired as chancellor he did not try to meddle in the business of his successor. That is an unusual trait.

A New Chancellor and a New President

In 1992 Hans Mark was succeeded by the president of UT-Austin, William H. Cunningham. Bill has a public relations background, and he is business oriented. As far as I was concerned, there were no other serious contenders for the job. If we had searched the world over, we could not have found anyone better suited to be chancellor than Cunningham. He was the right person for the times. Bill is a pragmatic, real-world man whose strong business sense was a huge asset and a major reason the university's budget did so well despite an era of tight state budgets. He was able to get things done because he's ambitious, competitive, energetic, and impatient.

He worked extremely hard, he put in long hours on the job, and he was liked and respected by lawmakers of all political persuasions. Cunningham was utterly dedicated to improving and expanding minority recruitment at the administrative, faculty, and student levels for the entire UT System.

> B and I bonded almost instantly after he became a member of the board. While I am perceived to be conservative and he is perceived to be liberal, we agreed that the future of Texas is directly related to the state's ability to provide a high-quality system of higher education to all of the state's citizens. B was as close to me as a father could ever be to an adopted son. We almost always came to the same solutions regarding the major higher educational issues of the day. On the occasions when we disagreed, I always knew that he wanted me to tell him exactly how I felt. If I was unable to convince him of the logic of my argument, we did it his way. He was the chairman, and he had the right and the obligation to make the final call.
> — *William H. Cunningham*

The board's decision to elevate Cunningham to the chancellor's office was easily made and totally expected. His promotion, however, meant that we now had to find a new president for UT-Austin. That did not turn out as I had expected.

After an exhaustive search and screening process by the appropriate university committees, the board was presented with a list of several well-qualified candidates. At the end of the search process, the board met to interview the finalists and to make an appointment. Mark Yudof, the dean of the UT-Austin law school, was among the finalists. Yudof is a gifted administrator and a great educator. As we began our interviews, Yudof was my firm choice for the job, and it seemed that he had the unwavering support of a majority of my board colleagues as well as that of the chancellor.

Yudof's closest competitor was Robert Berdahl, a historian who was serving as the provost at the University of Illinois. Eloquent, perceptive, and thoughtful, Berdahl made a good impression on everyone during his interview with the board. I knew that three or four of my fellow regents were strongly inclined to vote for him, but it was my understanding that Yudof still had enough votes to get the appointment. Yudof, however, made one mistake during his interview. Actually, it wasn't a mistake as much as it was a statement that was simply misinterpreted. Mario Ramirez asked Yudof if, as president, he would visit south Texas often to promote educational opportunities for Mexican Americans at the university. Yudof, being the honest guy that he is, said that he did not know if he would have the time to do things like that personally. That answer upset Ramirez, who apparently interpreted Yudof's answer as proof of his insensitivity toward south Texas and Hispanic Texans. At the time, I didn't realize how much Yudof had upset Ramirez. When we began the board meeting, I was certain that Yudof still had the votes. Ramirez, however, switched his vote, which made the count five to four in Berdahl's favor. I was shocked, but no one was more shocked than Mark Yudof was.

Bob Berdahl is a man of rare quality who made an excellent president. I think it was good for the university to have a historian as president. It gave us a different perspective. Berdahl demonstrated his brilliance and astuteness as an administrator as well as his personal self-confidence by making Yudof his provost. Bob did such an outstanding job that he was practically kidnapped in 1997 by the trustees of the University of California to be president of their Berkeley campus. Although I was pleased with Bob's performance as president and I hated to see him leave, I was extremely disappointed when he criticized Chancellor Cunningham at his last press conference as president. Bob claimed that Bill Cunningham had meddled in the day-to-day management of the Austin campus and interfered with other administrative activities that were the prerogative of the UT-Austin president. I disagree with Bob on that subject, but he has a right to his opinion. What I disliked was Bob's public criticism of the chancellor as he was departing for California. It was a cheap and ungrateful shot against the University of Texas System, which had given him such a great opportunity by appointing him president.

One of the sad ironies of recent university history is that Mark Yudof, who most probably would have succeeded Berdahl as president, accepted the presidency of the University of Minnesota a few weeks before California hired Berdahl. Our loss was Minnesota's gain.

The South Texas–Border Initiative

The most substantive issue I faced as a regent was the University of Texas System's relationship with the people of south Texas, most of whom are Mexican Americans. South Texas is the region of the state with the lowest per capita income. Some of our counties along the border with Mexico are among the poorest in the United States. Plagued by inadequate health services, poor public schools, and low incomes, some neighborhoods in south Texas have living conditions more characteristic of the Third World than of an advanced technological society such as the United States. The embarrassing historical truth is that the region has been terribly neglected by both the public and private sectors of Texas.

As I have stated many times, I view education as the drawbridge that offers an escape from poverty. I fervently believe that the regents of the university must make education available to every person who wants an education, and that is especially true in south Texas. That is why I vigorously supported a program Bill Cunningham conceived and drafted that became known as the South Texas–Border Initiative. One of Cunningham's primary goals when he became chancellor was to put in place a new UT System program to improve the quality of and access to higher education in south Texas. Bob Bullock, who at the time was the lieutenant governor and a powerful figure in Texas state government, also urged the UT System to take a leadership role in such an effort. The problem was how to pay for a costly new initiative when the State Legislature was continuing to reduce its financial support for higher education. Cunningham came up with the idea of financing the program with tuition revenue bonds, which used tuition income as collateral to back bonds bought by investors. Although tuition bonds had been used in the 1970s to build UT–San Antonio, they had not been used that often as a financing vehicle. I thought Cunningham's plan was masterful, and I worked hard to get it approved in the Legislature.

The basic goal of the South Texas Initiative is to make quality higher education available to tens of thousands of young people in the Rio Grande Valley and in San Antonio. The thinking behind the initiative is that Hispanics in south Texas need to be able to enter professions such as engineering and that they need access to training for high-tech jobs, especially in the computer industry. The South Texas Initiative was made possible by the passage of a legislative act in 1993 that provided more than $300 million in new higher education resources for those previously underserved areas of the state. One product of this funding is a new engineering school at UT–Pan American in Edinburg. Another vitally needed part of the South Texas Initiative was approved in 1995, this time for the enhancement and expansion of health education programs, including new medical residencies that will increase the number of physicians practicing in south Texas. These are investments of historic proportions in the future of Texas, for the entire state, not merely one region.

In San Antonio, the main UT campus is north of the heart of the city, a long distance from the areas where the less affluent people live, especially the Mexican Americans who live on the West Side. I have always believed in one-bus-stop education. Every youngster who lives on the West Side of San Antonio should be no more than one bus stop from a UT campus for higher learning. So we developed an adjunct campus in downtown San Antonio.

The San Antonio downtown campus may be the most effective part of our South Texas Initiative. The new campus is designed to make a lasting contribution to the renaissance of a section of San Antonio's central business district. More important, however, is the future that campus can offer to thousands of students who otherwise might not have had the opportunity to realize their dreams of seeking college degrees.

To me the South Texas Initiative is the most important general program the board started during my tenure. It is a positive, realistic type of affirmative action, not in words but in deeds. I think the initiative has demonstrated that the University of Texas is committed to helping that area of the state in meaningful and substantive ways.

Chairman of the Board

In February 1993 three new regents appointed by Governor Richards joined the board, Austin businessman Lowell Lebermann, Houston financier Peter Conway, and Austin attorney Martha Smiley. Conway soon determined that he had an investment situation that could be interpreted as a conflict of interest, so he resigned. Governor Richards appointed Thomas Hicks of Dallas, another financier, to replace Conway. I agreed to serve as the new chairman of the board. I must admit that when I accepted the chairmanship, I had no sense of how much of my time it would take. I could easily have made it a full-time job. Considering the amount of time I did devote to the chairmanship, my colleagues at American Income sometimes felt as though it was full-time.

It was a great personal honor for me to be elected chairman of the board of regents. In 1995, however, I received an even greater honor. My colleagues on the board elected me to a second two-year term. Historically, chairmen of the board of regents usually serve a single two-year term. Joining the small group of individuals who have been so honored was one of the highlights of my public life.

The Freeport-McMoRan Controversy

On June 1, 2000, Bill Cunningham left his position as chancellor to return to teaching. I think he was an outstanding chancellor. That is why it was so unfortunate that he had to spend much of his time and energy while I was board chairman dealing with an unpleasant and, I believe, unnecessary controversy about his relationship with prominent UT-Austin graduate Jim Bob Moffett, chairman of the Freeport-McMoRan company in New Orleans.

Moffett and his wife, Louise, have been generous donors and have promoted the university's welfare in significant ways. They provided a substantial portion of the money for a badly needed molecular biology building on the Austin campus, and they have established student scholarships and research endowments in natural sciences, law, business, engineering, computer sciences, architecture, and men's and women's athletics. They have also provided grants for basic research in the Department of Geological Sciences.

Nonetheless, Jim Bob Moffett is not a popular man in the city of Austin. Several years ago, his company acquired a property that John Connally and Ben Barnes had developed in the Barton Creek watershed in the hills west of Austin. Moffett turned the place into an expensive resort with a golf course and other upscale amenities. Unfortunately, Moffett's development and the sites for others nearby are in environmentally sensitive areas, the most significant features being Barton Creek and the aquifer that feeds beautiful Barton Springs swimming pool. Barton Springs has become a mystical place in the minds of some Austinites. To others, it is simply a wonderful place to go swimming and to get a cool break from the insufferable heat that besets Austin from May until October. Despite Moffett's having put in place costly pollution controls to protect Barton Springs, environmentalists claim that the controls are inadequate and that future development will destroy the springs. As a result, lawsuits were filed and fought, special referendums held, and a general state of impasse existed between Moffett and environmentalists.

In addition, Moffett's company, Freeport-McMoRan, has extensive mining operations and other interests in Indonesia and its territories. Those operations have generated much controversy, both from environmentalists who charge Freeport-McMoRan with raping the Indonesian landscape and from human rights activists who charge that the company is involved in the suppression and exploitation of the indigenous people in the territories occupied by Indonesia.

I'm not in a position to make a judgment one way or the other about Moffett and Barton Creek or Freeport-McMoRan and Indonesia. My interest in the affair stemmed from Bill Cunningham's position on the board of directors of Freeport-McMoRan and from his friendship with Jim Bob Moffett. That was enough to generate criticism of Cunningham by Austin's anti–Freeport-McMoRan gang, but the criticism was relatively minor compared to the firestorm that occurred after the board of regents agreed to name the new molecular biology building after the Moffetts. All hell broke loose. UT-Austin faculty leaders denounced Cunningham, and several student organizations went berserk. Of course, my favorite news journal, *The Texas Observer*, did what it could to stir up the pot.

> **When Rapoport went on the board of regents he suddenly became the establishment. Here was a man who had always been an outsider, a man who visualized himself as a revolutionary, and his life undergoes this transformation from the leader of the left to a defender of the Jim Bob Moffett deal.** —*Ben Barnes*

The critics charged that Cunningham's service as a Freeport-McMoRan director was a conflict of interest. I strongly disagreed, and I made certain that the press knew it. One way that ethical problems such as conflicts of interest arise is when a public official's various private business relationships are unknown to the public. That was never the case with Cunningham. His financial disclosure statements filed with the Texas Ethics Commission have always been complete, accurate, and in full compliance with the law.

Obviously, disclosure does not in itself eliminate all potential conflicts of interest. One must also avoid involvement in any decisions in which business relationships may conflict. Cunningham scrupulously adhered to that principle. He never had a financial interest in Freeport's relationships with the university, and his ability to carry out his official duties was never impaired by any of his business relationships, including his service on the Freeport board.

Some of the faculty charged that Freeport stood to gain financially from the results of the geological research that the company funded. Such a result would have been highly unlikely. The project allowed faculty and students to explore a remote region of the world that had never been studied in detail. It involved basic research, not applied research. The faculty and students were free to publish their research without any interference or prepublication approval from Freeport. The company employs its own scientists to conduct applied research, such as prospecting for minerals. Cunningham did not initiate or participate in the negotiations for the research contract. Faculty members and administrators in the Department of Geological Sciences and the College of Natural Sciences negotiated the agreement. The office of the executive vice president and provost reviewed and approved the contract. All the paperwork associated with the research contract bears this out, and those documents are part of the public record. Far from interfering with his public duties, Cunningham's association with Freeport and Jim Bob Moffett furthered his ability to fulfill a primary responsibility of any president or chancellor: securing private-sector support for academic programs and facilities and other critical needs.

Despite official explanations and clarifications, the controversy became a major distraction for the university administration, both at the system level and on the Austin campus. The situation reached a critical stage when Moffett threatened to sue several UT-Austin faculty members for statements they had made against him and his company. Suddenly the controversy jumped up a notch, with issues of freedom of speech and teaching looming over us all. At that point, I feared this affair was becoming a threat to the university's good health, and I encouraged Cunningham to resign from the Freeport-McMoRan board. I told him, however, that it was his decision and that I would back him no matter what he decided. Regardless of financial sacrifice, and it was a significant one, Cunningham rose to the occasion. He chose the university over personal gain, and that's the kind of man he is.

> The decision to resign from the Freeport board was very difficult for me for two reasons. First, I felt and continue to feel that Freeport not only had done nothing wrong in Indonesia or Austin, but, in reality, the company made very positive economic and social contributions to both Austin and Indonesia. Second, I believed that Jim Bob Moffett was being unfairly attacked by people who were willing to abuse the media and distort the truth. I am a very loyal person, and to be perceived as cutting and running from a friend who was in need was very difficult for me. However, both Jim Bob and B felt that it was appropriate for me to resign from the Freeport board. Reluctantly, I came to the same conclusion. It became clear to me that my resignation would be in the best interest of all concerned. — *William H. Cunningham*

I dealt almost daily with Bill Cunningham for six years, and I saw the totality of his commitment to the UT System evidenced in his every word and action. On a personal basis, I regret that so much attention and time had to be given to the Moffett affair. It was a waste because, based on my firsthand knowledge, there was no problem. Everyone's time would have been better spent dealing with substantive issues.

Funding the University

The most surprising thing to me about being a regent was the board's huge financial responsibility. Money dominated every discussion on the board. I had no idea it would be like that, but the UT System, which has 150,000 students, is in fact the largest entity in Texas state government.

It manages 2.2 million acres of land and a $4.5 billion budget, with approximately $1.8 billion allocated from state tax dollars. Every working day, the investment staff invests approximately $12 billion. With 69,000 employees, the UT System is the fifth-largest employer in Texas. In other words, the UT System is an enormously complex institution from an administrative and fiscal standpoint.

Years ago, my friend Ronnie Dugger argued in his book *Our Invaded Universities* that major universities should have ordinary working-class citizens and students on their governing boards. I agreed with him until I actually served on the board of regents. Now I know that ordinary citizens off the street cannot run a major, complex, multimillion-dollar operation like the University of Texas System. I have to tell you that the faculty can't run the University of Texas either. The average faculty member isn't equipped in terms of training, background, experience, and mind-set to handle university administration. That's why great scholars rarely make good administrators.

Students certainly are out of their league when it comes to membership on a university governing board. I make that statement fully knowing that it will not convince any twenty-one-year-old student. When I graduated from the university at the age of twenty-one, I was the smartest person that ever lived. Anyone who was around me for about twenty minutes would realize that I knew I was a genius. It takes several years and a ton of experience to learn the difference between knowledge and wisdom. I told one of the students who asked me to support having a student member on the board of regents that I opposed the idea. When he asked why, I replied that if a kid gets exposed to all of the problems we have to deal with as regents, that kid will become conservative much too young. I don't want that to happen.

The most frustrating problem I faced as a regent was that we did not have the level of funding we needed to make the breakthroughs to excellence that I think are possible. It is widely believed that the UT System is wealthy and has all of the money it needs to fulfill its diverse missions. That is a myth. In each legislative session from the mid-1980s through 1997 the State Legislature gradually cut back state support. Only in the 1999 session did appropriations increase. While I was on the board, the budget for the entire system had to be reduced because of a drop in investment income. We tightened our belts wherever we could. We did not use any Permanent University Fund money for new projects (the PUF is the university's endowment largely generated by oil revenue on university-owned land). We forged partnerships to get things done at little expense to the university.

Although we were fiscally responsible, we could never save enough money to meet the needs of higher education in a state that is growing and changing as rapidly as Texas. The salaries paid to most of our university employees are shamefully low. We need money to hire additional full-time faculty to teach all of the disciplines and fields at every one of our schools. We should be doing much more research. Additional facilities are needed, and we desperately need more money for libraries and electronic resources. There is so much that we could do, but the money isn't there.

That is why I am in favor of charging higher tuition at the University of Texas. That is a radical change in outlook for me. For many years, I spoke out against any raise in tuition at UT-Austin. A few days after my appointment to the board, I told the *Daily Texan,* UT-Austin's student newspaper, that it was my opinion that tuition should be eliminated or at least lowered in cost. I quickly learned how hopelessly uninformed I was on that subject.

Bob Berdahl noted while he was UT-Austin president that cheap tuition in today's economic environment leads to a cheap education. I now agree with him. Unfortunately, it takes a tremendous amount of money to educate a student in higher education today, and the legislative source of financial support is getting smaller and smaller. One of the only options we have for making up the loss in state support is to charge higher tuition. Raising tuition, however, will also require those of us with financial means to contribute to and help increase the size of our scholarship and loan programs. I am pleased that we implemented a system that allows us to redistribute our tuition revenue to subsidize the tuition of truly needy academically qualified students. I don't want any qualified student to be prevented from attending UT-Austin because he or she can't afford the tuition.

The Legislature is not anti–higher education or even anti–University of Texas. The problem is the antiquated tax system in Texas and the selfish attitude of some politically powerful conservatives who resent having to pay a dime in support of public programs. With no state income tax, Texas will always struggle to pay its bills, because other tax options such as the sales tax and the property tax are stretched to the limit. We need a change in public attitude as well. It seems that the only spending the general public will support is to build new prisons and highways. The constituents for those costly programs are so politically powerful that legislators who vote against them place their reelection in jeopardy.

Although the Texas Legislature has not been as supportive of higher education as I think it should, that doesn't mean that we didn't get the appropriate information about our fiscal problems in front of its leadership. As chairman of the board of regents, legislative relations was one of my most important duties. Because of my years of political activism in Texas, it was a job for which I was well prepared. I had an excellent working relationship

*B testifying in support of the UT System at a legislative hearing.
CN 10820, Rapoport (Bernard) Photograph Collection, Center for
American History, The University of Texas at Austin.*

with Lieutenant Governor Bob Bullock, Speaker of the House Pete Laney,
and the key committee chairpersons. I had a wonderful relationship with
state senator John Montford of Lubbock, who served as chairman of the
Senate Finance Committee during the years I was a regent. These and other
personal political relationships were extremely helpful to me in my efforts
on behalf of the university budget. When I called my friends in the Legislature on the telephone, they usually returned my call that day. I would have

my chance to talk to them, and they would listen and then do what they perceived to be right. They knew that I didn't need anything for myself; I was making a case for the university. Now, if John Doe came into a legislator's office, they would wonder if John Doe was trying to get them to do something that would help John Doe's business. Knowing me, they understood that I had nothing personal to gain. They knew that I was fighting for 150,000 kids.

Football and the University

What is going on in so-called amateur athletics today is a farce; too much money is spent on athletics. I love sports, but we should not get lost in this sport frenzy. We must remember that the university's real mission is to educate young people. If I had my way, universities wouldn't have major athletic programs. My model for athletics at a university is the Ivy League, where all the participants are truly amateur student-athletes.

Unfortunately, my views on the subject of collegiate athletics seem to place me in the extreme minority in this country. Currently, the boosters of big-time college football and basketball at most of the large state universities are too powerful for any group of college administrators or regents to fight. That was a lesson I learned as regents chairman when I had to deal with two controversies related to athletics. One was the decision to expand UT-Austin's football stadium, and the other was an initiative hatched in the State Legislature.

If I had never been on the board of regents it is likely that I would have opposed the plan to expand the football stadium at a cost of about $100 million. I really did not like the proposal. Bob Berdahl shared my feeling about that. He commented to me that spending $100 million for a facility that is used six days a year was absurd. But I learned as a regent that once you are in a position of power, you have responsibilities that must transcend your personal proclivities. When I became chairman and the expansion issue came up, an influential and powerful group of UT ex-students made it clear that they were very much in favor of it. Even though it went against my grain, I could see that much of the enthusiasm for higher education in Texas comes from people whose first concern is athletics. My guess is that the situation is the same in many other states, especially in the Midwest and the South. When I learned that most of the money for the expansion project would come from people who would not otherwise contribute to the university, I decided to go along with the proposal. I didn't feel prostituted by my agreement. I felt that the plan would not take anything away from the university.

UT faculty member and former member of Congress Barbara Jordan with B at a
UT-Austin women's basketball game. CN 10496, Rapoport (Bernard) Photograph
Collection, Center for American History, The University of Texas at Austin.

> While B never cared much about intercollegiate athletics,
> he realized that it brings many constituencies of the univer-
> sity together. Once he realized what intercollegiate athletics
> could do for the university, the university never had a more
> ardent supporter in the stands. We attended many in-town and
> out-of-town football games together. —*William H. Cunningham*

The second controversy about the proper place of athletics in college
occurred during the 1997 session of the Texas Legislature. Ron Wilson, a
Democratic state representative from Houston, filed a bill to require scholarship athletes at the state's public colleges and universities to achieve academic standards equal to the average of the rest of their class. When he filed
the bill, Wilson told the press that he was tired of watching athletes raise
the visibility and financial base of a school while no one seemed concerned

about their education. After that bill died, Wilson got another one through that required state schools to admit all students based on the same criteria used for scholarship athletes. Royce West of Dallas sponsored Wilson's bill in the Senate.

I could have supported the Wilson-West bill if they had written it to apply only if all of the other schools in UT-Austin's conference, the Big Twelve, followed suit. I would have led the fight for that bill. But if Wilson's bill had passed as written, it would have put the university at a tremendous disadvantage. The Wilson-West bill would have created conditions that would have kept us from competing in the Big Twelve. We would have to leave the conference. I believe that membership in the Big Twelve is a positive thing for the university. Leaving the Big Twelve would not suit most of the people who support the university and who are interested in it. The University of Texas System gave me information indicating that if the University of Texas at Austin left the Big Twelve, it would lose an estimated $16 million annually in football and basketball revenue and that the economic losses across the state would total $100 million. I wrote a letter criticizing the Wilson-West bill that was distributed to every member of the Legislature. I thought Ron Wilson's whole effort was political grandstanding. Royce West is a good friend of mine, and I think he is an outstanding member of the Texas Senate. But their bill made no sense as it was written. No one can expect the University of Texas to change the national problem with collegiate athletics by itself; we have to get everyone else in the country onboard.

The Open Meetings Controversy

My six years on the board of regents changed my perspective on a couple of other issues, most notably the open-meetings laws that most states have passed to govern the deliberations of public boards and commissions. Texas has one of the strictest open meetings laws in the United States. Before I became a regent, I thought the law was perfect as written. I was among its most ardent supporters when it was proposed in the Legislature. Later, as a member of a public board, I soon learned that the issue is far more complex than I had thought. My case was a classic example of the do-gooder who crusades for some cause without fully understanding or appreciating all of the ramifications.

In August 1996 the *Austin American-Statesman* launched an editorial campaign accusing the University of Texas Board of Regents of violating the spirit and the letter of the Texas open meetings law. The Austin newspaper, which is part of the Cox newspaper chain, published charges made by open government advocates that the regents were deciding important issues in advance of official meetings. The example cited was a meeting during which we made sweeping changes in the UT System's student admissions policies. The newspaper reported that before we accepted the policies in a unanimous vote, we held no discussion, asked no questions, and made no comments, despite the potentially controversial nature of the changes. We also passed a $4.5 billion budget without discussion. It was obvious to our critics that we had discussed the issues among ourselves in some manner or at some place away from public view.

Those votes occur without question or comment because the individual regents work hard to be as informed as possible about matters long before they come before the board. The chancellor's staff and the board secretary prepared most of the items on the agenda for board meetings many weeks prior to the meetings. During that process, the chancellor sent to each member a letter describing a specific policy that the UT System administration was planning to submit to the board at a future meeting. The letter included a ballot that each regent marked and returned to the chancellor indicating whether he or she supported the proposed policy. In addition, the chancellor and his staff presented background information to the board during executive briefing sessions.

The Texas open meetings law prohibits discussion about policy matters between members of a public board during closed or executive session meetings. Accordingly, while I was on the board, the regents were careful to avoid such discussions during the executive briefing sessions. We could and did ask the staff questions about the information they were presenting to us, but if it ever seemed to our general counsel Ray Farrabee that we were deliberating among ourselves, he would interrupt and stop the proceedings.

Because of advance notice and procedures such as the chancellor's letter and the executive briefing sessions, we always knew what topics and issues were to be considered many days before we came to the meeting. There were no surprises, so it was an unusual occasion when we had to discuss any items on the agenda.

Unequivocally, for all of my adult life, I have favored open meetings for our governing bodies. Now I wonder if our state laws have gone too far in requiring that every conceivable type of meeting conducted by government officials has to be open to the public. For example, the board's executive briefing sessions allowed each regent to address questions to the chancellor or his staff that he or she might not have been comfortable asking in a public forum. There is always the natural personal fear that one will be asking a stupid question or that the tone or content of the question will imply a prejudice or point of view contrary to the questioner's actual feelings. Playing the devil's advocate can be a useful way to examine an issue thoroughly, and these executive sessions made it easier to do that. I believe firmly that briefings are essential to a frank examination of policy issues. I would not want to see them open to the public.

I have been troubled also by another consequence of our open meetings laws. Although the university's board of regents has been blessed in recent years with outstanding members, such has not been the case with many of our city councils and public school boards. Unfortunately, open meetings requirements too often bring out the worst in some of the members of these boards and councils. Frequently these members abuse their public pulpit by vehemently expounding their singular point of view to such an extent that intelligent debate is foreclosed. Such individuals are more interested in demagoguery than in working with others to achieve the greatest good for the greatest number of citizens.

How best do we encourage cooperation and discourage demagoguery and factionalism? Would closed meetings take away the pleasure some elected officials receive from grandstanding and force them to get down to business? If the microphones and cameras were turned off and the audience was kept at a distance, would elected officials really put aside narrow differences and become more interested in forging a consensus? These are complex questions, and I can't say that I have any answers. I do know that our officials are no better or worse than we are. It is up to us to vote people out of office when they use open meetings as an opportunity to demagogue. So, no matter how much the system is abused, open meetings are essential elements of a democracy. I can't accept the idea of routinely closed meetings for our public officials. The public's right to know is one of the most important of all rights. The problem is how to protect the public's right to know without placing so many restrictions on our public officials that it makes it almost impossible for them to get the information they need to make decisions.

The Hopwood Case and Affirmative Action

Much has been written and spoken for and against the controversial public policy known as affirmative action. The philosophy has its origins in the civil rights movement of the 1960s, when President Johnson sought a method to make it possible for more African Americans to enter the professions and to compete more effectively in the managerial job market. Johnson and most of the civil rights leadership, especially James Farmer, president of the Congress of Racial Equality, supported a public policy that gave preference to African-American job and school applicants whenever they competed with equally qualified whites. According to Farmer, who was a native Texan, Johnson himself named the policy "affirmative action."

Affirmative action eventually became official policy at the federal, state, and local levels of government. By the time I became a regent, the University of Texas had developed and implemented admission and hiring policies that conformed to affirmative action policies used by most of the public universities throughout the country. In 1996 a federal appeals court decision in the *Hopwood* v. *Texas* case wiped out the affirmative action program at the University of Texas. Ruling that the university had discriminated against a white applicant for admission to the School of Law, the court banned the use of racial preferences by Texas public universities. The decision had an immediate and adverse effect on the university, setting back its efforts to attract more black and Hispanic students.

As a person who has supported the civil rights movement and who abhors racial prejudice, I believe fervently that this nation must be a land of equal opportunity for all. I have always opposed, however, any law, policy, or activity that has been created or has been administered to deny equal access to education, employment, public services, or any other aspect of life to anyone because of race, religion, or ethnicity. That is why I have not been enthralled with affirmative action as it has been practiced in the last several years. Many of the affirmative action policies that we have sanctioned, no matter how well intended, have tried to solve the problem of discrimination against blacks and Hispanics by discriminating against whites. Racial discrimination against anyone is wrong, no matter the reason for it.

To me the term "affirmative action" symbolizes a poverty of imagination that continues to afflict most university campuses. The term locks us into political patchwork thinking and blocks the creative solutions we so desperately need. I am committed to affirmative action, but to me real affirmative action means that every newborn child in this nation will have good nutrition. Affirmative action means that every child will be reared not only with love and care but also with discipline and direction. Affirmative action means that every school has a vibrant Head Start program and every resource necessary so that our children can be educated to be productive citizens of a new century. It means that we eliminate school district lines to ensure that every child has the same amount of financial resources for his or her education. That would be action that affirms, affirmative action that breaks the bonds of impoverished thinking.

Ben Barnes

One of the benefits of my service on the board of regents was being able to meet some wonderful people, such as Bill Cunningham and his talented wife, Isabella, who is a distinguished scholar and teacher in her own right. My service also gave me an opportunity to deepen my relationship with some people with whom I was already acquainted. A good example is Austin businessman Ben Barnes. I first met Ben in the late 1960s, but he and I did not become close friends until I became a regent.

A native of the west-central Texas town of De Leon, Ben was elected to the Texas Legislature in 1960 at the ripe old age of twenty-one. Barnes had a remarkable legislative career: Speaker of the Texas House at age twenty-six; lieutenant governor of Texas at age twenty-nine. As the wonder kid of Texas politics in the 1960s, Ben seemed to be on a path leading directly to the Governor's Mansion and beyond until the Sharpstown banking scandal derailed his political career in 1972. Barnes had nothing to do with the scandal, but the voters were so turned off by the affair that they tended to vote against anyone who had held an important state office. I never voted for Ben Barnes for anything in my life and he knows that. He was on the John Connally side of the Texas Democratic Party and I was on the Ralph Yarborough side. That was a canyon so wide that no bridge could span it at the time.

The university brought Ben and me together. He has some remarkable qualities, the most important of which is his commitment to things that are right and good. If I had to pick the most important supporters of higher education in the state of Texas (and I am talking about a very small group), no list would be accurate unless it contained the name of Ben Barnes. Another quality I admire in Barnes is his capacity for friendship. I might add something that testifies to the quality and magnitude of his character; he was the leader in having Ralph Yarborough, who is certainly one of the greatest public servants in the history of Texas, recognized as a distinguished alumnus of the University of Texas. Ben is no angel, and neither am I. When I hear his critics make outrageous and always unsubstantiated charges against him, I am reminded of Samuel Johnson's sagacious advice: "Be not too hasty to trust or to admire the teachers of morality; they discourse like angels, but they live like men."

Retirement from the Board

My term on the board ended in February 1997. My service as a regent of the University of Texas System was one of the most rewarding experiences of my life. I was given six years to contribute to the cause that means more to me than almost any other: the education of youngsters.

The month I left the board, Audre and I donated $5 million to help make a new UT art museum possible. I wanted to do something tangible to show my gratitude for the opportunity to experience six of the best years of my life. Our gift was a supplement to generous gifts for the museum of $10 million from renowned author James Michener and $12 million from the Houston Endowment. The new museum has been named for Jack S. Blanton, Houston oilman and former chairman of the UT board of regents. James Michener's collection of twentieth-century art is to be the centerpiece of the Blanton Museum. A preeminent art museum has long been an urgent need for the university. Now its magnificent collections will have an appropriate home.

I know that all who have served an institution such as the University of Texas System like to make reference to the great things that have been accomplished during their tenure. For me, I am satisfied with Mother Teresa's response when being awarded the Nobel Prize and hailed as an achiever of great deeds. She paralyzed that audience with a simple statement: "We don't do great things; we do little things with great love." All those with whom I have served have been imbued with this philosophy. We didn't want to shake up the world; we just wanted to make sure that the youngsters who were in attendance at the institutions that comprise the University of Texas System had an opportunity for a great education.

> **B brought a different perspective to the board of regents. B knows what it means to be poor. He also understands the value of education, and that combination made him a very good chairman for a state university board. His sympathies are always going to be with the students.** —*Ann Richards*

When I look back on my service as a regent, I see six major areas of achievement with which I am proud to be identified. Although I like to think that my presence on the board may have helped to realize these achievements, I want to emphasize that they were the result of the hard work and dedication of my colleagues on the board, the UT System administration, the administrations of the individual UT System institutions, and our friends in the Legislature working as one cohesive team.

First is the South Texas–Border Initiative for enhancement of academic programs and facilities. The young people who take advantage of the marvelous new educational opportunities made possible by the initiative will contribute to a Texas that is more prosperous and more just than ever before.

The second achievement was the work we did to assist the public schools. People are surprised when they learn that UT System institutions are spending more than $50 million each year on programs that range from tutoring and counseling to cultural enrichment for disadvantaged students to special professional development activities for teachers. In the past our nation has faced and defeated many formidable enemies; today the worst enemy we have is ignorance, and its weapons are prejudice, lack of opportunity, and human misery. We must fight this enemy with everything we have, beginning with the youngest pupils in the public school system and continuing through all levels. I am proud that the UT System has taken the initiative to work with the public schools on the side of hope and opportunity for all.

Third, one of the most important initiatives of recent years concerns a broad expansion in the area of information technology and telecommunications. We initiated a far-reaching expansion that includes exciting new realms such as telemedicine, interactive videoconferences, and steps toward what many people call the virtual university. I have often suggested that it would be a serious mistake to try to replace the person-to-person contact of traditional college campuses with computer terminals and television screens. I don't believe we can ever find a suitable substitute for the intellectual excitement and personal growth that students experience through face-to-face interaction with their peers and their teachers. Nevertheless, we should take advantage of the fantastic possibilities that new technologies offer for exchanging information, circulating ideas, and expanding the horizons of our culture.

Fourth, I have been gratified that during the past few years the bonds backed by the Permanent University Fund have received the highest possible ratings by all three major rating agencies. That may seem at first like a technical and arcane development, but I assure you it has extensive benefits for everyone who is served by the UT System's component institutions. The higher ratings have resulted in lower interest rates on future bond sales, thus increasing the purchasing power of the Permanent University Fund. The final result will be enhanced classroom, library, and laboratory facilities for students and faculty all across the system.

Fifth, I am proud of the creation of the University of Texas Investment Management Company (UTIMCO), which was created to manage the Permanent University Fund and other assets for which the board of regents has fiduciary responsibility. With this new entity, the UT System has become the nation's first public university to adopt the external investment corporation model implemented by leading private universities such as Harvard, Stanford, and Duke. As a separate corporation, UTIMCO is better able to respond quickly to market information and can thereby better control fund risk and return profiles.

A sixth area where significant progress was achieved concerns the overall efficiency of the UT System administration and of each of the campuses within the system. Working closely with the presidents of each UT campus, Chancellor Cunningham implemented measures that produced nearly $400 million in cost savings from 1992 through 1998. Regent Lowell Lebermann headed a system committee whose recommendations resulted in a major reorganization of the way the system does business, a streamlining of bureaucratic and regulatory procedures, and a massive reduction in paperwork. All of our institutions have continued to pursue a cost-cutting and cost-avoidance program that has been in place for several years.

Given the constraints on state funding for higher education throughout the 1990s, it is remarkable that the UT System has been able to streamline its operations and cut administrative costs while also expanding and enhancing educational services. On top of all that, we still have relatively low tuition and fees, ranking forty-second among the nation's state universities.

No doubt this is a wonderful success story, but the success of the UT System on behalf of the people of Texas will certainly be endangered without appropriate funding from the state, without a continued strong commitment to research by the federal government, and without expanded private-sector support. Despite everything that we achieved during my six years on the board, much more remains to be done. The new century will bring an intensification of the challenges facing Texas higher education, principally the need to maintain educational programs that are committed to excellence, while also continuing to ensure wide access to education for people from all regions and all backgrounds.

The Cost of Ignorance

The challenges facing Texas and the rest of our nation have never been more critical, and the choices we must make have never been more serious. The decisions we make about education at all levels of government at the beginning of the twenty-first century will, to a large extent, determine the ability of this nation to succeed as a viable and thriving society and as a vigorous competitor in an increasingly competitive world. The future happiness, security, and prosperity of the American people will depend on our achievement of those goals. None of this will be possible without a strengthened educational system at all levels, from prekindergarten through graduate school and postdoctoral studies.

Meeting these challenges successfully will require an increased public investment. To anyone who says that education is too expensive, I ask them, "What about the cost of ignorance?" If there is anything that we as a society most certainly cannot afford, it is to leave our citizens without opportunities for learning.

We are all being tested today, and long after we are gone from this earth our grandchildren and great-grandchildren will still be grading our work. Somehow we must surmount the concerns and distractions that are only for a day and, instead, concentrate on the long view, on the kind of world we are helping to build for our descendants. Keeping that perspective is difficult for all of us, but it is the measure of an effort to take life seriously, to accept our common responsibility, and to try to leave the world better than we found it, in at least some small way.

The Bernard and Audre Rapoport Building

Audre and I have received more honors and awards than we ever dreamed possible, and we have deeply appreciated every single one of them. In October 1998, however, the University of Texas Board of Regents honored us in a way that far exceeded any award or recognition we had ever received previously. The board named the economics building on the campus of UT-Austin the Bernard and Audre Rapoport Building. Having my name on the building that housed the offices and classrooms of the professors to whom I owe so much is an honor beyond anything I could ever have imagined. That it was a Republican-dominated board that voted to honor Audre and me — two dedicated and active Democrats — makes this recognition even more special. With that generous action, the regents demonstrated their sincere belief that political partisanship has no place on the university's board of regents.

I learned a lot as a result of my service as a regent. I guess the most important lesson was that it is possible to work constructively with people from different walks of life who have seemingly different, even opposite, points of view. When there is a common purpose, somehow differences diminish, almost disappear. My six years as a regent taught me that it makes no difference if one is liberal, conservative, or in-between when the cause is the university.

Individual political differences are dwarfed by the acceptance by one and all of a singleness of purpose: making the University of Texas System and all of its components outstanding educational institutions.

It is my hope that in the years to come the University of Texas will continue to be served by regents as dedicated and selfless as those who have served on the board in the recent past. The University of Texas has a record of greatness. I expect nothing less than continued greatness as the university faces the new century.

13 | ▶ *William Jefferson Clinton*

I have been a friend of Bill and Hillary Clinton's for more than twenty-five years. I met Clinton in 1972 when he was working for the McGovern campaign in Austin. He was just a kid at the time, but even then his dynamism, good humor, sharp intelligence, and driving ambition were strongly evident. After the 1972 presidential election, he returned to Arkansas, and I lost contact with him.

Early in 1974 Dan Powell, who was with the AFL-CIO in Memphis, told me that Clinton was a candidate in Arkansas for a congressional seat. He said that Clinton had persuaded the Arkansas AFL-CIO's political action committee to back him. Powell was really high on him. He believed that Clinton would be president of the United States someday. Aware that I had met Clinton during the McGovern campaign, Powell asked me to make a financial contribution to his campaign. I was happy to do it. Some of my political associates in Texas who had become friends with Clinton when he lived in Austin, including agriculture commissioner John White, land commissioner Bob Armstrong, and Garry Mauro (Armstrong's eventual successor as land commissioner), also sent contributions. Clinton lost the congressional election, but two years later he ran for Arkansas attorney general and won. I gave him money for that race also.

I contributed to every one of Clinton's campaigns after that, including the six times he ran for governor beginning in 1978. When Clinton was defeated for reelection as governor in 1980, I offered to put him on retainer with American Income. He did not accept my offer, because he was determined to win back the governor's office in 1982 and he wanted to spend his entire time making certain that happened. After he won that race in 1982, one of my protégés, Betsy Wright, served as his chief of staff. Betsy had worked in Sissy Farenthold's campaigns for governor and had been on the staff of the McGovern campaign in Austin in 1972, where she met Clinton. Hank Brown and I worked with Betsy on several projects. Before moving to Arkansas, she served as secretary of the National Organization for Women. Betsy's presence on his staff strengthened my ties to Clinton. I met with him several times in Arkansas while he was governor, and we developed a close relationship.

Clinton talked to me about the presidency as early as the late 1980s. It was clear that he wasn't ready in 1988, but I urged him to keep thinking about 1992 or 1996. I encouraged him to accept the offer to give the speech introducing Michael Dukakis at the Democratic National Convention in Atlanta in 1988. He wasn't a well-known national political figure, and I knew the speech would give him valuable exposure. Unfortunately, Dukakis's people revised the speech and insisted that Clinton read it word for word as revised. The speech was too long. Losing his sense of pace and timing, Clinton's delivery was awkward and stumbling. It was a disaster for him. Afterward, he called and asked for my reaction. I told him to quit worrying about the speech, that it was just an incident that would be discussed for a couple of days and then forgotten as the presidential campaign heated up. Clinton told me then that he was thinking seriously about running in 1992 if Dukakis lost to Bush. At the time, however, Dukakis looked strong and seemed to have a good chance of winning the election.

I supported and worked on behalf of Senator Paul Simon's presidential bid during the primaries of 1988. Simon is a terrific person who would have made a fine president. His campaign failed, however, so I attended the Democratic National Convention in Atlanta as an observer. Although I had supported Paul Simon all the way, I wasn't unhappy when Massachusetts governor Michael Dukakis won the nomination. I thought he would be an extremely strong candidate. He had an excellent record as governor, and he was energetic and articulate. I was delighted, of course, when he chose my friend Lloyd Bentsen to be his running mate. Bentsen strengthened the ticket substantially.

Immediately following the Democratic convention, I felt good about our chances, but it didn't take the Republicans long to destroy Dukakis. The Republicans ran one of the meanest and dirtiest campaigns in recent U.S. history. Directed by Lee Atwater, the Bush campaign did everything imaginable to frighten the voters into believing Dukakis was a radical, wild-spending liberal who was so soft on crime that he would release from prison every murderer and rapist in the country. It was an appalling performance.

Michael Dukakis, on the other hand, ran one of the most inept presidential campaigns in modern U.S. history. He sat back while the Republicans systematically destroyed him with demagoguery. I know it frustrated Lloyd Bentsen severely. As Lloyd has said, politics in Texas is a contact sport, so he was prepared to respond in kind to the shameful tactics of the Republicans. The Dukakis campaign was caught completely off guard, however, and never recovered. Bentsen's utter demolition of Dan Quayle in the vice presidential debate was the only bright spot for the Democrats in the entire campaign.

After the Dukakis debacle, I was among those who encouraged Bill Clinton to challenge George Bush in 1992. During the summer of 1991, Clinton came to Waco for a speaking engagement. I picked him up at the airport, and we stopped at my house to visit before the speech. We discussed the upcoming presidential campaign. When Clinton indicated that he would enter the race, I assured him that he could count on my full support. After the speech, we returned to my house so that he could call Hillary and give her a report on how the day had gone. He told her that his speech had gone well and that things looked promising because "our good friends Audre and B Rapoport have promised to be with us during the great adventure."

Clinton officially announced his candidacy on October 3, 1991. A few days later, I traveled to Little Rock to attend a meeting of people who Clinton hoped would play a financial role in the campaign. Among those in attendance were Dallas financier Jess Hay, Los Angeles attorney Mickey Kantor, and Clinton's Little Rock friends Webster Hubbell, Bruce Lindsey, and Mack McLarty. Together we pledged a total of $1 million for Clinton, and we agreed to serve as his fund-raising leaders.

My role from that point until Clinton's election more than a year later was to find as much money as I could to help pay for the campaign. Our fund-raising efforts went surprisingly well. It was a crazy campaign year that saw Clinton survive nearly every kind of personal attack imaginable, as well as the bizarre on, off, and on again candidacy of Dallas billionaire Ross Perot. The real surprise, however, was George Bush's fumbling and almost disinterested reelection effort. The result was that the Democrats finally recaptured the White House after a twelve-year electoral exile.

After Clinton was elected, we talked on the telephone several times, but I did not see him in person for several months. He consulted with me about some of the people he was considering for appointment to jobs in his administration. Of those, the one I had the most interest in was Lloyd Bentsen, whom Clinton was considering for secretary of the treasury. I hated to see Bentsen leave the Senate, where he was serving as the powerful chairman of the Finance Committee. As one of the most influential members of the Senate, Bentsen had served Texas well. It would take his replacement years to regain that influence, if it could be regained at all. My other concern was strictly political. Texas was becoming more and more Republican, and I was deeply concerned about the Democratic Party's chances in any special election to replace Bentsen.

Nevertheless, I was excited by the idea of Bentsen in the cabinet, in a position to influence policies in a wide range of national and international areas. I felt that the Clinton administration needed someone with Bentsen's experience and prestige in Washington. It certainly would give the administration more clout on Capitol Hill. I also knew that Bentsen had no desire to run for reelection when his term expired in 1994, so Texas Democrats would have to confront the problem of his replacement within the next two years anyway. I concluded that Bentsen should be offered the treasury post, and I passed that opinion on to Clinton. Bentsen received the appointment. Clearly, I was one of many whom Clinton consulted on the matter, and in many ways, Bentsen was an obvious choice.

One person who was not happy about Bentsen's appointment was Texas governor Ann Richards, who knew the Democrats would lose his Senate seat as a result. I wanted Ann to appoint former San Antonio mayor Henry Cisneros to the Senate as Bentsen's replacement, but Cisneros wasn't interested. There was also some concern about a marital problem Cisneros had experienced a few years earlier that had become a public scandal in San Antonio. Ann eventually appointed former congressman Robert Krueger, who had served as an ambassador at large for President Carter. Krueger is a former academician with a sharp intellect and a nice personality, but he's not a go-getter. He is a poor campaigner and he made a number of bad decisions during the brief period he served in the Senate. As far as I was concerned, it was a foregone conclusion that Krueger could not win the special election. The eventual result of these developments was the election of Republican Kay Bailey Hutchison as the junior senator from Texas.

I went out of my way not to bother Clinton after his inauguration in January 1993. As a new president, he obviously had pressing business that needed his full attention. I traveled to Washington several times in 1993, but I never saw the president. During that first year of his presidency, I watched in deep concern as Clinton seemed to wander from one unnecessary controversy to another. Most of the problems that first year stemmed from the president's attempt to do too much too soon, especially in the area of health care insurance reform.

Although the Clinton administration made many mistakes in formulating a plan, I basically agreed with the Clinton approach on health care reform. That was despite the nasty verbal attacks on the insurance industry by key members of the administration. The first lady, who was spearheading the effort to come up with a plan, was among those who attacked the insurance industry. Although I was unhappy with the tone of the rhetoric, the industry deserved some of the criticism. We will not have decent universal medical care in this country without socializing the health care industry. It is that

President Bill Clinton with B in the White House, 1994. CN 10489, Rapoport (Bernard) Photograph Collection, Center for American History, The University of Texas at Austin.

simple. I was one of the two or three presidents of life insurance companies who supported Medicare, and it has always seemed to me that intelligent people recognize those areas that lend themselves to the free enterprise system and those areas that fall to the province of government. It is ironic that after the massive scare campaign charging that *federally* managed health care would take our choices away from us, we are now saddled with a *private* system that takes our choices away from us.

I supported most of Clinton's initiatives during his presidency, but I have to confess that the North American Free Trade Agreement (NAFTA) put me in a tough position. I had good friends on both sides of that issue. Of course, the unions were strongly opposed to NAFTA. I finally took the position in public that some of my best friends are for NAFTA and some of my best friends are against NAFTA, and I always support my friends. Privately I was for NAFTA, provided provisions would be made for those whose employment was threatened, but I did not lobby for it. I sat that one out.

Late in January 1994 Speaker of the House Tom Foley and Senate majority leader George Mitchell invited me to attend Clinton's first State of the Union address to Congress. Foley and Mitchell were old friends of mine. Joint sessions of the Congress are held in the House of Representatives, so the night of the speech Audre and I were waiting in Speaker Foley's office by the floor of the House before we went to our seats in the visitors gallery. When President Clinton walked into Foley's office, he saw us and broke into one of his famous grins. He hugged and kissed Audre and then scolded me for not paying him a visit. I told him that I knew he was rather busy. Replying that he was never too busy to hear from old friends, he urged us to visit him in the White House.

The next month, the president appointed me to his Advisory Committee on Trade and Policy Negotiations. Mickey Kantor recommended my appointment. I accepted the post with some reluctance because I was afraid that my duties as chairman of the University of Texas Board of Regents would not let me attend meetings on a regular basis. That fear turned out to be legitimate. I was not a good committee member, missing several meetings because of my schedule as a regent.

Three months after we had seen him in Speaker Foley's office, the president invited Audre and me to spend the night in the Lincoln bedroom in the White House. We stayed up late talking to the Clintons upstairs in their private living quarters. I remember the president talked that night about how upset he was by the flood of vicious demagoguery that was spewing forth against him from right-wing hate mongers on talk-radio programs. During our discussion that evening, I was deeply impressed by Hillary Clinton's skillful analysis of the political mood of the country. Audre and I both returned to Waco with a heightened admiration for the first lady's intellect, knowledge, and practical good sense.

Audre and I are charter members of the Hillary Clinton fan club. We both feel that Hillary gets the worst press in a most undeserving way. Audre says Hillary's critics are jealous because she is as pretty as she is smart. She was one of the best first ladies this country has ever had. She is a kind and gracious person. A few weeks before Clinton's first inauguration, Audre and I went to a party for the Clintons in Little Rock at Mack McLarty's house. Audre had never met Hillary, and she knew few of the guests at the party. As Audre tells it: "At that gathering, Hillary came up to me and said, 'Audre, I know you don't know many people here.' So she took me around the room and introduced me, and she stayed by my side for a long while. She is a very nice and thoughtful person, and she didn't do it because Bill Clinton needed our money. They knew they had our support. She is a very warm person. I don't think she gets any credit for that."

In July 1994 we were in Washington for an American Income convention, and I was visiting at the Hilton Hotel with my granddaughters Abby and Emmy, who live in Williamsburg, Virginia, where my son, Ronnie, is a professor of political science at the College of William and Mary. I asked my granddaughters if they wanted to meet the president. To my surprise, they replied that they preferred to meet the president's daughter, Chelsea. So I called Hillary, and she arranged for Abby and Emmy to come over and spend some time with Chelsea. The girls had a ball. They even met Socks, the first family's cat. It was a classy thing for Hillary to do.

The 1994 Congressional Elections

The Clinton administration found itself operating in a significantly different political atmosphere after the first Tuesday in November 1994. Ultraconservative Republicans captured both houses of Congress that day. Dwight Eisenhower was president the last time the Republicans had enjoyed a majority in the House. There were a number of reasons for this enormous political shift. Among those reasons, perhaps one of the most powerful was the scurrilous rumormongering and unrelenting, vicious personal attacks on President Clinton and his wife by right-wing radio talk-show personalities and the narrow-minded hypocrites who run the Christian Coalition. Rush Limbaugh and Pat Robertson, of course, are the most obvious examples of the people who were responsible for the hate-Clinton campaign. The former is an irresponsible show-business personality simply hungry for high ratings, and the latter is a dangerous bigot who yearns for personal power in a nation that he wants to turn into a fundamentalist Christian theocracy. Another reason for that victory was the destructive and demagogic behavior of the Republican congressional minority angered by Clinton's election in 1992.

We Democrats also have to be honest with ourselves, for in many ways we have been our own worst enemies. We had contributed more than I like to admit to the formation of a regulatory state that by 1994 had created in a significant portion of the electorate an extremely hostile attitude toward governmental programs. A large number of the Americans who bothered to vote in November 1994 were reacting against the unacceptable standards we have in our public schools, the failure to address the problem of poverty except through give-away programs that require no commitment from the recipient, and the dictatorship of the governmental regulator. With respect to the last problem, we have to recognize that even when Congress passes a good law, it is implemented by people who have no responsibility to the electorate. We give lip service to democracy and always seem to end up with regulators who do not have to live in the real world telling those of us who do what they think is best for us.

Our lawmakers did not trust anybody; they did not trust the people they represent. They tried to dot the *i*'s and cross the *t*'s on everything. They wanted to encapsulate human behavior. They wanted to itemize what we can do and what we can't do. We have created a society where few people are willing to take risks. The idea that everything has to be equal for everybody actually makes a very mean society. When we even everything out, it makes everything unequal because we all start out at different levels.

> **I have watched and observed B moderate his political views over a period of time, and those political changes have been significant.** —*Ben Barnes*

There's a good reason why there was a conservative victory in 1994. There is cogency to the conservative position. I object to conservatives more than I do to the conservative philosophy. Most people who call themselves conservatives are not conservatives at all; they are monopolists. If you want to start a bank in Waco, everyone who has a bank will oppose you. If you want to start a savings and loan here, every savings and loan executive will oppose you. Well, now, if they are for free enterprise, that's not a consistent position, is it? If what they mean by "free" is providing access for people to get into all walks of life, then I'm the most conservative man who ever lived. The conservatives that I object to are opposed to competition, and I'm wholeheartedly for competition.

I also believe that the Democratic Party was guilty of extending the welfare system even though we know that much of the welfare state's programs don't address the fundamental causes of poverty and other social ills. The welfare state has created a system of entitlements that cause more problems than solutions. I don't think anyone is entitled to anything, and I think most Americans feel that way. Everything has to start with responsibility, and from responsibilities emanate rights. Many of the leaders of minorities today talk about entitlements rather than responsibilities. That is a destructive, dead-end attitude. We have to inculcate a sense of responsibility in people if we are going to make any progress in this struggle to alleviate poverty.

> **Rapoport has taken a turn against the bureaucratic exploitation of the welfare system, the fact that the welfare system is not helping people make it on their own.** —*Ronnie Dugger*

I have finally understood that labeling a person as liberal or conservative is a convenient way of maintaining prejudices. The so-called left can no longer think of me as a captive. Thoughtless giving is as unproductive as penuriousness. But so-called conservatives, please, do not think you have converted me. I'm still a liberal and I am as proud as I am loud about that fact.

I don't think Rapoport is the last standing liberal, but he may
be one of the last standing vocal ones. —*Ann Richards*

Being a liberal means that I still believe government has a positive role
to play in building and maintaining a just and equitable society. As I said,
government can't do everything for us, but that doesn't mean I'm antigovernment. People such as Texas senator Phil Gramm (who has lived his whole
life being supported by government) go around saying they hate government
and that government is evil. That's nonsense. Government is not evil, government is us. Government is what we have made it. It's not some foreign
thing. Government has a role in our society. It can be a catalytic force for
good. For example, one of the most important bills ever passed by the Congress was the G.I. Bill of Rights. It produced more money for the economy,
it broadened our talent pool, and it made a lot of people happy. What brings
out talent is education. That law helped bring out the latent talent that was
hidden among those who had not had an education.

I'm proud to call myself a liberal because, for me, it means I'm not going
to be constrained by yesterday's chains. I don't think I am any less liberal
today than I ever was, but I am more conservative than some people who
call themselves conservative. The infallible doctrine subscribed to by many
of those Republicans who were elected to Congress in 1994 is not conservative. That sort of commitment is unthinking and reactionary. The truth is
never final. There is a continuous process of searching for truth. There are
no absolutes.

Presidential Election 1996

President Clinton learned some valuable lessons as a result of
the 1994 congressional elections. He didn't abandon his fundamental belief
in social and political justice, but he did get the message that the American people don't want to be overregulated and dictated to. I think he did a
superb job of reorienting the Democratic Party accordingly. I also think that
the American people were displeased by the slash-and-burn tactics of the
new Republican congressional majority after 1994, and they were shocked
and appalled by the radical programs proposed by the extremists in the Republican Party. Many people, fairly or not, associated the tragic Oklahoma
City bombing in 1995 with the hate rhetoric from the right wing and the extreme antigovernment positions advocated by some Republican members
of Congress. For those reasons (along with a Clinton campaign that was as
masterful as Bob Dole's was inept), the American people decided that they

B and President Clinton's party on Air Force One. *CN 10497, Rapoport (Bernard) Photograph Collection, Center for American History, The University of Texas at Austin.*

had gone too far in 1994 and that it would be unwise to put a Republican in the White House who would leave the Republican Congress unchecked.

Democratic Party Fund-raising Controversy

Most of us on the Democratic side, of course, couldn't be certain that the 1996 presidential election was going to be dominated by such factors. We also knew that fund-raising was going to be even more difficult for the Democrats in 1996 than it had been in the past, because the party no longer dominated Congress. Money that normally went to the people in power in Congress would no longer go to the Democrats. The Republicans, who were accustomed to campaign chests bulging with money, were going to be richer than ever. Accordingly, those of us responsible for raising money for the party had to work harder to make certain that the Republicans did not spend us into oblivion.

For my part, I raised $1 million for President Clinton in Texas, while the combined contributions of my family and company to the Democratic Party totaled $282,000. Our success at raising enough money to be competitive, combined with Clinton's reelection, created deep resentment and

WILLIAM JEFFERSON CLINTON ◀ 267

frustration in the Republican Party. The result was their decision to launch congressional hearings to uncover alleged illegal or unethical fund-raising activities by the president and vice president.

The Republicans made their accusations about illegal fund-raising a few days before the election. Those allegations included the charge that the Clintons had allowed a number of people to spend the night in the White House in return for political donations, which was portrayed as a violation in spirit of the law against soliciting campaign donations in the White House. When my name was spotted on the list of overnight guests at the White House that was subsequently published in the newspapers, my telephone began to ring off the hook. Reporters called to ask what it was that I had done for Clinton to be able to spend the night in the White House. If there ever was a tempest in a teapot, that was it. I didn't give money to the president's campaign or to the party because he invited Audre and me to spend the night in the White House. That's absurd. The president invited us because we have been his friends for nearly twenty-five years. On that score, he is no different from any of his predecessors. I don't know of any president who didn't have some of his friends spend the night at the White House.

> B Rapoport was my friend twenty-five years ago. When I was a defeated candidate for Congress with a campaign debt that was almost twice my annual salary, he was my friend. When I was the youngest former governor in the history of the Republic and nobody felt I had any political future, he was my personal friend. I don't think there is anything wrong with having people like that spend the night with you. I just simply disagree that it is wrong for a president to ask his friends and supporters to spend time with him. This job . . . can be a very isolating job. I look for ways to have genuine conversations with people. I learn things when I listen to people. —*President William Clinton, White House press conference*

I don't know how much money Audre and I have given to politicians, but it is a substantial amount. It is in the millions of dollars. But political fund-raising is a dirty, filthy process. Politicians aren't dirty. I have never had a politician ask me to do anything even close to being illegal. An American can give a federal candidate no more than $25,000, but we can give additional money to the state Democratic Party, which it can then use to help the candidate. We can give more money to political action committees that will also use it to help the candidate. It is all perfectly legal, but it circumvents the intent of the law. It can and does add up to millions of dollars donated by someone for a particular candidate. That is a corrupting influence.

I think the campaign finance reforms were silly. It doesn't matter to me that it was my own Democratic Party that was responsible for those reforms. They hurt the liberals more than they hurt conservatives. That was something Congress did not take into account when it passed the reforms. If a conservative Republican wants to run and needs $250,000 to get started, then he can go to the big corporations and get ten, fifteen, twenty executives to put together that $250,000 easily. So the restriction really is hurting the liberal candidate more than it is the conservative candidate. As far as eliminating corruption, it doesn't do that. I'm never concerned with corruption. We can ferret that out.

We always want to legislate ethics. The reality is that there are only two ways to handle this problem of campaign financing. One option is to have unlimited contributions and total disclosure. If an individual wants to give $100,000 or $1 million to a candidate, then blast it in the papers, give it publicity, and let the other side tear them apart. Let people do what they want to do, but make certain that the public has access to the information. Let everything else go by the wayside and have tough penalties for not reporting. I think the only serious approach to campaign financing is for the public to be fully informed. For people who hide or launder money as they did in the Nixon affair, there ought to be an automatic jail sentence.

I prefer another option, however, which is total public financing. All campaign support should come from the government, with absolutely no private contributions allowed, including the candidates' own money. If the average citizen wants to run for an office, and someone with my financial resources is the opponent, what chance does the average citizen have? Everyone should start on the same level and then compete on the basis of ideas, programs, and personal competency.

It was clear that the Lincoln-bedroom allegations and the fund-raising hearings in Congress were simply an extension of the Republicans' systematic effort, dating back to the beginning of the first term, to destroy Clinton's effectiveness as president, if not his presidency. The never-ending Whitewater investigation, of course, had the same purpose.

The Hubbell Affair

I never dreamed that I would have any connection with the investigation of Clinton's role in the Whitewater affair, the controversy over an Arkansas real estate deal associated with the failure of a savings and loan institution. In late March 1997, however, I received a federal subpoena calling me to testify before the Whitewater grand jury in Little Rock, Arkansas.

The story behind the subpoena began sometime in April 1994, when Truman Arnold, an oilman who operates out of Texarkana, called and asked me to do him a favor. Truman and I had become good friends when we were raising money for Bill Clinton's campaign in 1992. He said that associate attorney general Webster Hubbell, a former law partner with Hillary Clinton, was resigning from the Justice Department because of some dispute over his billing practices back when he was with the Rose Law Firm in Little Rock. He said that Hubbell was looking for work and that he was not in good financial shape. He had a couple of children in college who were depending on his support. Truman said he was helping Hubbell, and he wondered if I could also. He told me that he thought Hubbell could be useful to my business. He asked if I could put him on retainer at $3,000 a month for a period of six months.

Although I have a close relationship with Bill Clinton, he had never asked me to do anything for Hubbell. I want that to be clear. On the other hand, because we are so close and I knew that Hubbell was one of his favorite people, I was open to helping Hubbell. Would I have helped Hubbell if the president had not been my friend? I honestly don't know. I did not know him well at all. I met him at that first fund-raising meeting in Little Rock soon after Bill Clinton announced his candidacy for the presidential nomination. I knew that Hubbell was resigning from his position in the Justice Department, but I had no knowledge of the legal problems that had led to his resignation. Hubbell had not been indicted at that point.

I put Hubbell on retainer for a total of $18,000 for six months. I didn't think another thing about it. For one thing, $18,000 spread out over six months is an insignificant amount of money in the context of a business as large as ours. I also did not know that there was a general effort to help Hubbell and that several other people were being called. It was only after the investigation of Hubbell's work arrangements began that I learned that former White House chief of staff Thomas "Mack" McLarty had made several calls on Hubbell's behalf. That's all there was to it.

Truman Arnold had not said how Hubbell could help my business, and the truth is that I didn't give much thought to it. I just wanted to be helpful to someone that Truman said needed help. Hubbell did do some work for us, however. Just a few days after I hired him, in May 1994, Hubbell monitored a bill in the Pennsylvania Legislature for us that proposed to regulate the amount of commission an insurance agent could negotiate with a company. In June Hubbell submitted a report to me that outlined his ideas about potential new markets for American Income, especially in Arkansas. Hubbell also monitored insurance regulation in Congress for us.

Four months after I hired him, Audre and I took Webster and his wife,

Suzy, out to dinner in Washington, and we talked on the telephone several times, but that was the extent of our personal relationship. He never came to Waco. Throughout that time, Hubbell contended that he was innocent of any wrongdoing. All of a sudden, in December 1994, Hubbell pleaded guilty to two felony counts of mail fraud and tax evasion, and he went to jail. I was shocked. I certainly would not have hired him as a consultant to my company if I had known or even suspected that he was guilty of fraud. But I still didn't turn my back on him. I had no sense of guilt about my relationship with him, because I had no reason to feel guilty. I contributed $5,000 to a fund raised by Mickey Kantor to help his children, and I wrote Hubbell while he was in prison to keep his spirits up.

Then, allegations appeared in the press charging that the purpose behind the effort to help Hubbell after he had resigned from his government post had been to pay him off to keep him from testifying against the Clintons in the Whitewater investigation. The help I had given Hubbell put me right into the middle of the thing. The *New York Times* was the first to report my arrangement with Hubbell. After that there must have been 10 million words written in the press about our relationship. It was incredible. Every time a reporter called, I told the same story, which was the truth. Each one asked me what I knew, and I said that I didn't know anything. I just told them that Truman called and I agreed to hire Hubbell for what I considered to be a modest amount of money, and that was that.

What did B Rapoport want or expect in exchange for helping out Webb Hubbell? Nothing. I know because one of my hobbies is keeping a running count on the people who have been helped by B Rapoport. One of the many subsets of B's generosity is people who have been chewed up and spit out by the vagaries of political morality in this country, starting at least as far back as the late John Henry Faulk, who was blacklisted in 1956. And B never asked for a thing in return. Never asked for a thing from former House Speaker Jim Wright, either, whom he supported when Wright was in power and supported when Wright came home in disgrace. Never asked for anything from at least a dozen Texas liberals I can think of off the top of my head who were felled in electoral combat and needed jobs.
—*Molly Ivins,* Texas Observer

I always figured it would be a cold day in hell when I agreed with anything Molly Ivins said, but I'm wrong. Her comments about Bernard Rapoport could not be righter. I'm not impartial—thanks to his generosity, I'm very comfortably seated in the Audre and Bernard Rapoport Chair of Jewish Studies at the University of Texas at Austin—but I also know what I know. What has he ever asked me to do for him, either as liberal arts dean [1979-1993] or as a UT professor? Nothing. He doesn't even expect me to vote right, which from his point of view, I hardly ever do. To paraphrase Plato on Socrates, B Rapoport is the best and wisest and most righteous man I have ever known. —*Robert D. King,* Texas Observer

In late March 1997, I received that federal subpoena. My attorney, Pat Beard, went with me to Arkansas, although he couldn't be in the room while I met with the grand jury. When I arrived at the Federal Building in Little Rock on the morning of April 3, I was taken into a small anteroom to wait my turn to testify. Also waiting in that room was James McDougal, who had been convicted for his role in the supposedly illegal financial schemes surrounding the Whitewater real estate development in northern Arkansas. McDougal had decided to present information to the grand jury, so my appearance was delayed until the afternoon. I had never met McDougal, although we both knew about each other. After we had engaged in small talk for about twenty minutes, McDougal suddenly said, "Well, I have a lot to tell the grand jury." I looked at him straight in the eye and replied that I had nothing to tell them. I also told him that I thought the whole investigation was a waste of everyone's time and money.

I was finally called into the jury room, where the federal investigators questioned me for about two hours. Although they asked me the same questions over and over again, the investigators weren't at all hostile. They were nice and polite. There must have been forty or fifty people on the grand jury. At one point during the proceedings, my prison correspondence with Hubbell was brought out and I was questioned about it. The letters surprised me, but they shouldn't have. I had given them to the investigators when they asked for all of our files related to Hubbell. I was a little embarrassed when they read some of the letters out loud. They were full of my private thoughts to Hubbell about how he needed to keep his spirits up and that he needed to look forward to the future for his sake and the sake of his family, that sort of thing. When I'm trying to help someone who is in jail, I always write compassionate letters. The following passages from my letters to Hubbell are typical:

OCTOBER 3, 1995: "First things first, my friendship with you is as solid today as it was the day that we met. I know

the inner goodness of you—I really do. I want to begin sending you books and magazines—the kind of things that are so
important in your life."

JUNE 26, 1996: "It has been too long since I have written
you, Webb, and too long since I have heard from you. We all
miss you and miss you very much. Do you have any idea what
the opportunities for shortening your stay is? Do let me hear
from you."

JULY 18, 1996: "I think very seriously about what is possible
for you after your situation is concluded which I am pleased
to see is in the offing. What do you think about the insurance
business? With your personality, you could really do well in
the selling field and it would be a profession in which you
could be in control of your time. Anyway, remember, there are
so many of us who know who Webb Hubbell really is. We like
what we see and even more what we know."

In cases such as this, I'm not as interested in truth as I am in making the
person who is in a difficult situation feel better. So when the investigators read those letters to the grand jury, they didn't sound good, and I was
embarrassed.

As I was walking out of the room after the completion of my testimony, I
overheard one of the jurors say to another, "He must be honest, he wasn't
nervous." Well, that is certainly true. I wasn't nervous, because I had nothing to hide. I actually enjoyed the experience. What I did not enjoy, however, was the newspaper coverage. For example, when I was walking up the
steps to the Federal Building in Little Rock, some reporter asked me what
I was going to say to the grand jury. I just laughed and said that I would
be "lecturing them." It was a joke—a bad one, I agree—but a joke nonetheless. I couldn't believe it when that statement was quoted in most of the
newspapers as a serious, confrontational remark. I also think it's crazy when
newspapers across the country, including the *Los Angeles Times,* put a person's picture on the front page even though it has nothing to add to the story.
It says a lot about the state of American journalism.

All my life I have tried to help friends who were having a difficult time.
In the 1960s, when John Henry Faulk was trying to get back on his feet after
being blacklisted, I hired him as a speaker and entertainer for company conventions and sales meetings. Don Yarborough needed financial help in 1968,
so I hired him as a legal consultant and union meeting speaker. I hired Ralph
Yarborough as a consultant for a brief period in 1971 after he left the U.S.
Senate. When Jim Wright resigned from the House of Representatives in

1989, I hired him as a management consultant for American Income. I lent $50,000 to Bert Lance, President Carter's budget director, for a house when he was in trouble. And there have been others. I'm not citing these examples to prove that I'm a great guy. It's just that I don't write off friends because they are down or under a cloud. I never have. I'm not an angel, and I hate people who pretend to be virtuous, but I've never done anything illegal, and that includes my relationship with Truman Arnold and Webster Hubbell. The truth is that a friend called and asked me to do a favor for him, and I did, and that was all there was to it. Everything else is superfluous.

> **B is with you as a friend. You can count on him at the lowest moments of your life.** — *Garry Mauro, former Texas land commissioner*

Is there anything that Clinton could have done for me in return for my helping Hubbell? No. I've never asked the president for anything. He did ask me early in his first term if I would be interested in having an official position in his administration. I said no because I then had the best public service job I could think of, as a member of the University of Texas Board of Regents. I wouldn't trade that for anything he could appoint me to. The silliest thing I saw in the newspapers was a statement implying that the president gave me a ride on *Air Force One* after hiring Hubbell as a consultant. The truth is that the president accepted my invitation to speak at the University of Texas at Austin in 1996, and I rode with him on *Air Force One* when he flew from Austin to Houston after the speech.

> **And what did Rapoport want? He's already been invited to the White House so many times that he can't remember. He has almost as much money as God.** — *Molly Ivins,* Texas Observer

> **Bernard has incredible potential power but never uses it — at all. I'll say, "Look, Bernard, my god. You have the president's ear and here is this bad thing that is happening that could be prevented or corrected or whatever. Why don't you use your influence with him to do what we think is the right thing?" Well, of course, he will not. He will not bother the president about any issue. It's that simple.** — *Charles Cooper*

Webster Hubbell could have done much better with his life acting honestly than he did crookedly. What he did at his law firm was inexcusable in the sense that there is no reason for anybody who has good friends and the intelligence he has to do the things that he did to earn a living. It was the worst kind of thievery, taking advantage of position.

I guess the saddest result for me from that ridiculous affair was that after a close relationship with Bill Clinton that goes back to 1972, I could not go to the White House and the president and I could not have telephone conversations for a period of several months. That's not because we had a falling out. It's because our attorneys counseled us not to communicate. If I went to the White House, it was likely that the president and I would be besieged by the press with questions about what we discussed or if I was giving him money or whatever. To say that I was just paying a courtesy call to a friend of twenty-five years wouldn't satisfy them. If we had no contact, we didn't have to explain ourselves to the independent prosecutor and we avoided hassles with the press. That is sad.

Like the Pharisees at the Front of the Temple

As I write this, my friend Bill Clinton is no longer president. The years that he lived in the White House were among the most prosperous in the history of this country. Yet, he will go down in history as only the second president to have been impeached. More than enough has been said on television and radio about this sorry episode. Undoubtedly, in the future there will be a large library of books written about the impeachment, the Senate's refusal to remove him from office, and all of the personalities involved. There is no need for me to add much to the story. I do want to go on record, however, about how I felt about the president's troubles.

During the impeachment process, some reporters called and asked my reaction. I quoted the late psychologist Abraham Maslow: "Love is loving someone so much you don't want to change anything about them." That's exactly how I feel about Bill Clinton as a human being.

I knew about Clinton's affairs and his weakness for women. I talked to him about it from time to time, so the affair with Monica Lewinsky was no surprise to me. How do I feel about his relationship with Monica Lewinsky? I think Clinton's private life before taking office is no one's business, but the president of the United States has no private life. Everything a person does while occupying that office is the public's business. The president is in that job twenty-four hours a day. Anyone who wants the job has to accept that. It's not a question of being pure, it's a question of being responsible. It is part of the price of getting the job.

In my view, no one of sound mind can defend what he did. Do I think the president lied? Yes. Do I think he took inappropriate actions to obscure

Vice President Al Gore with B in 1996. CN 10498, Rapoport (Bernard) Photograph Collection, Center for American History, The University of Texas at Austin.

what really happened? Of course I do. Any man in the country who ever crossed the line of acceptable behavior might well have lied and been guilty of some of the same responses as those of the president. That doesn't absolve him; it only explains his subsequent actions and places them in some reasonable human perspective. He was certainly wrong and was justifiably blamed and humiliated for his actions. Yet the relentless national flogging of the man was entirely out of proportion, both to his offenses and to the persistent needs of the country.

The president's indefensible actions, lamentable as they were, are simply dwarfed when set against the seriousness of our continuing social and educational problems. While those problems were going unnoticed and unattended, it seemed that every politician beat his breast on television, proclaiming his overwhelming shock and outrage at Clinton's sins. It was an obscene, compulsive circus. Like the Pharisees at the front of the temple, such hypocrites hoped thereby to convince the viewers that they and they alone are untouched fountains of purity and virtue. Most of the president's loudest critics can only be described as hand-wringing, hypocritical orators, who adopted the ridiculous posture of moral self-immolation. In my opinion, the Republican leaders, including Tom DeLay and Bob Barr, who single-mindedly pursued the president were simply trying to distract the nation from our real public issues and to diminish even further any meaningful concern for the large social problems that we have, problems that so badly need addressing.

The worst result of the entire Lewinsky scandal is that a lot of good people are not going to run for office. I think our pool of potential leaders is going to be much smaller now.

As I write this, Texas governor George W. Bush has become president as a result of a shameful political decision by the Rehnquist majority on the U.S. Supreme Court. I supported Al Gore's candidacy with much enthusiasm, so I am disappointed and frustrated by the court's unprecedented decision. Nevertheless, I do not want my associates in the Democratic Party to behave as the Tom DeLay wing of the Republican Party behaved during the Clinton administration. It is my sincere hope that my party and the media will treat President Bush with more respect and decency than the media and the Republican right wing ever treated Bill and Hillary Clinton.

My disappointment over the results of the 2000 presidential election has been much alleviated by the Democratic Party's gains in the U.S. Senate, especially Hillary Clinton's wonderful victory in New York. Hillary will be an energetic and vocal advocate for children, the elderly, the economically disadvantaged, and other members of our society who lack a strong voice in the new Republican administration. Her presence in the Senate with Ted Kennedy, John Kerry, Patrick Leahy, Harry Reid, and Tom Daschle gives me hope for the future.

14 ▶ *American Income in the 1980s and 1990s*

I started American Income in 1951 with a $25,000 investment. Today it is one of the most profitable small insurance companies in the country, with more than $1 billion in assets. One reason I was able to achieve this is that I really searched for those things that I perceived were possible and discarded those things that were not.

American Income started with a hospitalization policy sales campaign that produced a 15- to 20-percent response from the people we targeted in a direct-mail effort. When the response to that solicitation eventually fell to about 1 percent, we implemented an entirely new strategy using gimmick leads, which gave an inducement to the respondent. That approach sold policies to one out of five leads. Our agents barely made a living at that rate. So we changed directions again and concentrated on the union market. That's when American Income really grew. Later, I saw that Medicare was going to be a reality, so I gave up our hospitalization business and entered the disability field. When disability insurance became unprofitable in the early 1970s, I changed the company again. At that point, my management and I did something that no other company has ever done in the insurance industry. In virtually one day we converted American Income from an accident and health insurance company to a life insurance company. A few years later, we decided to enter the credit union market. Then we entered the association market, such as the cosmetologist association, the truck drivers association, and veterans groups. The point is that we were not afraid of change, and we were not timid about taking risks. I believe those characteristics were critical to American Income's success.

> To a fault, Bernard is in favor of action. Action in business is everything. You can afford to make incredible mistakes if you keep acting over and over again, because most of the competition is not acting. They are sitting around thinking about how

> to avoid mistakes. Bernard will run four or five inconsistent
> directions all at once, when only one way is really possible, but
> he will stir up a lot of stuff while he's running in those different
> directions. — *Charles Cooper*

Another key to American Income's success was our decision to expand the management structure at our state agencies. We created an intermediate level of agents, which enabled the state general agents to divide responsibilities with lieutenants. The expansion of our management team allowed us to increase the size of the sales force. That structural change also made it possible for us to expand into Puerto Rico, Canada, and New Zealand.

I really do believe that there was an intangible human element that also played a significant part in American Income's great success. That element was simply my policy of treating employees like human beings. Under my direction, American Income never had a layoff. I was committed to upsizing, not downsizing.

> Rapoport is one of a very few rich people who still gives a
> damn about workers and what happens to the working class in
> America, and ninety-nine times out of a hundred he'll be on
> their side in an issue. — *Hank Brown*

I read in the paper every week about how some company has made the most money ever in its history. Then I hear that those companies are laying off thousands of employees to cut costs because the stockholders are demanding even larger profits. That kind of corporate behavior is irresponsible and inhumane. It affirms the perception that our society ignores loyalty and only recognizes performance. As bigness increases, it seems that loyalty becomes less important. Being nice to one another also becomes less important.

The problem with performance as it is interpreted today is that it does not take into account possibilities. The essential force behind the growth and success of American Income Life was my understanding from the beginning that it was not important what the stockholders earned, or what the officers earned, or what the staff earned. What was critical to our success was the ability of our sales agents to do their jobs. I knew that if we could create a climate in which the agents could earn more money at American Income than they could at any other place, it would trickle all the way up. I knew that our success depended on successful implementation of this philosophy.

I was able to give our sales force the confidence that I knew what was best for them and that I understood what was needed for them to have more opportunity with me than they could get in any other place in the world. I believe that was another reason for American Income's success.

> Rapoport is the greatest selling insurance executive I've ever known, and the greatest sales manager. Bernie developed his people, and he developed the contacts that led them to business. He never put layers between himself and his salespeople.
> — *Charles Terrell*

When I was running American Income, I had a telephone talk with each one of my state general agents every Saturday morning. I made the first telephone call at 6:45 in the morning and the last at 11:45 A.M. I talked to fifty or more people every Saturday for about five minutes. The discussions were well organized. We didn't waste time with gossip. We tried to solve specific problems every week. I believe that if I had stopped the Saturday morning calls American Income would have lost 20 or 25 percent of its production. I didn't have serious problems with any of the state general agents, because if they had something on their mind I was in a position to hear them out and to get it resolved. That's why the Saturday morning calls were vital.

> Bernie's telephone never stops ringing. He may call you out of the blue and just start talking or asking a question. "Do you know," or "What do you think about so-and-so," and then he'll give you some warm feeling about yourself, or ask some real nice question, and then you're sitting there still holding the telephone because he's gone. I think in all the years I've known Bernie, he's never said good-bye. When he gets through, he's through. But at the same time, he's got ten more phone calls coming in. — *Charles Terrell*

I had plenty of face-to-face as well as telephone contact with our agents. I visited every agency at least once a year, and I had an annual national convention where I could see everybody at one time. We had two national meetings a year with our state general agents.

> I have been to one of his sales meetings, and believe me, he knew everybody there. He has so much energy that it's astounding. I mean, he's go-go-go, and it would wear out most twenty-five-year-old people. I really don't think I ever have known another person who goes full throttle all the time like he does. — *Charles Terrell*

I think the personal touch is so important to everything you do in life, even in the business world. I believe in feeling. When I meet people, I will generally put my arm around them. I loved those long-distance telephone commercials that said, "Reach out and touch someone." It makes people feel better when you touch them. I know people who look down on that kind of behavior. They think there is something phony about a person like me who is exuberant and gregarious. It's because they are envious, basically, of people who care about other people and, in caring, want to show it.

> When B enters a room, you know he's in the room. I mean, he's the tornado, the cyclone, coming into the room, but instead of everyone running away, they run toward him. They know that talking to him will be worthwhile and challenging and that good ideas will be coming out of his mind at a mile a minute. —Senator Patrick Leahy

Many people in the business world are too lazy in the way they relate to other people. They are so lethargic, they don't even like to stand up when somebody walks in the room and shake hands with them. That kind of behavior on the part of top management can really slow a company down. If you are the president or CEO of a company, how can you expect to motivate your employees if you aren't openly exuberant and excited about the company and the people who work for it? In corporations as well as in other hierarchical organizations, enthusiasm and energy have to come from the top.

> I have been on a plane or two with Bernie coming back from Washington. When I'm coming back on an airplane, I'm ready to relax, but he's working the whole first-class cabin. I mean, literally, he's working: talking to people, asking questions, getting information, and whatever. Bernie could've been a stand-up performer, you know. He feeds on it, and he never stops. He's immensely entertaining, particularly even to strangers, and very gracious for the twenty seconds that he is able to focus on you. —Charles Terrell

> When you meet B Rapoport you know immediately that you have met a person the likes of which you will never meet again. In some respects he is bigger than life. He is a warm, caring, gregarious person. He is one of those people that you meet, and then you meet again, and before you know it, you have a friend in this person. You soon have the sense that he has been your friend for most of your life. —Senator Thomas Daschle

We had to be good to our agents, but they, likewise, had to be good to the company. There has to be a complete understanding between the agency force and the executives of an insurance company. The company has to protect the interests of its agents, but the company also has to decide what's good for itself.

I stressed to our people at the company that I wanted them to operate like they were in a glass house speaking through megaphones. I told them that they had to act at all times as if the insurance commission was on their left shoulder, the SEC was on their right shoulder, and Ralph Nader was watching from up above. As long as they made decisions within those parameters, I would defend them to the death.

Whenever I interviewed a new sales agent, I pointed out that in the old days a person worked until the age of sixty-five and then got a gold watch at retirement. By working at American Income as a sales agent, though, they would make so much money they were going to give *me* a gold watch. I am delighted by the knowledge that my company created many millionaires.

> If a guy was seeking a job and he was in Bernard's office for half an hour, Bernard would be on the telephone for fifteen minutes and for the other ten minutes he'd be talking. The candidate might be able to say half a dozen words, and out the door he went. Then I interviewed the guy for two hours, and I would learn his entire life history. I would have him all figured out. Later, when I met with Bernard to discuss the guy, Bernard would also have him figured out. But he did it in fifteen minutes, when it took me two hours of intense discussion. It drove me crazy. I think he watches you very closely while he is talking and carrying on. He looks closely at your eyes and how you react to him while he is in this constant state of movement. He gets a very good read on certain aspects of a person. He is very perceptive that way. — *Charles Cooper*

My wife, Audre, was another reason for my success with American Income. She is deeply involved in everything I do, she is charming and highly sociable, and she is interested in people. My debt to her is great indeed.

> It's amazing how Audre's kept up and done her stuff all these years. A lot of women say, "Hey, wait a minute, I'm gonna slow down. I don't have to do all that you do." They go and just sit with the grandchildren or whatever. But if you look around and he's working a party, she's holding her own, too, and always has. Or if he's trotting all over Washington, so

is she. That is unique, when you get a couple that's been together that long and they still approach it with that energy and enthusiasm. — *Charles Terrell*

The Leveraged Buyout

It was in the early 1980s that American Income began to make substantial profits. Annual earnings had risen 50 to 60 percent during the late 1970s, and our stock price increased enormously. Because I owned about 20 percent of the stock, my personal financial worth soared as well. For the first time since we started American Income, my holdings in the company were worth much more than my debt. I was now worth substantially more in terms of assets, but I remained cash poor. Being in that condition had never bothered me before, but I now realized that there were some things I really wanted to do, and I needed cash to do them. I was deep into my sixties, and I had not done enough to take care of my family's future. I also wanted more money for my political and philanthropic interests. It seemed to me that the time was ripe to sell the company, pay off my debt, and use my cash to accomplish some of those goals.

> It was a constant battle to keep Bernard from selling the company. I had argument after argument with him about it. I fought off a number of those buyout deals, but it finally came down to the point where I knew he was driven to sell the company. — *Charles Cooper*

Throughout most of the 1980s, Charles Cooper and I worked with two or three investment banking firms to market the company, but nothing came of our efforts. Finally, in the summer of 1988, Mike Lang, the CEO of Beta Financial Corporation of Dallas, came forward with the concept of a leveraged buyout. Lang told us that he could put together enough funding to take the company private. He, Charles Cooper, and I would join with some other investors and split up the stock. Essentially, we would buy all of American Income's stock at a price that an investment banker would determine to be fair. I liked the idea. I was getting frustrated at our failure to find a buyer for the company, so I agreed to work with Lang. We made a formal leveraged buyout bid early in the fall of 1988.

When our bid became public knowledge, four others quickly materialized. The most attractive bid was from a California firm called Golder, Thoma, and Cressy (GTC). Their top management came to Waco, and we had some discussions. I liked them as people, and I was impressed by what they said. It was clear that the firm was more substantial than Lang's Beta Corporation. GTC also had a lot of experience with leveraged buyouts.

With American Income attracting new attention, Cooper and I decided to hire Bear Stearns, an investment advising firm, to review and evaluate the bids. In September 1988 our board of directors appointed a special committee composed of former Texas Board of Insurance chairman Lyndon Olson, Jr., Austin attorney Sarah Weddington, and former secretary of labor Ray Marshall to work with Bear Stearns to review and analyze the various bids. The committee was responsible for recommending which of the bids, if any, the company should pursue.

Although the bids differed in their financial terms, they all expressed a desire for Cooper and me to remain in our management positions and for the company to maintain its business plan and method of operations.

> **Our job was to see to it that whatever deal was cut protected the interests of the stockholders and the policyholders. It was then that I began to learn from the professionals in the insurance business how good Rapoport really is. We had maybe seven or eight investment companies that wanted to buy American Income Life. Every one of them said they would not buy it unless Barney Rapoport remained as chairman of the board. I questioned these companies about why they wanted to buy American Income Life. They all said that it's extremely well run, it's very profitable, and it's mainly because of Barney Rapoport—that he has this kind of business sense that few people have. Nobody could replace him.** —*Ray Marshall*

After several weeks of work, the special committee decided in favor of the bid from GTC. Not only did GTC offer the highest cash price for our stock, but it was also clear to our directors that GTC's detailed proposal was more consistent with the interests of American Income's policyholders, employees, and agents. Most significant was GTC's method of financing its purchase. In a leveraged buyout, a company is acquired largely with borrowed money. Usually, that debt is paid with funds generated by the sale of some of the acquired company's assets. Instead of using any of our company's assets to pay for the deal, however, GTC bought our stock with its own bank loans and surplus debentures. The dividends that GTC received from American Income's earnings were used to pay GTC's debt. In addition, the Indiana Department of Insurance restricted the percentage of American Income dividends that GTC could take on an annual basis.

In other words, this was not one of those infamous deals so typical of the 1980s when investment holding companies bought out successful businesses and sucked them dry of their cash and other assets and left their loyal and hard-working employees in unemployment lines.

GTC put in $15 million of its own cash and borrowed $250 million from the banks. I put $5 million in the deal, which gave me about 20 percent of the company. That was as much of the company as I had owned prior to the deal. I gave 20 percent of my holdings to Charles Cooper because he had contributed so much to our success. Charles Cooper, GTC, and I then owned 41 percent of American Income's stock. I had to set aside about $10 million to pay the capital gains tax. That left me with about $25 million in cash. For the first time in my life, I had real money.

From 1951 until 1984, I had owed the banks millions of dollars. I still owed Sam Klein's bank in Louisville for the loan he had given me in 1970. I had not made a payment on principal for the eighteen years it carried the loan. After the leveraged buyout, I went to the bank and wrote one check for the entire debt, something like $16 million. Imagine that: the son of a penniless Jewish Russian socialist immigrant writing a check for $16 million! Signing that check gave me a lot of pleasure. Sam Klein's loan to me turned out to be a good deal for his bank.

Torchmark and the Foundation

In the early 1990s Cooper and I put American Income back on the market. Our earnings had paid down GTC's leveraged buyout debt, and we seemed once again to be in a position to sell the company for a good price. I was seventy-eight years old, and I knew that I was not going to live forever. I wanted to improve my estate tax situation, and I wanted to be as financially liquid as possible. I did not, however, want to retire. I looked for a purchaser who would respect my role in developing American Income and who would understand how valuable my political and labor union relationships were to the continuing growth of the company.

Beginning in late January 1994 I had a series of discussions with Ron K. Richey, chairman and CEO of Torchmark Corporation, about acquiring American Income. Torchmark is a publicly traded insurance and diversified financial services holding company chartered in Birmingham, Alabama. It has $12 billion in assets. Richey and I have been good friends for more than thirty years, so the discussions were easy and enjoyable.

A merger of Torchmark and American Income seemed to be a natural to me. Richey made it clear that he had no interest in tampering with the operations of the company in the event of a merger. He emphasized, in fact, that a merger would be attractive to Torchmark only if the present management stayed in place. Richey was especially insistent that I continue my leadership of the company. After a number of meetings with Audre and myself, Charles Cooper, and our partners at GTC during that spring and summer, Torchmark's management worked out a purchase agreement, which its board of directors approved on September 15, 1994. We sold American Income to Torchmark for $563 million. That's not bad for a company that started out with $25,000.

I received about $150 million from the sale. I put $43.7 million of that money into the Bernard and Audre Rapoport Foundation, which we had established in October 1987 with a $3 million gift. I now had the luxury of working with my foundation while I was living, which allowed me to develop clear policies for its future direction.

The folks who ran Torchmark in 1994 were wonderful people. Ron Richey understood our unique qualities as a business, and he appreciated the way we treated our people. Although we became a wholly owned subsidiary of Torchmark, I did not run the company any differently after the merger.

Ron Richey retired, however, a couple of years after Torchmark bought American Income. To be candid, I would not have made the deal if I had known that Richey was going to retire that soon. Charles B. Hudson succeeded Richey as CEO. Unfortunately, Hudson and I had a personality clash almost from the beginning. There was nothing ugly between us, we just didn't warm to each other. It seemed to me that Hudson had certain perceptions about insurance that were predicated on what he was familiar with, which was primarily the Medicare supplement business and life insurance sold by direct mail. The genius of American Income, however, was its sales force, and that was a kind of operation Hudson didn't understand.

In August 1999 Hudson informed me that I would no longer be the CEO at American Income. He wanted changes! Yes, he wanted to run the company his way. So Charles Cooper and I left American Income. As I said, I resented C. B. Hudson, especially when he made that decision. I soon realized, however, that I had been wrong about him. It is true that he is a number-oriented person, but there is another side to him. Several months after he took my place as CEO, he called to apologize, saying that he had been fed a lot of misinformation about me. Our relationship changed, and he demonstrated a degree of sensitivity that surprised me. Today we are good friends. There are no hard feelings on my part.

As of September 1, 1999, I was no longer an employee of American Income. I was retained as a consultant at a substantial salary because of my good relations with the unions. I am free to do anything I want to do in business, except that I can't compete in the union market with another company for a couple of years.

I'm not that surprised by what happened with Torchmark. It is typical of the business climate today. The problem with the corporate culture now is that it is all number oriented. There is little concern for people. The pressure is all on the bottom line. If I had been under the umbrella of a holding company such as Torchmark when I began my business career, I would never have been able to build American Income. As an entrepreneur, I made a lot of mistakes, but I didn't have to account to anyone for them. I could just keep going until I either failed or succeeded. You can't do that as part of a huge conglomerate. You make a mistake, and you are out. That has a chilling effect on innovation and risk taking, which are both necessary ingredients for building a business. The only thing holding companies are interested in is a profit at the end of each quarter.

If I were someone who was consumed by business and business alone, the Torchmark situation would have made me angry and miserable. But business is not my entire life. I have my family, my friends, and my foundation.

I'm now in my eighties, but I'm still not interested in retirement. I'm in good health and I feel great, so why stop working? I get too much satisfaction and happiness from the active life that I lead to stop. I'm the kind of person who needs to be building something all the time, so I decided to acquire another insurance company. I worked hard to build this new company, which is based in Dallas. After a year of difficult work, I sold the company in April 2001 for a substantial profit. Most of that profit will go to my foundation. My goal is to increase the funding of the Rapoport Foundation to a point where it can be a significant factor in support of the various causes in which Audre and I believe so fervently.

> Years ago when we would see Bernard increasingly involved in business, Mother and I would really be concerned and really wish that he did not work so hard. It has only been in the last few years that I have stopped telling him not to work so hard. It took me many years to realize how much he really enjoys business, and I think he would miss it dreadfully if he did not do it. —*Idel McLanathan*

A few years ago I became interested in Zen Buddhism, so I decided to do some reading on the subject. I came across a story about a man who was digging a well with a spade. His neighbor came to him and said that if he would use an ox he could do it ten times faster. Rejecting this advice, the man replied, "But you don't understand, the joy is in the doing." People say to me, "B, you have all of this money and you only have one house, you drive a Ford car, and you don't wear fancy clothes, and you don't do this and you don't do that, and you give so much money to charity. You really don't enjoy yourself. Why don't you retire and spend the rest of your life on a yacht in the Caribbean?" I look at them and I feel sorry for them. I'm having a ball. I'm doing what I want to do. The joy is in the doing.

Rapoport is a cheerful workaholic, a chronic optimist, a tennis nut, and an avid bibliophile who can't quite understand why other people don't get as much of a thrill out of working as he does. —*Jim Wright*

15 ▶ To Save the World: The Rapoport Foundation

Audre and I were raised in the spirit of giving. We want that spirit to continue through the Rapoport Foundation long after we are gone. In a broad sense, the mission of the Rapoport Foundation is to promote peace, justice, and education. Audre and I have specified that one-sixth of the annual contributions must be for the benefit of the state of Israel. We give special emphasis to Jewish concerns because Jews are so few in number and their problems are so seemingly insurmountable. The allocations for Israel will always be in the areas of education and child care. Another one-sixth must benefit the University of Texas at Austin. One-third will be reserved for the community of Waco, Texas, and the remaining one-third can be allocated on a discretionary basis.

Everything we do in the foundation must bring people together without regard to race, religion, ethnic background, or finance. I want the foundation always to stand for something and not to avoid involvement because "it is just not the thing to do." I always want the foundation in its physical appearance to be simple. I do not want it to seek recognition and visibility through an impressive building or offices with fancy furnishings. The foundation's assets should always be used to provide direct benefits to those it is to serve, whether it is the people in Israel, the students at the University of Texas, or the citizens of Waco or other areas that receive grants from the discretionary allocation.

I want the Rapoport Foundation to be involved in the effort to eradicate poverty in Waco. I want to improve the lot of people who do not perceive that there is opportunity. I want to try to show them that life indeed is worthwhile and there is a reason for having hope. I'm also particularly interested in educating young people. Camus said, "Poverty is imprisonment without a drawbridge." In my mind, that drawbridge is education. We must never forget that. Feeding without educating will ensure starvation later. Somehow as a society we have had a hard time learning that. I want the foundation to do whatever it can to ensure that pregnant women and newborn babies have good nutrition. Instead of concentrating on prisons, I'll concentrate on the other end, so we won't need prisons.

I have one caveat. I came out of a generation that believed virtue and being a do-gooder were one and the same. That isn't true; any social organization that seeks to ameliorate the quality of life must first accent responsibility. We want to get people on their feet so they can take care of themselves.

Other than the University of Texas, some of the organizations and institutions that I want the foundation to continue to help include the United Jewish Appeal, the Jerusalem Foundation, Oberlin College, Baylor University, the Institute for Policy Studies, the Waco Independent School District, and the University of Texas Southwestern Medical Center. Audre has had a special interest in Planned Parenthood. She has always believed that high-quality reproductive health care and education should be readily available to all women who want and need such services.

> Planned Parenthood is something I believe in. I believe that a woman has the right to plan childbearing. A woman is more than a female who exists to reproduce. A woman is a person first, and she needs somewhere to go to help her be that person. —*Audre Rapoport*

I don't know if I am really philanthropic or if I just want to get rid of my money. The truth is that I have hated money all my life. I hate money because it caused so much misery when I was growing up without it. I don't think there was a day when my parents didn't argue about money. I only wanted money so that I could do things with it. Money must be your servant, not your god. I can't ever remember wishing I had a better car or a bigger house or a more expensive watch.

> Barney's living in the same house today that he was when he first came back to Waco. Now, he's made some improvements and stuff, but he doesn't put on airs. He drives a run-of-the-line car, and money doesn't mean anything to him like that. He's not trying to put on the dog. —*Fred Schmidt*

> I had known B for a number of years, but I had never visited him in Waco. He kept after me to come down, so I went down there to see this big wealthy Texan. He and Audre were in the process of redoing their house. They were living in two modest adjoining rooms at the Holiday Inn. When I got there, I

> thought, so this is how wealthy Texans live? Poor Vermonters live this well. But living in a motel didn't seem to matter to them at all. They didn't care. These are two people who are the same no matter where they are, whether it is in the halls of the Capitol or in a friend's living room in Waco. —*Senator Patrick Leahy*

Don't get me wrong, I don't deny myself anything I really want. When I fly to London or Israel, I fly first class. I don't care how much it costs. I stay in the best hotels. I want special service when I travel. I want to be comfortable. That is using money as your servant. I don't care about and I don't need material objects. My son, Ronnie, is even less interested in material things.

Ronnie is the most Veblenized person I have ever known. He has no material yearnings. Conspicuous consumption is anathema to him. He has money, but he refuses to live better than his faculty colleagues. Ronnie has always been the most important thing in my life. Like most fathers, I have lived vicariously in the life of my son. I always tried to give my son the same advice that my father gave me: protect your name, cultivate a sense of outrage at injustice, and always have a book in your hands. That is advice that he seems to have accepted wholeheartedly.

Ronnie was a great student all the way through. He earned his undergraduate degree at Oberlin and his doctorate in political science at the University of Michigan. As a professor at the College of William and Mary, Ronnie has the job that I always wanted, and that pleases me immensely. He has brought great joy to my life in so many ways. He is the best son and the best father. He married a wonderful girl named Patricia. Audre has said that if we wanted to draw a picture of the kind of daughter-in-law we would want, we would draw a picture of Patricia.

The births of my grandchildren, Rebecca Abigail (Abby) and Emily Palmer (Emmy), brought about a truly profound change in my life. I call my granddaughters every day. I wake up in the morning and I'm excited because I know I am going to talk to them during the day. I think about them all the time. Abby wrote in a school composition that I was the greatest influence in her life. You can just imagine how that makes me feel. I'll never be old, because I've got Ab and Em. They have preserved my sense of youth. It is exciting to love without reservation, and that is what those two have given me.

Having grandchildren has given Audre and me something else. It has reminded us of how critically important it is to provide young children with the best education possible during the most formative years of their lives.

The Rapoports' son, Ronnie, and his bride, Patricia Williams, on their wedding day. CN 10755, Rapoport (Bernard) Photograph Collection, Center for American History, The University of Texas at Austin.

Visiting our grandchildren's schools in Virginia opened a whole new world to us. Ab and Em have always attended public schools. My visits to their classrooms made me aware of the vast differences among their classmates in terms of preparation and family attitudes about education.

On one of my visits to my granddaughter's second-grade class, I discovered that a child to whom I had been reading a story did not know how to read. It bothered me so much that I came home and did some research. I found out that the vast majority of children who drop out of high school fall behind in their learning between the ages of five and eight. It is during those crucial early years that learning patterns are formed. The experience motivated me to find out more about the condition of early childhood education in this country.

The picture is not a pretty one, not in Waco, not in Texas, not anywhere in the country. I learned that too many young people today do not have the same hope for the future that I did when I was growing up. When I was a child, I was full of hope and expectation. Today, there are far too many children in this country who feel trapped in hopeless poverty. They have no expectations. One of the primary goals in my life has been to take people who were without hope and motivation and instill that desire to utilize their potential. Of all the challenges that I wanted to meet outside of business, that was one that I set out for myself.

Illiteracy and undereducation are the key contributing causes of poverty in this country. Addressing the root causes of poverty will require a commitment to an educational system that begins with a Head Start program for all children who need it, continues with a comprehensive K-12 curriculum, and from that point moves on to higher education. We have to understand that we can't fix the problem at the end level of education until it is fixed at the beginning. We don't need money for handouts—welfare, that is—that allow us to sweep people under the rug to get them out of the way. We need more money for childhood education.

When we cut teachers' pay increases and reduce support staff, who is going to be hurt? Our children. Teachers work ten-, twelve-, and even fourteen-hour days. The principals who lead them also work hard. These dedicated folks have a tremendously important job—educating our children. Neither group is compensated anywhere near the extent that they would be were they employed in business or in industry. We're getting more than we're paying for, but for how long? Would you be a teacher or a principal, working those long hours for their level of pay? How can we expect top performance from top people when we are unwilling to pay for either?

When we don't put our children first, all of us, even those of us without children at home, are sowing the seeds of trouble. A couple of years ago I was talking with someone about my concern for our school system, and he somewhat sarcastically said to me, "Your child is not in school, is he?"

I said, "No, he is fifty years old."

He then asked, "So why are you concerned about the public school system?"

Let me tell you what I told him. If we cannot look beyond ourselves to the best interests of our children, we are a threat to our community. When we cut education budgets, we increase taxes for those who come after us, because every uneducated child is someone for whom taxpayers—you and I—will pay and pay and pay. Funding programs such as remedial training so children can be brought up to speed in the educational process is not spending money, it is investing it. Though money alone is not the answer to what ails education, when we think about the trade-off, the hidden taxes that come with neglect, we must acknowledge this: What do we get for investing in our children? In the end, lower taxes. If we had all the resources available for the education of our children that we spend on security today, we wouldn't have to worry about crime to the extent that we do. There would be no need for a goodly portion of the social agencies that we now must support. Neglected social problems don't just get progressively worse, they increase at an exponential rate.

The jeremiad, one tale of woe after another, as to why public education is failing can be summed up as a lack of seriousness, a lack of commitment. The appearance is that we don't care. If we did, we would have succeeded. Perhaps we thought there was an easy way and there wasn't. One supposedly easy route is vouchering, wherein we surrender the democratic approach and substitute elitist myth, the surest corrosive ingredient in destroying a society. Vouchers are not the answer for the education of American youth. Vouchers are just another piece of patchwork that doesn't work. If public education is not equal or superior to private education, then we might as well fold up our democratic tent and settle for a dictator, we hope a benevolent one. I have no complaints about private schools, but our first responsibility to all of our children is to provide them access to a first-rate public education. Without it, there can be no democracy. We must never forget that equal with the vote, public education is the other most essential ingredient for those who are concerned with the continuation of a democratic society. Vouchering is the worst way of trying to solve our educational problems for the simple reason that whenever we diminish our commitment to public education and seek ways to avoid accepting responsibility for it, it further debases what we seek to correct.

During the Democratic National Convention in Chicago in 1996, I attended a meeting with a group of CEOs of the largest, most powerful companies in the country. I can tell you this: early childhood education meant nothing to most of those business leaders. They didn't have the faintest idea of its value, its potential, its true meaning. They still believe that the failure of public education lies with our teachers, that they are not good enough, don't care enough, and don't work hard enough. They do not see, as I have come to see, that the reason education is in crisis today is that parents aren't there. Families have changed, and so children have changed. In the typical good homes—those with a mommy and a daddy—the children are rushed off to school every morning—lucky to have a good-bye kiss. Both Mommy and Daddy are rushing off to work as well, because some women want to work and some have to work to make ends meet. When school is out, too many of these children come home to an empty house with no one there to see that the homework gets done.

Those are the good homes. What about the others? What about those homes where there is no Daddy? What about those homes where Mommy is a teenager? We are now in the third generation of children having children, of children unable to teach their children anything, not because they don't want to but because they don't know how. What of those little children today? They are not simply poor. They live in poverty. What's the difference? I know what it is like to be poor. My family didn't have money, but we always knew that things would get better. We always knew, my sister and I, that we would get a good education because that was important. We didn't have money, but we had everything else, especially hope. Our parents told us how wonderful we were. We were told we could do anything. Our parents believed in us, and so we came to believe in ourselves. That's the difference between being poor and living in poverty.

Poverty is about hopelessness. Poverty is having nothing and never once believing that you will ever have anything. Poverty is having no one to believe in you. Poverty is never learning to believe in yourself. Too many children today don't talk about what they are going to be when they grow up. They talk about if they grow up. They know no peace, security, or stability. Some of them don't know where they are going to sleep from night to night. No one believes in them. How can they believe in themselves? Is it any wonder that little boys carry guns? That little girls carry babies because some older boy or man has taken advantage of them? Is it any wonder that drugs are everywhere in that world? How can a human being face that kind of hopelessness without being on drugs?

> I think what is close to B's heart are children. I believe that he sees our country through the eyes of children. He wants us in the Senate to do everything we can to make absolutely certain that his and everyone's grandchildren have a secure future. He expects the president and the Congress and everyone in a position of power regardless of party to have the goal of making this a better place for our children and grandchildren. His clear message to us in Congress is for us to do all that we can to insure that our children are educated and that they are healthy. — *Thomas Daschle*

Although our families have changed, our schools remain the same. By and large, they are still teaching children the same way they taught me so many years ago. The problem is that the public school system we all knew so well was never designed to reach each child on an individual basis. It was designed to reach all children. Those who could learn easily that way were considered the best students. Remember? Those who just about got along in that system were the average students. Those who couldn't seem to get it were the slow students.

The Need for Individual Attention

Educational researchers report that the old system never gave any of us more than one and a half minutes a day of individual attention, a total of three hours each school year on average. That was okay if you were among the best or even among the average, because most of us came into school with about three thousand hours of what these researchers call preliteracy. That meant we were ready with some basic information about numbers and letters and colors that we had learned at home. When we came into school, teachers had something to work with. Today's children enter school knowing "absolutely nothing." That's what Diedre Hayes, the principal of the Frazier School in Dallas, told us. Her statement is supported by current research, which indicates that today's children have only about 200 hours of preliteracy when they start school.

What is it that these children don't know that they should know? They don't know their letters or the sounds letters make. They don't know the alphabet song. They don't know their numbers. Now that's starting out way behind. Tests show us that unless these children receive special attention, they improve only about half a grade each year, which means they come into school behind, leave kindergarten still behind, and then have trouble doing first-grade work.

Teachers teach the basics and reteach the basics. Special labs are developed to teach the basics again. Everybody's trying, but little is accomplished. Students lose confidence in themselves and in their teachers. Teachers feel the same way about themselves and their students. The truth is that a minute and a half of individual instruction a day will never solve these problems.

Forty-five minutes or ninety minutes of individual instruction a day would make an enormous difference to both teachers and students. The problem is that no teacher can spend forty-five minutes a day with each child. That's impossible. Even the best volunteer program will never recruit even the most caring volunteers for forty-five minutes a day.

There is something that is possible: bringing individualized, personalized, interactive computer-assisted learning into our classrooms so that each child can receive the individual instruction contained in some of the most creative educational software ever produced. Yes, I am talking about the computer, but not as technology for technology's sake, not as a new toy, and not as a way simply to teach children how to use a computer or with the purpose of getting them on the information superhighway. I'm talking about providing the computer as a tool our teachers can use to teach our children how to read and to write and do arithmetic.

The existence of today's computer hardware and some new and extraordinary software programming means that for the first time in our history, we have the means for providing teachers with a tool that has not existed before. It is a tool that will enable teachers to reach and to teach to each child's needs and abilities. Some of the new software programs are so interactive, so personal, that even a little kindergarten child can simply click a mouse and get the individual instruction needed to learn to read.

I first heard about this new educational approach after it was used for a full academic year by one of our Waco elementary schools. The school set up a computer laboratory for children who badly needed remedial help. These children were not learning at grade level and were falling farther and farther behind. At the conclusion of their first year with these special programs, the children improved their reading and math skills by almost two grade levels.

Fired up by the results, I decided to fund projects at two elementary schools in Waco to demonstrate its possibilities if used in all classrooms, not just in a special laboratory. We provided funds for the schools to buy six computers for each classroom in grades one through five and to hire a classroom aide for each class who works only on these special software programs under the teacher's supervision. Each child needing help will spend forty-five minutes a day working with either a reading or arithmetic software program created to provide individual instruction. If the child needs help with both reading and math, he or she will spend ninety minutes a day with these individualized programs. If the child has trouble with a problem and the program cannot help, the computer voice tells the child to bring the teacher over to the computer.

My hope and expectation is that the new computer programs will result in the widespread adoption of an extremely promising approach to dealing with one of our most serious educational problems.

The Waco 1000 Program

Ours is a society in which there is an increasing lack of community and a corresponding loss of dignity. Community and dignity are requisite for a sustainable society. I have always believed that every member of a community should give whatever they are capable of giving to help that community be a better, more dignified place to live. Those of us who have more to give than others have a special obligation in that regard. It means more than giving money, although that certainly is an important part. It also means serving as a volunteer in the schools, hospitals, museums, and libraries. It means serving on the boards of community agencies that serve the larger good.

I have tried to practice what I preach in Waco. My community involvement has included work with the United Way, United Negro College Fund, Central Texas Sickle Cell Anemia Association, Waco Boys Club Foundation, and Paul Quinn College. Audre has been just as involved in community work as I have. She served on the board of Planned Parenthood of Central Texas for a number of years, and she has helped raise money to support its programs. Its board of directors recognized her contributions in December 1995 by naming its Waco clinic the Audre Rapoport Women's Health Center and Library.

> I have deep admiration for the people who direct and manage Planned Parenthood. We don't need more unwanted children in this world. The work they do in trying to prevent these unwanted pregnancies is vital to the health of our society, and once an unwanted pregnancy does occur, a woman — especially a very young woman — should have the option of an abortion. I am fiercely prochoice. — *Audre Rapoport*

Through our foundation, Audre and I are trying to involve more of our citizens in the community. That is why we created and funded the Waco 1000 program in December 1995. The purpose was to put 1,000 volunteers in Waco schools to tutor children in the elementary grades. The program recruits people from the business and retirement communities to devote time to disadvantaged children by helping them with reading and arithmetic. Each volunteer spends one hour per week in an assigned school. One hour a week is an ideal commitment. It means that for one hour, volunteers are committing themselves to helping one child, perhaps helping him or her so much they can save that child's life.

When the program began I wondered, "How can I give up one hour a week?" As so many of us do, I overestimated how busy I was and assumed I could find little time for anything other than business and my already planned personal commitments. I had a good time feeling sorry for myself. I even considered paying someone to do this for me. However, it didn't take long for me to realize it was a truly important issue and one hour a week would have to be found. So, I shook myself and admitted, with some disgust, that I was overestimating my importance and feeling sorry for my heavy work schedule. I took the plunge and agreed to invest that one hour a week with third graders at an elementary school in Waco.

My first hour was amazing. I had three children read to me. I fell in love with each one of them. Most of the kids I met came from single-parent homes, some from homes where aunts or grandmothers raised them. By the second week, I knew I had a lot more time than I thought I had. The third week, I walked into that room and twenty-one children descended on me, hugging and wanting to be hugged. I have never experienced such sincere loving in my entire life. These were kids who wanted to be loved, and I wanted to love them, too.

> One of the things about B Rapoport that appeals to me the most is the fact that this busy man, who dines with presidents and senators and who travels around the world and who has made millions of dollars, has the time almost daily to read to the elementary schoolchildren in his community. I believe that sets an example, not only for people in Texas but for the whole country. —*Daschle*

It's a wonderful experience. Audre and I are having a good time. We can see, every time we come, how much love and attention these children need. We have learned that there is a lot more to be done in terms of educating our youngsters than we thought before we initiated our reading with the kids. We can help them learn to read or learn to do addition and subtraction. More important, we are paying attention to them. They have become important because someone is coming every week just for them. That importance translates into hope, self-esteem, and self-worth.

The Waco 1000 program has touched the hearts of its volunteers as well as the minds and souls of the students. I think of Dorothy Progar, a retired librarian, who became "Miss Dorothy" to a third-grade class. After months of telling her kids that "readers are leaders" and that they should always aim for the best, Miss Dorothy stated that she had ended the school year with her heart full of joy as a result of the progress that she had seen among the students. During the summer vacation, she even taught one of the children how to swim.

Lonzo Degrate, a maintenance technician at the Waco Regional Airport, met his student every Tuesday to help with his reading. His student had an attitude problem at first, but after three months, Lonzo could see a distinct change. "He started really getting interested in his work," Lonzo said. "The moment I'll remember is when I realized that he wanted to learn. He told me he'd started studying at home by himself."

At first, Harvey Zigel, a retired real estate broker, thought that he had nothing to offer. "How can I tutor anyone if I haven't been to school in fifty years?" he asked. A few weeks later, however, Harvey had a different feeling. "I found that I was looking forward to my one hour with my student," Harvey said. "I hope the experience was as rewarding to him as it was to me."

The success of Waco 1000 has given me hope. I saw kids who could not read in September and could read darn well in May. We can erase the attitude that there is no hope. Believe me, all children want hope. We need more schools, better schools, and better pay for our teachers. Don't ask, "Where is the money coming from?" There is plenty of money. How we allocate resources determines the quality of our society. Our number-one priority as a society should be the education of our youngsters. Every day we delay in addressing the problems we face will take a week to correct. We are many decades behind. Let us begin, or it will not be an ending that any of us likes.

> **I don't know of a man that cares more about educating children than Bernard Rapoport. I don't know of a man that gives more of his time and energy and resources to serve other people than Bernard and Audre Rapoport.** — *Don Evans, U.S. Secretary of Commerce*

The Heart Attack and Immortality

When I woke up on the morning of September 14, 1979, I had a terrible bout of what I thought was indigestion. I took something for it, showered and dressed, and went to my office. I felt weak and tired. When one of our executives came in to see me about a business matter, he suddenly had an alarmed look on his face and said that I looked very ill. I called Audre, and she drove me to Scott and White Hospital in Temple, which is just a few miles south of Waco. I knew all the doctors there. It is one of the best hospitals in Texas. The minute the nurses took my blood pressure, they knew I had suffered a heart attack. I was sixty-two years old, but I had never had heart problems before then. After I was stabilized, the doctors determined that the attack had cost me about 20 percent of my heart.

My doctor was Per Langsjean. I had been a chain smoker for many years before my heart attack. I had started smoking a pipe when I was in college. Dr. Langsjean told me that I had to quit smoking if I wanted to recover. I replied that I was sixty-two years old and if I died from smoking so be it. I wasn't afraid of dying. I was heavily addicted to nicotine. The truth was that

I didn't think I was strong enough to give it up. Dr. Langsjean responded that he wasn't worried about my dying. The problem was that I was going to have a stroke and probably be in a vegetative state for several years before I died. That got my attention. It wasn't easy, but I did quit smoking. I haven't missed it since.

Naturally, my heart attack forced me to confront the fact that I wasn't getting any younger. The more I thought about it, the more I came to feel that people who worry about age are silly. It seems clear to me that there are two kinds of problems, those you can do something about and those you can't. Obviously, age is something you can't do anything about, so why worry? As I write this I am well into my ninth decade of life. I don't want to be forty, and I don't want to be twenty, and I don't want to be sixty-four. This year I want to be eighty-four, and next year I will want to be eighty-five. There is no doubt that as we get older we don't run as fast as we did when we were younger, but we have a little more wisdom, and that wisdom can make up for a lot. I have always been an optimist. I understand what the Indian philosopher meant when he said, "Believing may be difficult, but the need for believing is inescapable." I hope that I will always retain my ability to believe in the future. If I can, I know that I will be productive until the day I die, and I still have a lot that I want to do.

One thing I want to do is be more successful in following through on the ventures in which I participate. I have a short attention span. If a person doesn't get my interest in the first fifteen seconds, he's going to lose me. I've handled millions of problems with people, so when people start talking to me, I just anticipate that I already know what they're going to ask me.

> **Bernard has a habit. He does not want to talk to you unless you go to Waco, and if you go there you have to go to dinner with him. And you do not ever talk business until two seconds before you are ready to leave. Then he asks what you came for, and if you can say it in two seconds then okay. Otherwise, forget it. Friendship comes first.** —*Hiram Friedsam*

I want to be more involved in the things I have an interest in because I think that I could contribute more and be more effective. I want to be helpful to the University of Texas. That's one of my challenges. I want to help make certain that the university continues to excel. And there are other challenges. I want to be a better husband, and I want to be a better father. I want to be a better citizen.

I don't worry about death, and I'm not concerned about my personal immortality. When alluding to immortality, I am always reminded of an inter-

B and Audre with Abby and Emmy. CN 10481, Rapoport (Bernard) Photograph Collection, Center for American History, The University of Texas at Austin.

view with Rabbi Heschel. The question to the rabbi was, "What do you think your mission on earth is?" The rabbi quickly responded, "To do God's work on earth." Then, when asked about the hereafter, the rabbi responded, "I am so busy doing God's work on earth that I will let God worry about that."

Those are my feelings as well. I just want to do whatever I can in the time left to me on this earth to help make a difference in matters that concern me, such as bringing hope to children who are without it by giving them an opportunity to be educated. I'll let God worry about the hereafter.

My view of immortality was captured succinctly by the great CBS newsman and author William Shirer. Shirer observed that the concept of immortality originated "in the greed of unsatisfied people who make unwise use of the time that nature has allotted us." The wise person understands that the natural life span is enough time to enjoy the full range of pleasures to be found in this world. When death comes, that person leaves this world satisfied, freeing a place to be taken by the newly born. "For the wise man," Shirer argued, "one human life is sufficient, and the stupid man will not know what to do with eternity."

I want that last sentence chiseled on my tombstone.

Index

Note: Page numbers in italic refer to photographs.